本书获广西民族大学教材

INTRODUCTION
TO PUBLIC POLICY

"十四五"普通高等教育公共管理精品规划教材

公共政策分析导论双语教程

王　波 ◎ 主　编
叶兴艺 ◎ 副主编

大连理工大学出版社
Dalian University of Technology Press

图书在版编目(CIP)数据

公共政策分析导论双语教程/王波主编. -- 大连：大连理工大学出版社，2024.1(2024.1重印)
ISBN 978-7-5685-4097-1

Ⅰ.①公… Ⅱ.①王… Ⅲ.①公共政策－政策分析－双语教学－教材 Ⅳ.①D035-01

中国国家版本馆CIP数据核字(2023)第003546号

GONGGONG ZHENGCE FENXI DAOLUN SHUANGYU JIAOCHENG

大连理工大学出版社出版

地址：大连市软件园路80号 邮政编码：116023
发行：0411-84708842 邮购：0411-84708943 传真：0411-84701466
E-mail:dutp@dutp.cn URL:https://www.dutp.cn
大连天骄彩色印刷有限公司印刷 大连理工大学出版社发行

幅面尺寸：185mm×260mm 印张：12.75 字数：310千字
2024年1月第1版 2024年1月第2次印刷

责任编辑：邵 婉 责任校对：朱诗宇
封面设计：奇景创意

ISBN 978-7-5685-4097-1 定 价：50.00元

本书如有印装质量问题，请与我社发行部联系更换。

Preface

    If you are reading this book, you probably want to work in some form of public service and are hopefully politically active and vote. You can benefit from understanding the public policy process. It is a process of making decisions that has much to teach people to help them in their individual lives. In addition, the overall process is basically the same no matter what sort of government and policy rule in your jurisdiction, whether you are from China or some other countries. This is because the public policy process is a technical process that is compatible with any national value system.

    The public policy process requires clarification of values. This is done through political processes where different public actors weigh in and contributeto a collective definition and sense of meaning. While values need to be clear, they may be clear implicitly through the nature of the system, rather than explicitly through formal statements. There is no requirement for what the values must be. The process applies in any country. The policy process is a systematic process for making quality decisions within a given values framework. The emphasis of the process is on making decisions of the highest quality with the most efficient use of resources in a policy — making framework.

    Residents and citizens are part of this system, consume media, and participate in the political process. When you do not participate, you assert that your values are not important and hand over the process to others and let them make the decisions that affect your life. An understanding of public policy can help you evaluate the information you take in, clarify public debates, and make informed citizen decisions that are consistent with your individual values.

    This process is analogous to the decision—making process you use in your private life. Your decisions at work and at home are not always consistent and so do not reinforce each other. Everyone can benefit from a systematic approach to decisions. The successful student of public policy will start to improve their personal life as a systematic approach to problem—solving takes the place of the haphazard approach that results from a lack of consideration.

This course can help you live a better life, be a better and more effective citizen, and prepare for the real world of work, whether in the corporate or public sector. Take it seriously and the benefits will be significant.

Finally, no book belongs to the authors alone. A listing of the many people who provided us support and advice would be a listing of the many friends who encouraged us. However, our publisher Dalian Universityof Technology Press deserves special mention for supporting and advancing our work despite difficulties in the publishing business. In addition, Prof. Jongyoul Lee and Prof. Chad Anderson made a critical contribution to the basis for this book. To them and to all who have helped and advice, we owe a deep gratitude.

Wang Bo

Ye Xingyi

2023.11

Contents

Chapter 1　Introduction ·· 1
　1.1　What's Public Policy? ··· 1
　1.2　Why Do We Need Public Policy? ··· 3
　1.3　A Look at the Study of Public Policy ··· 4

Chapter 2　The Study of Public Policy ··· 12
　2.1　Why Do We Study Public Policy? ··· 12
　2.2　The Context of Public Policy ··· 13
　2.3　Market Failure: Rationale for Public Policy ··································· 16

Chapter 3　Actors and Their Roles in Public Policy ································ 26
　3.1　Official Actors and Their Roles ··· 27
　3.2　Unofficial Actors and Their Roles ·· 29

Chapter 4　Models and Theories ··· 39
　4.1　Policy Theories ··· 39
　4.2　The Policy Process Model ·· 46

Chapter 5　Policy Instruments ·· 61
　5.1　Definition of Policy Instrument ··· 61
　5.2　Policy Typologies (tools) ··· 62
　5.3　Elements for Selecting Policy Instruments ··································· 64

Chapter 6　Analyzing Public Policy ··· 74
　6.1　Defination and Nature of Policy Analysis ······································ 74
　6.2　Types of Policy Analysis ··· 76
　6.3　Framwork of Policy Analysis ·· 78

Chapter 7　The Public Policy Process ……………………………………… 97
- 7.1　Defining Problems and Agenda Setting ……………………………… 97
- 7.2　Policy Formulation …………………………………………………… 100
- 7.3　Policy Legitimation …………………………………………………… 102
- 7.4　Policy Implementation ………………………………………………… 103
- 7.5　Policy Evaluation ……………………………………………………… 108
- 7.6　Policy Termination …………………………………………………… 117

Chapter 8　Public Problems and Policy Alternatives ……………………… 143
- 8.1　Public Problems: Definition and Components ……………………… 143
- 8.2　Constructing Alternatives …………………………………………… 149
- 8.3　Assessing Policy Alternatives ………………………………………… 151

Chapter 9　Creative Thinking about Policy Action ………………………… 161
- 9.1　Brainstorming ………………………………………………………… 161
- 9.2　Quick Surveys ………………………………………………………… 162
- 9.3　Literature Review …………………………………………………… 163
- 9.4　Comparison with an Ideal …………………………………………… 163

Chapter 10　Policy Failure and Learning from It ………………………… 169
- 10.1　Explanations for Policy Failure …………………………………… 169
- 10.2　Policy Success, Failure, and Learning …………………………… 170

Chapter 11　Policy Capacity and Participation …………………………… 178
- 11.1　Improving Policy Capacity ………………………………………… 178
- 11.2　Citizen Participation in Decision Making ………………………… 179

Bibliography …………………………………………………………………… 186

前　言

公共政策学是第二次世界大战后兴起的一个新型研究领域，以一系列独特、新型的范式对决策科学化、民主化、法制化及社会发展起到促进作用，是当代社会科学以及管理科学的一个重要而又充满生机的跨学科的新领域。公共政策关心的问题是在生活中"谁获得"、"为什么"以及"带来什么影响"。在公共政策分析中，应该将做得更好与做好的事情结合起来，这样才能更好地维护公共利益。而学习公共决策的意义是让每个人都可以从系统的决策方法中受益。

目前国内各高校中，行政管理、公共事业管理、城市管理等专业均将"公共政策分析"作为专业必修课，并列为双语教学的课程，但却苦于没有一本合适的用双语编写的公共政策分析的教材。因而，出版一本适应国内教学需求的"公共政策分析"双语教材势在必行。在英语语言的应用上，本教材吸收国外同类教材的语言特点，同时考虑非母语学生的情况，尽量采用简单英语语法和标准词汇，做到言简意赅，深入浅出。一方面便于学生掌握公共政策分析的英语语汇，为学生阅读专业英语材料和培养学生用英语学习、科研和工作的能力打下良好的基础；另一方面，它能体现管理国际化的要求，为培养具有国际化视野的公共管理类专业人才提供较好的知识平台。

本教材基于政策过程的视角，系统地介绍了公共政策的政策主体、政策执行的理论与模型、政策议程、政策制定、政策执行、政策评估、政策创新、政策终结等的基本知识。在对公共政策分析的各个步骤依次进行介绍的基础上，展现公共政策分析系统的知识体系和公共政策分析过程的基本脉络。

本教材从撰写到出版，历时三年多，得到了大连理工出版社特别是邵婉老师的大力支持和帮助，再次表示衷心的感谢。教材难免存在疏漏之处，敬请批评指正。

王　波

叶兴艺

2023.11

目 录

第1章 导 论 ··· 7
  1.1 什么是公共政策？ ··· 7
  1.2 为什么需要公共政策？ ·· 8
  1.3 公共政策研究 ··· 9

第2章 公共政策研究 ·· 20
  2.1 为什么需要研究公共政策？ ·· 20
  2.2 公共政策环境 ·· 21
  2.3 市场失灵：公共政策的合理性 ·· 23

第3章 公共政策主体及其权力 ··· 33
  3.1 官方决策者及其权力 ··· 34
  3.2 非官方参与者及其权力 ·· 35

第4章 政策执行理论与模型 ·· 51
  4.1 政策执行理论 ·· 51
  4.2 政策执行的模型 ··· 57

第5章 政策工具 ·· 68
  5.1 政策工具的内涵 ··· 68
  5.2 政策工具的分类 ··· 69
  5.3 政策工具的选择 ··· 70

第6章 政策分析 ·· 87
  6.1 政策分析的定义及本质 ·· 87
  6.2 政策分析的类型 ··· 89
  6.3 政策分析过程的框架 ·· 90

第 7 章　政策过程 ·········· 123
7.1　问题定义和议程设置 ·········· 123
7.2　政策制定 ·········· 125
7.3　政策合法化 ·········· 127
7.4　政策执行 ·········· 128
7.5　政策评估 ·········· 131
7.6　政策终止 ·········· 138

第 8 章　公共问题与政策备选方案 ·········· 153
8.1　公共问题：定义及基本要素 ·········· 153
8.2　构建备选方案 ·········· 157
8.3　政策备选方案评估 ·········· 159

第 9 章　政策分析的创造性思维 ·········· 165
9.1　头脑风暴 ·········· 165
9.2　快速调查 ·········· 166
9.3　文献研究 ·········· 166
9.4　与理想愿景的比较 ·········· 167

第 10 章　决策失误与误区 ·········· 174
10.1　对政策失误的解释 ·········· 174
10.2　决策成功、失误和教训 ·········· 175

第 11 章　公共决策能力与公民参与 ·········· 182
11.1　提高公共决策能力 ·········· 182
11.2　公共决策中的公民参与 ·········· 183

Chapter 1

Introduction

Summary

> Public policy consists of actions made in the public's name, made by government or at least initiated by government. Public policy is interpreted and implemented by public and private actors. It includes both what government intends to do and what government chooses not to do. It is defined as in the public interest. Public policy is studied for scientific purposes of learning truth or for more practical professional and political reasons.

1.1 What's Public Policy?

Public policy is normally thought of as government action to address a problem or problems. The central focus is who gets what when and how. Policies are revealed through texts, practices, symbols, and discourses that define and deliver values through goods and services as well as regulations, income, status, and other positively or negatively valued attributes. Public policy is basically government action or inaction taken in response to social problems.

Social problems are conditioning the public widely perceives to be unacceptable that require intervention. Personal or private problems like bad grades or low sales are not the same as social problems such as environmental degradation, workplace safety, or access to health care that can be addressed through government action, private action (meaning that individuals or private organizations like businesses and NGOs take the responsibility), or a combination of the two. Any level of government (central, provincial, urban, local) may be involved in a policy effort. This is because social problems, and the public demand for action to address them, manifest themselves from the local to the national level, or even internationally. At the local level there are problems like traffic congestion. At the national level there are issues like power generation and the response to climate change.

Defining Public Policy

Birkland speaks to the difficulty of defining public policy, noting that there are many different definitions that vary depending on the perspectives of the users (Birkland,2001). Therefore, Table 1-1 presents several such definitions. However, public policy can be defined by five traits (Birkland, 2001):

— Policy made in the "public's" name

— Policy generally made or initiated by government

— Policy interpreted and implemented by public and private actors

— Something government intends to do

— Something government chooses not to do

Sabatier speaks to the complexity of defining public policy as part of the policy process:

"In short, understanding of the policy process requires knowledge of the goals and perceptions of hundreds of actors throughout the country involving possibly very technical scientific and legal issues over periods of a decade or more while most of those actors are actively seeking to propagate their specific spin on events" (Sabatier, 2007: 4).

Therefore, there are a broad variety of potential definitions that depend on the technical, scientific, legal, political, and institutional orientation of the actors in the process advancing the definitions. At any rate, public policy is related to government and public institutions or organizations recognized as acting on behalf of the public interest. It is related to formal and informal rules and laws and implicit and explicit intents.

Table 1-1　　　　　　　　　　Defining Public Policy

Definition	Author
"Whatever governments choose to do or not to do."	Dye (1992)
"Public policy is the outcome of the struggle in government over who gets what."	Cochran et al. (1999)
"In studying policy, then, we look at the broader sweep of politics, not simply the written laws and rules themselves."	Birkland (2001)
"The combination of basic decisions, commitments, and actions made by those who hold or influence government positions of authority."	Gerston (2010)
"Public policy is defined here as what government ought or ought not to do, and does or does not do."	Simon (2009)

1.2　Why Do We Need Public Policy?

　　The dominant ideological foundation of modern constitutional systems following the American Constitution is known as classical liberalism. Among the many beliefs stemming from liberalism is the belief that power is derived from the consent of the governed. This means that "the people" are the governed, but they also provide their consent to the government. As a result, when policy advocates seek to induce the government to make policy (by taking an action or refusing to do so), proponents of the new policy will claim that the government does so in the "public interest."

　　However, controversies arise because there is disagreement over what constitutes "the public interest." For example, those who argue that need more government workers to match the average size of OECD governments claim to do so to bring the proper level of public services to national citizens. On the other hand, some argue that lay off government workers can avoid waste and provide efficient government, this is another definition of the public interest. Some policy advocates claim that laws that relieve tax burdens on the rich are in the public interest because they create overall public wealth. On the other hand, those who argue that the rich should be taxed at a higher rate than the poor claim that taxation based on ability to pay is more in the spirit of the public interest.

　　Another example of disputes over what policies should be made in the broader public interest is the issue of the minimum wage. Recent controversies regarding the minimum wage have emerged in South Korea regarding publicizing, enforcing, and raising the minimum wage, including a petition campaign for a 10,000 minimum wage. Each side of the argument has reasonable advocates who speak for the public interest. Minimum wage opponents argue the public interest is advanced through lower wages that help keep small businesses open and allow them to hire more workers. On the other hand, proponents argue that more money improves the welfare of poorer workers and circulates more money through the economy. Are small business owners acting against the public interest by opposing a higher minimum wage that might put them out of business? Are low-wage workers acting against the public interest by asking for more money that could improve their lives? Indeed, every area has many citizen groups that promote their interpretation of the public interest or the "national interest." When a group is making a normative claim for what might be called the "public interest", the public interest is highly variable depending on who is defining it.

　　In the minimum wage example, how would you define the public interest? If you were a small business owner, you would likely define it in a very different way from a low-wage worker or a representative of a union. You might say that the public really has no clearly stated interest in setting wages, but they do display a preference for lower prices, and low prices have to come out of someone's earnings. Low-wage workers, on the other hand, might argue that more equality would benefit everyone, while higher prices might not be opposed and seem so bad if people at the bottom had enough money to pay them. These different arguments reflect the difficulty in defining a universal, agreed-upon public interest.

Public policy is related to the public interest because it affects all of us in some way. However, not everyone is necessarily affected by the same policy in exactly the same way. Nor is intensity of feeling about a particular issue necessarily equal among different members of the public. Most people care about their everyday lives but not too much about government because the activities of government seem removed from daily interests and needs. Still, the government plays an important role in every aspect of people's lives, from the power efficiency labeling on electrical appliances to registering and regulating hotels. As oppressive as government is claimed to be by some interests, at least some government activities are benign and beneficial to most people, and people tend not to dwell on those policies until something goes very wrong with them.

You may be interested in public policy because you care intensely about a particular area of public policy—the economy, or the environment, or the promotion of morality and ethics in government. Even people who are intensely interested and are participants in the policy process are not concerned with every issue, though. There is considerable division of labor in democratic politics. Different positions have different constitutional responsibilities, and the vast array of issues that government handles on the people's behalf requires that even members of assemblies need to be specialists in fairly narrow fields.

The people delegate the power to make policies in their name (or, more precisely, the system is designed this way) because it is the people's government. The people cannot all be concerned with the day-to-day multitude of issues that government must address, so the people have delegated decision-making to people who specialize in making the complex decisions that modern government must face. By delegating this power, the people do not abandon their interest in what the government does or how it does it (and sometimes the procedures government uses are at least as important as the goals to be achieved), nor do members of the public give up their right to promote their individual ideas of what constitutes the public interest.

1.3 A Look at the Study of Public Policy

Academics, policy analysts, and advocacy organizations, and citizen activists are not united by any single purpose. Instead, many interests move individuals and organizations to deal with public policy, and distinct aspects of its study reflect their interests. Academics, study public policy for scientific purposes. In other words, they work to build a general understanding of public problems and the policy-making process. They seek "truth" through scientific methods, regardless of whether the knowledge is relevant or useful in some immediate way. Their goal is to explain the causes and consequences of public policies, quite apart from what governments ought to do.

Some people study public policy for professional reasons, such as conducting policy analyses for government agencies, think tanks, or interest groups. Their objective is to examine public problems and policy alternatives and produce usable knowledge that can help policy makers, interest groups, or citizens choose those policies that are likely to achieve their desired outcomes. Some analysts are committed to specific policy values and goals and sometimes to ideological and partisan agendas. Not surprisingly, they try to emphasize the studies and findings that help to advance their values and goals. This kind of policy study can be described as political, rather than professional or scientific.

Discussion Questions

1. How would you define public policy?
2. How would you define the public interest? Can you give an example that conflicts with your definition?
3. Why do people study public policy?

Vocabularies

public
private
public actor
private actor
public interest
private interest

References

Birkland, Thomas A. 2001. An Introduction to the Policy Process: Theories, Concepts, and Models of Public Policy Making. Armonk, New York: M. E. Sharpe.

Cochran, Clarke E., Mayer, Lawrence C., Carr, T. R., Cayer, N. Joseph, McKenzie, Mark J., and Peck, Laura R. 1999. American Public Policy: An Introduction. 6th ed. New York: St. Martin's Press.

Dye, Thomas R. 1992. Understanding Public Policy. 7th ed. Englewood Cliffs, New Jersey: Prentice Hall.

Gerston, Larry N. 2010. Public Policy Making: Process and Principles. Armonk,

New York: M. E. Sharpe.

Kraft, Michael E. and Furlong, Scott R. 2004. Public Policy: Politics, Analysis, and Alternatives. Washington, D. C: CQ Press.

Peters, B. Guy. 1999. American Public Policy: Promise and Performance. Chappaqua, New York: Chatham House/Seven Rivers.

Sabatier, Paul A. 2007. "The Need for Better Theories," pp. 3-17 in Sabatier, Paul A. (ed), Theories of the Policy Process, 2nd ed. Boulder, CO: Westview Press.

Simon, Christopher A. 2009. Public Policy: Preferences and Outcomes, 2nd ed. New York, New York: Routledge.

第 1 章

导 论

公共政策是由政府制定或由政府发起的以公众名义制定的议案,并由公共和私有部门来解释和实施。它既包括政府计划做什么,也包括政府选择不去做什么。它的定义需要符合公共利益,但在公共利益的构成上存在争议。对公共政策进行研究的目的源自其科学性,以了解真相或出于更实际的、专业的和政治的原因。

1.1 什么是公共政策?

公共政策通常被认为是解决社会问题的政府行为。关注谁在何时何地获得了什么。通过文本、实践、符号和话语揭示政策,通过商品和服务以及法规、收入、地位和其他正面或负面价值的属性来定义和传递价值。公共政策基本上是针对社会问题采取的政府作为或不作为。

社会问题是公众普遍认为不可接受或者需要进行干预的情形,社会问题(环境恶化,工作场所安全或医疗保障等)不同于个人问题(如成绩不好或销量减少),需要通过政府部门和私营部门(个体或私营组织,如企业和非政府组织),或两者的合作来加以解决。任何层级的政府(中央政府、省政府、城市政府、其他地方政府)都可以参与政策的制定,因为社会问题从地方到国家,甚至是国际社会都是普遍存在的,公众会要求政府采取行动来解决这些问题,如地方层面的交通拥堵,国家层面的能源和气候变化应对等。

公共政策的定义

伯克兰谈及定义公共政策的难度时指出,不同主体对政策的定义会有所不同(见表1-1)但是公共政策可以依据以下五个特征来加以定义(伯克兰,2001):

——以"公共"的名义加以制定

——一般由政府制定或发起

——由公共或者私有部门解释和实施

——政府计划做的事情

——政府选择不去做的事情

萨巴蒂尔谈到作为政策过程一部分的公共政策定义的复杂性时指出:"对政策过程的理解需要了解参与者的目标及其看法,其中可能涉及技术手段上的科学性及合法性问题,而且应是大多数参与者正在积极试图去倡导的内容。"(萨巴蒂尔,2007:4)因此,存在各种各样的潜在的定义,这些定义取决于定义完善的过程中参与者的技术、科学、法律和政治取向。无论如何,公共政策被认为与代表公共利益的政府和公共机构或组织有关。它涉及正式和非正式的规则、法律以及各种隐含的和明确的意图。

表 1-1　　　　　　　　　　　　公共政策的定义

定　义	作　者
"政府决定做或者不做的事情"	戴伊(1992)
"公共政策是政府决定谁得到什么的斗争的结果"	科克伦等主编(1999)
"在研究政策时,我们会考虑更广义范围内的政治,而不仅仅是法律和规则本身"	伯克兰(2001)
"拥有或影响政府权力的人的基本决定、承诺和行动的组合"	格斯顿(2010)
"公共政策在这里被定义为政府应该或不应该做什么,做什么或不做什么"	西蒙(2009)

1.2　为什么需要公共政策?

美国宪法之后的现代宪政制度的主要意识形态基础被称为古典自由主义,认为统治者的权力来自被统治者的授权。认为统治者的权力来自被统治者的授权。这意味着"人民"虽然是被治理者,但是需要他们向政府授权。因此,当政策倡导者试图促使政府制定政策(通过采取行动或拒绝这样做)时,新政策的支持者会声称政府这样做是为了"公共利益"。

然而对"公共利益"的构成存在着争议。例如,主张需要更多政府工作人员以匹配经合组织规定的政府平均规模的人认为这样做可以提供更高质量的公共服务。另一方面,主张裁减政府工作人员的人认为这样可以避免浪费和建设更有效率的政府,这是对公共利益的另一种定义。一些政策支持者认为,减轻富人税收负担的政策符合公共利益,因为创造了整体的公共财富。但是那些认为应该对富人以高于穷人的税率征税的人则认为基于支付能力的税收政策更符合公共利益。

另外一个同样存在争议(政策制定如何体现更广泛的公共利益)的例子是最低工资标准的设定问题。韩国提高最低工资标准的提议引起了很大的争议,甚至发生了大规模的请愿活动。争论的双方都有合理的为公共利益诉求的理由。提高最低工资标准的反对者认为,通过降低工资可以增加公共利益,因为有助于小企业雇用更多的工人从而维持其生存。另一方面,支持者则认为,更多的税收可以改善贫困工人的福利状况,并通过经济的发展带来更多的资金。小企业主反对可能让他们破产的更高的最低工资标准是否违背公共利益?低收入的工人要求更多可以改善其生活的收入是否违背公共利益?现实中,每个地区都有许多公民团体,可以阐述他们对公共利益或"国家利益"的解释。当一个群体对所谓的"公共利益"做出规范性主张时,公共利益的多样性取决于由谁来给出定义。

在最低工资标准的例子中,如何定义公共利益?如果你是小企业主,你可能会以与低收入的工人或工会代表截然不同的方式进行定义。你可能会认为公众对确定工资标准没有太多的兴趣,但事实是他们表现出对较低价格的偏好,低价格来自其收入的需要。另一方面,低收入的工人可能会说,平等可以让每个人受益,如果底层的人有足够的钱用来支付,那么更高的价格可能就不会遭到反对。这些不同的观点反映了在界定公共利益方面的困境。

公共政策同公共利益相关,因为从某种程度上说,它会影响到我们所有人。但是,"同一政策并非以相同的方式影响所有人",而且对于特定问题的感受体验在不同的成员之间也有所差异。大多数人更多关心的是自己的日常生活,而不是政府,因为政府的活动似乎脱离了人们的日常利益需求。尽管如此,政府仍在我们生活的各个领域都发挥着重要作用,从电器的电源效率标签到酒店入住及管理。尽管一些利益集团断言政府具有压迫性,但至少政府活动对大多数人来说是有益的,在这些政策出现严重问题之前,人们倾向于不去纠结。

你可能对公共政策感兴趣,因为你非常关注公共政策的某一特定领域——经济、环境,或政府关于道德和伦理的宣传。即使是那些对政策过程非常感兴趣并且参与政策过程的人也不是关心每一个问题。民主政治中存在相当多的分工,不同的立场有不同的责任,代表人民的政府处理大量的问题,要求其成员要成为某一领域的专家。

人民授权政府制定政策(或者更确切地说,制度是这样设计的),因为它是人民的政府。但是人们不可能关心政府必须解决的全部日常问题,所以人们将决策权委托给那些专门制定现代政府必须面对的复杂决策的人。通过这种授权,人们并没有放弃他们对政府所做的事情或如何做的兴趣(政府采用的程序至少与要实现的目标一样重要),也不会放弃他们要求改善公共利益的权利。

1.3 公共政策研究

学者、政策专家和倡议组织以及公民团体的活动家不是为了任何单一目标而联合起来的。相反,不同的利益诉求促使个人和组织参与到公共政策中来,其研究也从不同侧面反映了其各自的利益诉求。学者出于科学的目的研究公共政策。换言之,他们致力于建立对公共问题和政策制定过程的一般理解。他们通过科学方法寻求"真理",不介意这些知识是否以某种直接的方式相关或有用,他们的目标在于解释公共政策的因果关系,而不是政府应该做什么。

部分人出于职业原因研究公共政策,例如为政府机构、思想库或利益集团进行政策分析。他们的目标是检验公共问题和政策选择,并提供有用的知识以帮助决策者、利益集团或公民选择那些可能实现预期目标的政策。

一些专家致力于具体的政策价值和目标,有时也致力于意识形态和党派议程。毋庸置疑,他们试图强调有助于推进其价值观和目标的研究及发现。这样的政策研究可以被描述为政治行为,而不是专业或科学研究。

思考问题

1. 如何定义公共政策?
2. 如何定义公共利益?你能给出一个与你的定义相冲突的例子吗?
3. 人们为什么要研究公共政策?

词 汇

公共
私有
公共部门
私有部门
公共利益
私有利益

参考文献

Birkland, Thomas A. 2001. An Introduction to the Policy Process: Theories, Concepts, and Models of Public Policy Making. Armonk, New York: M. E. Sharpe.

Cochran, Clarke E., Mayer, Lawrence C., Carr, T. R., Cayer, N. Joseph, McKenzie, Mark J., and Peck, Laura R. 1999. American Public Policy: An Introduction. 6th ed. New York: St. Martin's Press.

Dye, Thomas R. 1992. Understanding Public Policy. 7th ed. Englewood Cliffs, New Jersey: Prentice Hall.

Gerston, Larry N. 2010. Public Policy Making: Process and Principles. Armonk, New York: M. E. Sharpe.

Kraft, Michael E. and Furlong, Scott R. 2004. Public Policy: Politics, Analysis, and Alternatives. Washington, D. C: CQ Press.

Peters, B. Guy. 1999. American Public Policy: Promise and Performance. Chappaqua, New York: Chatham House/Seven Rivers.

Sabatier, Paul A. 2007. "The Need for Better Theories," pp. 3-17 in Sabatier, Paul A. (ed), Theories of the Policy Process, 2nd ed. Boulder, CO: Westview Press.

Simon, Christopher A. 2009. Public Policy: Preferences and Out-comes, 2nd ed. New York, New York: Routledge.

Chapter 2　The Study of Public Policy

Summary

> People study public policy for theoretical and academic scientific reasons. It's studied for political reasons, for more effective participation, and for better-insight into choosing political candidates.
>
> Public policy takes place in a social and cultural context. It's also affected by the political and governing context as well as by an economic context that has concerned with inflation and unemployment. Public policy is a response to market failure, and can include the provision of the public goods, the addressing of externalities, the maintenance of natural monopolies, and the balancing of information asymmetries.

2.1　Why Do We Study Public Policy?

There are many different reasons to study public policy. They include theoretical reasons (Cochran et al., 1999) or scientific reasons (Anderson, 2000). Analysts, practitioners, and academics want to understand the theory in order to comprehend the public policy process. Understanding the theory can allow analysts and practitioners to apply theory for practical purposes. Academics use theory to help with scientific understanding.

Therefore, people may study public policy in order to know more about the process both in pursuit of knowledge for its own sake and to inform practitioners. This is a question of so-called "pure" science versus "applied" science. Scholars at universities and in research institutes also have some of the same interests as policy analysts, but scholars are more often concerned with building general knowledge of the policy process instead of affecting the process more directly. This is more related to pure science, of knowledge for its own sake.

Examples of applied science include using the science for practical political reasons, for more efficient participation, or for facilitating the democratic process by selecting candidates wisely.

Political Reasons

People with political goals study public policy so as to learn about how to promote the policy options that they prefer. Their purpose is to advance their political interests through the policy process. One group of people using knowledge of public policy for political purposes is the policy analyst. Policy analysts work inside and outside of government to understand and influence policy. Therefore, they have a professional concern for public policy as part of their job.

Another group of people interested in policy for political purposes is made up of concerned citizens. For citizens, strong personal interest by itself should be a good reason to study public policy. Studying public policy may help citizens:
— sharpen their skills
— decide what political positions and policies to support
— evaluate democratic governance

It may also encourage students to consider and/or to prepare for careers in public policy, law, or government.

More Efficient Participation

In a democracy, citizens choose representatives to act on their behalf, but that is not the last step of citizen participation. Citizens may speak out during the policy development process and in response to government actions. People are not usually restrained by a lack of knowledge about public problems, policies, government decisions, or politics. However, they can participate more effectively and have greater leverage by improving their understanding of these issues.

Selecting Candidates Wisely

Candidates for public office state their positions on the issues during political campaigns. They do this through speeches and advertisements to persuade voters to support them. Voters who study public policy are better equipped to understand the candidates, their policy ideas, and are more prepared to evaluate them.

2.2 The Context of Public Policy

Public policy is affected by social and economic conditions. In addition, the structure of government and national and local cultural norms are some of the variables that shape the policy process. As a result, a description of the context of public policy is important. Next is a discussion of the social, economic, political, and cultural context of public policy.

Social Context

Social conditions affect policy decisions in numerous ways, as is evident in controversies over phenomena as diverse as urban sprawl, internet privacy, and getting the economy going. Social conditions are dynamic and in a constant state of change although you may like to imagine society as unchanging. The population changes because of immigration, growth in non-traditional households, and lower or higher birth rates. These social changes alter how the public and policy makers view and act on problems ranging from crime to the rising cost of health care. The elderly currently makes up the fastest growing segment of the total population. Their needs are different from the needs of the rest of the population, and they are more likely than younger citizens to demand that government pays close attention to them.

As the elderly population continues to increase, policy makers face difficult challenges. In particular, there is the question of how to ensure the pension system's solvency as greater numbers of people begin to draw benefits. In the past, the national pension system posed no special risk to budgetary resources. Public officials recognize that they must find politically and economically realistic ways of dealing with an aging population.

Other parts of the social context include the lower birth rate, the insecurity of forced early retirement, the increase in women in the workplace, as well as the increasing emigration (moving to other countries and working and studying in other countries). All of these represent variables that can affect the policy-making process. How citizens relate to one another in their communities also influences public policy making.

Economic Context

The economy has a major impact on the policies governments adopt and implement. Economic policy deals with inflation and unemployment, but the economy itself affects the development of many other programs. For example, a strong economy often leads to lower unemployment, which, in turn, reduces the need for welfare and comparable assistance programs. China shift to a less regulated economy featuring more transparency along with the growth of service and IT sectors has had and will continue to have many impacts on public policy. Another way to appreciate the influence of the economic context is to consider unemployment.

International Labour Organization (ILO) published report *Global Employment Trend for Youth* 2020: *Technology and Future Work* that analyzed global employment trend for youth and stated one out of five young people in the world is unemployed due to the epidemic this year, and working hours of serving young people reduced by 23%. The global youth unemployment rate is 13.6% which is higher than other groups in 2019. The epidemic has further exacerbated the unemployment problem of young people around the world. The economic crisis caused by the epidemic has hit the employment of young people, especially young women, faster and more seriously than other groups. The report recommends that countries should make the protection and promotion of young people's employment an important component of future epidemic response policies.

Political Context

Politics affects public policy choices at every step, from the selection of policy makers in elections to shaping how conflicts among different groups are resolved. To appreciate the political context, one must be aware of the relative strength of the major parties. The influence of minor parties, the ideological differences among the public, especially the more attentive public groups such as committed liberals and conservativess, the ability of organized interest groups to exert pressure are also important factors.

Liberals and conservatives, regardless of the names of the current parties they belong to, often hold sharply different views about the legitimacy of government action and which policies are acceptable. Ideological polarization between the parties makes government action difficult on many policy issues. The student of public policy also needs to recognize that political labels such as liberal and conservative are not always a reliable guide to predicting specific policy positions.

It is simplistic to think that conservatives always want a smaller government and that liberals favor the opposite. Most conservatives argue against more government regulation of the economy and for decision making by business and industry. They often also favor a strong government role in achieving certain social goals, such as maintaining the traditional social order. Liberals, on the other hand, tend to call for government regulation of business activity to protect consumers and workers or to control air and water pollution.

Party labels, may be a poor indicator of positions taken on policy issues, especially as party labels change so fast, with some politicians associated with different parties almost every election. Within the major political parties one can easily find ideological differences among members. For example, the New Politics Alliance for Democracy of South South Korea is a merger blending several strains of liberalism.

Cultural Context

Political culture refers to widely held values, beliefs, and attitudes, such as trust and confidence in government and the political process, or the lack of it. Political cultures not only vary from nation to nation but from region to region within South Korea, and even from one community to another, as one might expect in a modern society. These cultural differences help to explain the variation in provincial (and municipal) policies across the nation. Different cities adopt different approaches to development, some city governments invest in people and welfare while many other cities develop through investments in places like stadiums, housing, and parks. Policy makers in these different communities make different policy calculations on the basis of very different political cultures.

Cultural conflicts also affect public judgments about government officials and their conduct and many influence the policy-making process.

2.3 Market Failure: Rationale for Public Policy

In a market economy, private actors are supposed to provide for the needs of people. However, they are not always able to do so. Such market failure is a major rationale for government action. Four commonly recognized kinds of market failure include public goods, externalities, natural monopolies, and information asymmetries. They provide the traditional economic rationales for public participation in private affairs.

Public Goods

The terms *public goods* and *collective goods* appear frequently in the economics and policy analysis literature. The blanket use of the term, however, obscures important differences among the varieties of public goods. These differences include the nature of the market failure and, consequently, the appropriate public policy response. A basic question should be raised when considering any market failure, that is: Why does the market fail to allocate this particular good efficiently? The simplest approach to providing an answer involves contrasting public goods with private goods.

Two primary characteristics define private goods, rivalry in consumption and excludability in ownership and use. Rivalrous consumption means that when a thing is consumed it cannot be consumed by anyone elses. A perfectly private good has complete consumption rivalry. Excludable ownership means that only one person or entity has control over the use of the goods. A perfectly private good is completely excludable. For example, shoes are private goods because when one person wears them, no one else can wear them (rivalrous consumption) and the person who owns them can determine who gets to wear them at any particular time (excludable ownership).

Pure public goods, on the other hand, are either *non-rivalrous* in consumption, *non-excludable* in use, or both. In other words, any goods that is not purely private is considered to be a public good. A good is non-rivalrous in consumption when more than one person can receive consumption benefits from some level of supply at the same time. For example, policing and national defense are non-rivalrous in consumption because all citizens benefit from them without reducing the benefits of others—a new citizen enjoys the same benefits without reducing the benefits of those already defended. A good is non-excludable if it is impractical for one person to maintain exclusive control over its use. For example, species of fish that range widely in the ocean are usually non-excludable in use because they move freely between national and international waters so that no individual can effectively exclude others from harvesting them.

Externalities

An externality is any impact (positive or negative) resulting from any action (that may be related either to production or consumption) that affects someone who did not fully agree to it through participation in a voluntary exchange. Price changes in competitive markets are not relevant externalities because buyers and sellers engage in voluntary exchange by participating in the market. Pollution that hurts people who live near a factory and are exposed by chance is an example of a negative externality.

Table 2-1   Examples of Externalities

	Positive	Negative
Producer-to-Producer	Recreational facilities attract people who purchase from nearby business	Toxic chemical pollution harms downstream commercial fishing
Producer-to-Consumer	Private timber forests provide scenic benefits to nature lovers	Factories pollute the air harming lungs of people living nearby
Consumer-to-Consumer	Immunization against contagious disease helps to reduce risk to others	Cigarette smoke hurts the health of non-smokers
Consumer-to-Producer	Letters from consumers provide information on product quality	Trespassers damage private property by taking a shortcut

Natural Monopoly

Natural monopoly occurs when the average cost declines over the range of demand. This definition is in terms of both cost and demand conditions. In the case of a natural monopoly, a single firm can produce the output at a lower cost than can any other market arrangement, including competition. Even though the basic definition of a natural monopoly sounds static, markets in the real world are dynamic. Technological changes may lead to different cost characteristics, or high prices may force the replacement of goods by close or even superior substitutes. The result may be the elimination of a natural monopoly or the supplanting of one natural monopoly technology by another. For example, cellular phones may be direct substitutes for line-connected phones, providing competition for traditional telephone systems.

Information Asymmetry

Information itself has the characteristics of a public good. Consumption of information is non-rivalrous. One person's consumption does not interfere with another's. The basic question is primarily whether exclusion is or is not possible. Thus, the production and consumption itself is of interest in the public goods context. Second, there may be situations where the amount of information about the characteristics of a good varies between people. The buyer and the seller in a market transaction, for example, may have different information about the quality of the good being traded. Similarly, there may be differences in the level of information relating to the attributes of an externality between the generator of the externality and the affected party. Workers, for instance, may not be as well informed about the health risks of industrial chemicals as their employers.

Traditional market failures indicate possibilities for improving the efficiency of market outcomes through collective action. Market failures and unsatisfied distributional goals are necessary but not sufficient grounds for public intervention. The costs of the proposed intervention must always be considered. Just as markets fail in fairly predictable ways, government failures may contribute to the costs of policy interventions. They may also be a cause of policy failure.

Discussion Questions

1. Why are you studying public policy?
2. How can the study of public policy improve government and the democratic political process?
3. How can the study of public policy be useful?
4. Identify and explain the different policy contexts.
5. Identify and explain the different types of market failure.
6. Give examples of public and private goods and explain how they differ.

Vocabularies

inflation
unemployment
public goods
collective goods
rivalrous consumption
excludable ownership
non-rivalrous consumption
non-excludable ownership

References

Anderson, James E. 2000. Public Policy Making. 4th ed. Boston: Houghton Mifflin.

Birkland, Thomas A. 2001. An Introduction to the Policy Process: Theories, Concepts, and Models of Public Policy Making. New York: M. E. Sharpe.

Cochran, Clarke E., Mayer, Lawrence C., Carr, T. R., Cayer, N. Joseph, McKenzie, Mark J., and Peck, Laura R. 1999. American Public Policy: An Introduction. 6th ed. New York: St. Martin's Press.

Elazar, Daniel J. 1984. American Federalism: A View from the States. 3rd ed. New York: Harper and Row.

International Labour Organization. 2020. Global Employment Trends for Youth 2020: Technology and Future Work. International Labour Office: Geneva

Kim, Heejin. 2015. "Jobless Rate for Young South Koreans Rises to 11.1%." South Korea Joong Ang Daily. March 19, 2015 from http://South Korea joong ang daily. joins. com/news/article/Article. aspx? aid=3002087

Kraft, Michael E., and Furlong, Scott R. 2004. Public Policy: Politics, Analysis, and Alternatives. Washington, D. C: CQ Press.

Mazmanian, Daniel A., and Kraft, Michael E. eds. 1999. Toward Sustainable Communities: Transition and Transformations in Environmental Policy. Cambridge: MIT Press.

Putnam, Robert D. 1995. "Tuning In, Tuning Out: The Strange Disappearance of Social Capital in America." PS: Political Science and Politics, 28 (December): 664-683.

Weimer, L. David and Vining, R. Aidan. 2005. Policy Analysis: Concept and Practice. 4th ed. Upper Saddle River, New Jersey.

第 2 章

公共政策研究

　　人们或者出于理论的学习和学科发展的需要研究公共政策,或者出于更有效的政治参与,更好地选择政治候选人而研究公共政策。公共政策需要一定的社会、文化背景,也会受到政治、治理环境以及与通货膨胀和失业率相关的经济环境的影响。公共政策是对市场失灵的应对,包括公共产品的提供、解决外部性问题、维持自然垄断、平衡信息不对称等。

2.1 为什么需要研究公共政策?

　　研究公共政策基于不同的理由,包括理论上的需要(科克伦等人主编,1999)或学科发展的需要(安德森,2000)。政策专家、政策实践者和学者希望在掌握理论的基础上,更好地理解公共政策过程。理论可以帮助政策专家和实践者更好地将理论应用于实践。学者可以利用理论来促进学科的发展。

　　因此,人们为了更好地了解政策进程而研究公共政策,既为了追求知识本身,也可以为从业者提供信息。这是一个所谓的"纯粹"科学与"应用"科学的问题。大学和研究机构的学者有一些与政策专家共同的兴趣,但学者们更多关心的是建立政策过程的一般意义上的知识,而不是直接地影响政策过程。这与纯科学和知识本身有关。

　　在实践中的应用包括将其用于实际的政治活动、更有效的参与,或通过明智地选择候选人来促进民主进程。

政治原因

出于政治原因而研究公共政策的人是为了了解如何推广他们的政策选择,通过政策过程来实现他们的政治利益。政策专家是将公共政策知识应用于政治实践的人,在体制内外工作以了解和影响政策过程。因此,作为工作的一部分,他们对公共政策有着专业的关注。

另一出于政治目的对政策感兴趣的群体由公民组成。对于公民来说,强烈的个人兴趣是研究公共政策的一个很好的理由,研究公共政策可能有助于公民:

——提高自身的技能。

——做出采取怎样的政治立场和政策支持的决定。

——对民主治理进行评价。

这也可以鼓励学生为将来从事公共政策、法律或政府相关工作做准备。

更有效的参与

在民主国家,公民选择代表表达自己的意愿,但这并不是公民参与的最后一步。公民还可以在政策制定过程中以及对政府行动的回应中畅所欲言。人们通常不会因为缺乏对公共问题、政策、政府决策或政治的了解而受到限制。然而,通过提高他们对这些问题的理解,他们可以更有效地参与并产生更大的影响力。

明智地选择候选人

候选人在竞选期间就一些问题表明立场,他们通过演讲和宣传活动来说服选民支持自己。而关注公共政策的选民可以更好地了解候选人,理解他们的政策理念,并且更愿意对他们做出评价。

2.2 公共政策环境

公共政策受到社会和经济因素的影响。此外,政府结构以及国家和地方的社会文化惯例也是影响政策过程的一些因素。因此,对公共政策环境的了解很重要。接下来我们将探讨公共政策的社会、经济、政治和文化环境。

社会环境

社会环境以多种方式影响政策决策,这一点可以从对城市蔓延、互联网隐私和经济发展等各种现象的争议中看出来。虽然我们可能认为社会环境没有发生变化,但实际上社会环境一直处于动态的、不断变化的状态中。例如由于移民、非传统家庭的增长以及较低或较高的出生率,带来了人口的变化。这些变化改变了公众和政策制定者对从犯罪到医疗保障成本上升等各种问题的看法和行为。目前,老年人是许多国家人口增长最快的人群。他们的需求与其他年龄段的人口需求不同,也更需要政府对他们的关注。随着老年人口的不断增加,政策制定者面临着更为艰难的挑战。尤其是,如何确保养老金体系的偿付能力，让越来越多的人从中获益。过去，国家养老金制度没有面临特别的财务风险，现在政府已经认识到需要找到处理人口老龄化的政治和经济的现实途径。

社会环境的其他影响包括较低的出生率，提前退休带来的不安全性，职业女性的增加，以及增加的移民（移居其他国家，在其他国家工作和学习的人）。所有这些有代表性的因素都可能成为影响政策过程的变量。公民在社区内的相互关系也会影响公共政策制定。

经济环境

经济环境会对政策的实施产生重大影响。经济政策需要考虑通货膨胀和失业因素，而且经济本身也会影响许多其他计划的进展。例如，强劲的经济往往带来失业率下降，进而减少对福利和类似援助计划的需求。随着服务业和信息技术的发展，我国转向透明度更高且监管较少的经济发展，已经并将继续对公共政策产生影响。了解经济环境影响的另一个途径是失业。我国的就业挑战依然存在，尤其是青年、女性和老年群体。

国际劳工组织（ILO）发布了《2020年全球青年就业趋势：技术与未来工作》的报告，该报告分析了2020年全球青年就业趋势，称全球五分之一年轻人因疫情失业，仍在职年轻人的工作时间减少了23％。2019年全球青年失业率为13.6％，大约2.67亿年轻人没有工作或没有接受教育、培训的机会，失业率高于其他群体。疫情进一步加剧了全球年轻人失业问题，疫情造成的经济危机对年轻人特别是年轻妇女的就业打击比其他群体都更迅速、更严重。报告建议各国将采取必要措施保障和促进年轻人就业作为今后疫情应对政策的重要组成部分。

政治环境

从政策制定者的选定到不同群体之间的利益冲突的解决，政治因素影响着公共政策选择的每一步。要了解政治环境，必须了解主要政党的相对实力。小党派的影响，公众的意识形态差异，尤其是公共团体，如坚定的自由主义者和保守主义者，以及有组织的利益集团施加压力的能力也是重要因素。

自由主义者和保守主义者，无论其政党归属如何，往往对政府行为的合法性以及哪些政策可以接受持有截然不同的观点，各方之间在意识形态上的分歧增加了政府在许多政策问题上采取行动的难度。学习公共政策的学生也需要认识到，自由主义者和保守主义者等政治标签并不总是预测具体政策立场的可靠指南。

认为保守主义者总是想要一个较小的政府，而自由主义者有着相反的政治诉求，都过于简单化了。大多数保守主义者反对政府对经济以及工商业决策的更多监管。他们通常也倾向于政府在实现某些社会目标方面发挥强有力的作用，例如政府传统的维持社会秩序的功能。另一方面，自由主义者倾向于要求政府对经济活动进行更多的监管，以保护消费者和工人，或者控制空气污染和水污染。

政党标签可能无法很好地反映在政策问题上的立场，尤其是在政党标签变化如此之快的情况下，一些政客几乎每次选举都与不同政党有关联。在主要政党内部，人们很容易发现成员之间的意识形态上的差异，如韩国的新政治民主联合是一个融合了几种自由主义的合体。

文化环境

政治文化指的是公众持有的价值观、信仰和态度,例如对政府和政治议程的信任或缺乏信任。政治文化不仅因国家而异,而且各个国家内部不同地区之间也可能有所差异。这些文化差异有助于解释国家各省(市)政策上的变化。不同的城市采用不同的发展方式,如一些城市热衷提升市民的福利,而许多其他城市则通过对体育场馆、住房和公园等方面的投资来发展城市。这些不同地区的政策制定者根据其截然不同的政治文化制定相应的政策。

文化冲突会影响公众对政府官员及其行为的判断,并影响政策制定过程。

2.3 市场失灵:公共政策的合理性

在市场经济中,私有部门被期望满足人们的需求,但是在现实中往往不能实现。市场失灵也成为需要政府作为的主要理由。公认的四种市场失灵包括公共物品、外部性、自然垄断和信息不对称,这为公众参与私人事务提供了传统的经济理论基础。

公共物品

公共物品和私人物品这两个术语经常出现在经济学和政策分析的文献中。然而,对这两个术语的不加区别的使用掩盖了各种公共物品之间的重要差异。这些差异包括市场失灵的本质,以及适当的公共政策应对等。在考虑市场失灵时存在一个基本问题,即为什么市场未能有效地对某一特定物品进行分配?提供问题答案最简单的方法是将公共物品与私人物品进行比较。

私人物品具有两种属性:消费的竞争性和所有权的排他性。消费的竞争性意指只要增加一个消费者,就需要减少任何其他消费者对这种产品的消费。纯私人物品具有完全的消费竞争性。所有权的排他性意味着只有一个人或实体可以控制该物品的使用。纯私人物品是具有完全排他性的。例如,鞋子是私人物品,因为当一个人穿着它们时,其他人则不可以穿(消费的竞争性),拥有鞋子的人可以决定谁在任何特定时间穿着它们(所有权的排他性)。

另一方面,纯公共物品要么是消费的非竞争性的,要么是非排他性的,或两者兼而有之。换言之,任何不纯粹的私人物品都可以被视为公共物品。当多于一个人同时从某种物品的供应中获得消费利益时,这种商品的消费就是非竞争性的。例如,警务和国防在消费方面是非竞争性的,因为所有公民都可以从中受益,且不会减少他人的利益——公民享有同样的福利而不会降低既得利益者的利益。如果一个人对某种物品的独占使用是不切实际的,那么该物品是非排他性的。例如,在海洋中广泛分布的鱼类通常在使用中是非排他性的,因为它们在国家内部和国际水域之间自由移动,没有人能够有效地禁止其他人捕捞它们。

外部性

外部性是指行为(可能与生产或消费相关)对一些没有完全同意参与自愿交换的人所产生的影响(正面或负面)(表 2-1)。竞争市场中的价格变化不具有外部性,因为买卖双方通过参与市场进行自愿交易,污染使得住在工厂附近的人受到影响则是负外部性的一个例子。

表 2-1 外部性的例子

	正外部性	负外部性
生产者-生产者	娱乐设施可以吸引更多居住在附近的人到商家购物	有毒化学污染会危害下游商业捕鱼
生产者-消费者	森林为大自然爱好者提供了美景	工厂污染了空气,而对附近居民的肺造成了伤害
消费者-消费者	传染病的免疫接种有助于降低传染给他人的风险	二手烟对不吸烟者的健康的伤害
消费者-生产者	消费者的邮件反馈可以提供有关产品质量的信息	不法进入者通过"走捷径"破坏他人私人财产

自然垄断

当平均成本在需求范围内下降时,就会发生自然垄断,该定义同时考虑成本和需求条件。在自然垄断的情况下,个别厂商可以以比任何其他市场安排(包括竞争)更低的成本生产和出售。尽管自然垄断的基本定义看上去是静态的,但现实世界中的市场是动态的。技术变革可能带来成本的变化,或者高价格可能迫使通过相似的甚至更优质的替代品来替换。其结果可能是消除了自然垄断,一种自然垄断技术被另一种技术所取代。例如,手提电话可以直接替代线路连接的电话,从而与传统电话形成竞争。

信息不对称

信息本身具有公共物品的属性,信息消费是非竞争性的。一个人的消费不会影响到另一个人的消费,问题关键是排他性是否存在。因此,生产和消费本身在公共物品背景下是有意义的。其次,可能存在关于商品特征的信息量在人与人之间变化的情况。例如,市场交易中的买方和卖方掌握的关于所交易的商品的质量信息有所不同。与之相类似,与外部性的生成者和受影响的一方之间的外部性的属性相关的信息的级别也可能存在差异。例如,雇员可能不像雇主那样充分了解工业化学品带来的健康风险。

传统的市场失灵表明可以通过集体行动提高市场效率。市场失灵和对分配目标的不满意是政府干预的必要条件而不是充分条件。我们始终需要考虑干预的成本,因为正如市场以可预测的方式失灵一样,政府失灵也可能会带来政策干预的成本,进而可能带来政策的失误。

思考问题

1. 为什么要学习公共政策？
2. 公共政策研究如何改善政府和民主政治过程？
3. 如何让公共政策研究变得更有意义？
4. 辨析并解释不同的政策环境。
5. 辨析并解释不同类型的市场失灵。
6. 解释公共物品和私人物品以及它们的异同。

词 汇

通货膨胀
失业
公共物品
集体物品
竞争性消费
排他性的所有权
非竞争性消费
非排他性所有权

参考文献

Anderson, James E. 2000. Public Policy Making. 4th ed. Boston: Houghton Mifflin.

Birkland, Thomas A. 2001. An Introduction to the Policy Process: Theories, Concepts, and Models of Public Policy Making. New York: M. E. Sharpe.

Cochran, Clarke E., Mayer, Lawrence C., Carr, T. R., Cayer, N. Joseph, McKenzie, Mark J., and Peck, Laura R. 1999. American Public Policy: An Introduction. 6th ed. New York: St. Martin's Press.

Elazar, Daniel J. 1984. American Federalism: A View from the States. 3rd ed. New York: Harper and Row.

Kraft, Michael E., and Furlong, Scott R. 2004. Public Policy: Politics, Analysis, and Alternatives. Washington, D. C. CQ Press.

Mazmanian, Daniel A., and Kraft, Michael E. eds. 1999. Toward Sustainable Communities: Transition and Transformations in Environmental Policy. Cambridge: MIT Press.

MOEL (Ministry of Employment and Labor). 2015. "Major Statistics," August 10, 2015, from http://www.moel.go.kr/english/pas/pas Major.jsp

Putnam, Robert D. 1995. "Tuning In, Tuning Out: The Strange Disappearance of Social Capital in America." PS: Political Science and Politics, 28 (December): 664-683.

Weimer, L. David and Vining, R. Aidan. 2005. Policy Analysis: Concept and Practice. 4th ed. Upper Saddle River, New Jersey.

Chapter 3
Actors and Their Roles in Public Policy

Summary

Public policy actors refer to individuals, groups or organizations that directly or indirectly participate in the whole process of public policy. Public policy actors not only participate in and influence the formulation of public policies, but also play an active role in the implementation, evaluation and monitoring of public policies. Due to the differences in political systems, economic development and cultural traditions among countries, the components of public policy actors and their modes of action are also different.

Official actors refer to the government in a broad sense, that is, the legislature, the executive and the judiciary. In the modern political system, these three systems respectively hold the legislative, administrative and judicial powers, perform their respective duties, formulate various public policies according to the powers granted by the Constitution, and restrict each other to maintain the balance between the three powers. The party in power in China has a very important position in public policy making. The official actors in China include legislature, executive and judiciary and the party in power.

The players in the public policy process are divided into two main categories:

— Official Actors
— Unofficial Actors

Official actors are involved in public policy by virtue of their statutory or constitutional responsibilities and have the power to make and enforce policies. The legislative, executive, and judicial branches are clearly official institutions. Unofficial actors include those who play a role in the policy process without any explicit legal authority (or duty) to participate, aside from the usual rights of participants in a democracy. Thus, interest

Chapter 3 Actors and Their Roles in Public Policy

groups are involved in politics not because they are sanctioned by law, but because interest groups are an effective way for people to express their collective desires for policy. The media have rights to freedom of the press because of their implicit roles as provider of political information and as watchdogs over government, but the news media have no formal guaranteed role in policy making. Under certain conditions, such as matters of national security or personal privacy, the media can be denied access to policy making information and processes.

3.1 Official Actors and Their Roles

The Legislative Branch

The legislative branch is the subject of a lot of research as political scientists continue to work to understand how the legislature works and why it does what it does. In the People's Republic of China, the National/Local People's Congress and their Standing Committee Members play the role of the national legislature.

What does a legislature do? The very name of this branch suggests lawmaking, and this is assumed to be the primary function of the legislative branch. In fact, though, the constitution gives the National People's Congress broad powers. These include legislative power, decision-making power, appointment and removal power, and oversight power over the national administration.

Legislative power includes the right to propose and decide upon putting up amendments to the constitution. It also includes the right to reject or to agree to and ratify foreign treaties. Finally, it includes the lawmaking function implied in the name legislature that is assumed to be the main job of the National People's Congress.

The Executive Branch

The executive branch is a branch that implements the laws and policies of the state and manages the internal affairs of the state, such as the internal affairs of the country. It grasps the state's administrative power and uses public policies to manage social public affairs. It is the executor of the national will established by the legislature.

The executive branches of China are the State Council and its constituent parts and the local people's governments at various levels. They are the executive branches of the state power and exercise the state administrative power. As the central government, the State Council's power mainly includes administrative legislative power, legal proposal rights, authorized legislative power, administrative management, economic management, social management, and diplomatic management.

Government provide public goods and services that the private sector is unwilling or unable to provide, or people demand from the government rather than the private sector. In general, any good that carries with it major free-rider problems is a public good (see the previous chapter for a discussion of public goods). Public goods are goods that are indivisible (non-rivalrous) and non-exclusive (non-excludable).

The Judiciaries

As an important part of the government, the judiciary is also an important subject of public management. In China, the people's court and the people's procuratorate as judicial branches are an important part of the state power structure. According to the Constitution, the people's court is a judicial branch, the judicial power is exercised independently, and the people's procuratorate is the judicial supervisory authority that exercises the procuratorial power independently.

What role has the court played in public policy making? In a long-accepted practice, most public policy scholars have divided the courts from the other branches under the notion of separating law from politics. Woodrow Wilson (1887) argued that the American Congress makes public policy and the bureaucracy simply carries out that policy without exercising discretion. Thus, the Wilsonian perspective established a distinction between law and politics in relation to policy making. Politics created policy, and the law ensured that such policy was implemented justly.

As Edward Levi (1949) notes, legislatures and executives initiate public policy, while the court reacts to the practical effects of such policies. These choices in determining the outcome of the policies in the real-world act to further draw the courts into policy making.

The Communist Party of China (CPC)

The current political system in China is the system of the integration of People's Congresses. From the perspective of institutional norms, the National People's Congress is the supreme power, exercising the legislative power of the country; from the perspective of government process, the CPC is the leading core of China's government system, controlling the government operation process and leading the formulation of public policies.

As the party in power, the CPC plays a leading role in the process of public policy in China. Political, organizational and ideological leadership reflects the role of the CPC as the party in power in the process of public policy and its way of realization.

3.2 Unofficial Actors and Their Roles

Unofficial actors indicate those actors who are not official because their participation in the policy process is not a function of their duties under the constitution or the law. This is not to say that these actors have no legal rights or standing to participate in the process; rather it means that their mode of participation is not specified in law. These unofficial actors include:
— individual citizens
— interest groups
— political parties
— think tanks and other research organizations
— communications media

Individual Citizens

How do individuals play a role in policy making? If one believes in broad-based political participation as a key feature of democracy, it may be heartening to realize that people have been and can be mobilized. In other words, anyone can be persuaded to care about particular issues. Non-voters and relatively uninterested people can still be sufficiently motivated to join an interest group or take other political actions. People will often act when something threatens, or appears to threaten, their livelihood or their lifestyle, such as when commercial development disturbs their neighborhood, or when government is unresponsive to local needs for education or public safety. While some people will mobilize to try to get the government to do something about a problem, other people will often organize to get the government not to do something—not to approve a new waste dump, not allow obscene material on the Internet, not allow unethical political campaigning. The decision not to approve a program or not to do something is as much a policy as is the decision to act affirmatively to do something, and it is often true that blocking an action is more easily achieved than actually moving a policy idea forward.

Interest Groups

Interest groups are made up of a number of individuals sharing a common purpose. A social movement is created when interest groups come together and create broader demands for change. A social movement involves far more people—although not all at a higher degree of activity than the membership of relevant interest groups. Social movements often involve a coalition of groups with similar goals, while other people support movements without a formal group affiliation. However, there are many ways to categorize interest groups. An institutional interest group, whose members belong to a particular institution can be distinguished from a membership group, whose members have chosen to join. If you are a student at a university, you are a member of an institutional interest group, university students, because you share some interests with your fellow students, such as affordable tuition and quality education. If you join an NGO, you are part of a membership group because you have chosen to join. Interest groups can also be categorized as economic or private interest groups versus public interest groups. Public interest groups, such as environmental groups, seek to create broad benefits for the society not simply for their members.

Political Parties

Political parties serve important functions in the policy process. First, party labels provide voters with cues for voting. Voters know, in general, that the Democratic Party tends to be a more socially liberal party. Second, political parties provide a way for the electorate to transmit rough political preferences to the elected branches of government. Third, political parties help elected officials and their supporters create packages of policy ideas that can be used to appeal to voters and then shaped into legislation. Finally, political parties are crucial to organization of the legislative branch. National and local assemblies elect their leadership along party lines, and committee assignments are made based on party.

Think Tanks and Other Research Organizations

The development of more complex government problems and the need for greater analytical ability have led to the growth of independent research organizations, or what are often called think tanks. Research organizations and think tanks can provide valuable input into the policy process.

Communications Media

The news media are important actors in the policy process. Indeed, the freedom of the press (which today includes radio, television, the Internet, and other new media) provides for a vigorous, activist press that serves as a "watchdog" over government. Journalists and academics have reinforced the belief that the news media play an important role in informing citizens about issues and what their government is doing about them. There are many history examples of the media exposing some of the troubling activities and shortcomings of business and government.

The Korean media were roundly criticized for failing in this watchdog role in the case of the Sewol ferry disaster. In particular, the media came under fire for uncritically accepting inconsistent and inaccurate government announcements while intruding on the privacy of grieving families still in shock over their loss. Newspapers remain important to policy elites and to some mass audiences. many are widely read in policy making circles. In addition, their audience is multiplied over the web. Subway advertising (such as lightboxes, wall stickers, handrails) is another new form of media. Television is the primary source of news for most South Koreans who consume news. The particular importance of the media is in its agenda-setting function. They help elevate some issues to greater public attention.

Discussion Questions

1. What are the differences between official and unofficial actors? Give examples of each.
2. What are the three branches of government? What are their powers in South Korea?
3. What are the two high courts in South Korea? What are their policy roles?
4. What are some ways citizens can get involved in the policy process? How have you participated?
5. Which official and unofficial actors have the most power to set the agenda?
6. What are the advantages of political parties?
7. What are some problems with the exercise of influence by different unofficial actors?

Vocabulary

official actors
unofficial actors
legislative
executive
judicial
National Assembly
individual citizens
interest groups
political parties
think tanks
research organizations
communication media

References

Birkland, Thomas A. 2001. An Introduction to the Policy Process: Theories, Concepts, and Models of Public Policy Making. New York: M. E. Sharpe.

"Constitution of the Republic of South Korea" from http://South Korea. na. go. kr/-res/low_01_read. jsp

Kingdon, John W. 1995. Agendas, Alternatives and Public Policies. 2nd ed. New York: Harper Collins.

Kraft, Michael E. and Furlong, Scott R. 2004. Public Policy: Politics, Analysis, and Alternatives. Washington, D. C. : CQ Press.

Levi, Edward. 1949. An Introduction to Legal Reasoning. Chicago: University of Chicago Press.

Olson, Mancur. 1971. The Logic of Collective Action. Cambridge: Harvard University Press.

"Powers of the National Assembly" from http://South Korea. na. go. kr/ int/aut_01. jsp? leftid=CA

Ripley, Randall and Franklin, Grace. 1991. Congress, the Bureaucracy and Public Policy. 5th ed. Pacific Grove, California: Brooks-Cole.

Wilson, Woodrow. 1887. "The Study of Administration," pp. 22-37, in Shafritz, Jay, Hyde, Alan, and Parkes, Sandra (eds). 2004. Classics of Public Administration, 5thed. Belmont, California: Wadsworth.

Wood, B. Dan. 1991. "Federalism and Policy Responsiveness: The Clean Air Case." Journal of Politics, 53(3): 851-859.

第 3 章

公共政策主体及其权力

公共政策主体是指直接或间接地参与公共政策全过程的个人、团体或组织。公共政策主体不仅参与和影响公共政策的制定，而且在公共政策的执行、评估和监控等环节都发挥着积极的能动作用。由于各国在政治体制、经济发展和文化传统等方面的差异，公共政策主体的构成要素及其作用方式也有所不同。

官方决策者是指广义的政府，即立法机关、行政机关和司法机关。在现代政治体制中，这三大系统分别掌握着立法、行政和司法三种权力，各司其职，依据宪法赋予的权力制定各类公共政策，同时相互制约，保持三种权力之间的平衡。我国执政党在公共政策制定中有着极为重要的地位，我国官方决策者包括立法机关、行政机关、司法机关和执政党。非官方参与者包括利益集团、政治党派、大众传媒、思想库和公民个人等。它们作为体制外的力量，通过游说官方决策者，施加压力，从而影响公共政策过程。

公共政策主体可以分为两类：

——官方决策者

——非官方参与者

官方决策者因其法定或宪法责任参与公共政策过程，并有权制定和执行公共政策。立法机关、行政机关和司法机关显然是官方决策者。非官方参与者同样在政策过程中发挥重要作用，包括除了民主社会中参与者普遍具有的权利外不具有任何法律权威（或责任）的主体。因此，利益集团参与政治不是因为它们法律上的合法性，而是因为利益集团是人们表达集体意愿的有效途径。作为隐性角色——政治信息提供者和政府的监督者——媒体享有新闻自由的权利，但在政策制定方面没有正式的保障。在某些情况下，例如国家安全或个人隐私问题，媒体可能无法获得这些政策制定的相关信息和流程。

3.1 官方决策者及其权力

立法机关

为了了解立法机构的运作方式及运作机理,立法机构成为许多政治学家持续研究的主题。在我国,全国及地方人民代表大会及其常务委员会履行国家立法机构的职能。

立法机关做什么?顾名思义,其主要职责是立法。实际上,全国人民代表大会具有立法权、决定权、任免权和对国家行政部门的监督权等职权。其次,它还包括拒绝或同意和批准对外条约的权力。最后,它包括立法机构中隐含的立法职能,该职能被认为是全国人民代表大会的主要职责。

行政机关

行政机关是贯彻执行国家的法律和政策,管理国家的内政、外交等行政事务的机关,它掌握国家行政权力,运用公共政策对社会公共事务进行管理,是立法机关所确立的国家意志的执行者。

我国的行政机关是国务院及其各部门和地方各级人民政府,它们是国家权力机关的执行机关,行使国家行政权。国务院作为中央人民政府,其权力主要包括行政立法权、法律提案权、授权立法权、行政管理权、经济管理权、社会管理权、外交管理权等。

简单来说,政府机构提供的是私人部门不愿意或没有能力提供的公共物品和服务,或者人们要求由政府而非私人部门提供的产品或服务。总的来说,任何存在重大搭便车问题的产品都是公共物品(参见前一章关于公共物品的讨论)。公共物品是不可分割(非竞争性)和非排他性的产品。

司法机关

司法机关作为政府的重要组成部分,也是公共管理的重要主体之一。在我国,作为司法机关的人民法院和人民检察院是国家权力结构中的重要组成部分。按照宪法规定,人民法院是司法审判机关,独立行使审判权,人民检察院是司法监督机关,独立行使检察权。

法院在公共政策制定中扮演什么角色?在长期的实践中,大多数公共政策学者在法律与政治分离的观念下将法院与其他机构分开。伍德罗·威尔逊(1887)认为,美国国会制定公共政策,官僚机构只是执行该政策而不行使自由裁量权。因此,威尔逊主义的观点在政策制定方面对法律与政治加以区别。政治制定了政策,法律确保这种政策得到公正执行。

正如爱德华·莱维(1949)所指出的那样,立法机构和行政机构制定并执行公共政策,而法院则对这些政策的实际效果做出回应。在确定政策的实际效果时,这些选择有助于进一步将法院纳入政策制定中来。

中国共产党

我国现行的政治体制是人民代表大会制度。从制度规范层面来看,全国人民代表大会是最高权力机关,行使国家的立法权;从政府运作的过程来看,中国共产党是当代中国的领导核心,左右政府运行过程,主导公共政策的制定。

中国共产党作为执政党,在我国公共政策过程中发挥着主导性作用。政治领导、组织领导和思想领导体现了中国共产党作为执政党在公共政策过程中发挥的作用及实现方式。

3.2 非官方参与者及其权力

非官方参与者是指那些非官方的行为主体,他们参与政策过程不是在履行宪法或法律的职责的功能。但这并不意味着这些行为主体没有合法的权利或地位参与这一过程;相反,这仅仅意味着法律没有规定他们的具体的参与模式。非官方参与者包括:
——公民个人
——利益集团
——政党
——智库和其他研究团体
——媒体

公民个人

个人如何在政策制定中发挥作用?如果人们确信广泛的政治参与是民主的一个重要特征,那么令人振奋的是人们已经并且可以行动起来了。换言之,任何人都可以被说服去关心某一特定问题。非选民和相对不感兴趣的人也有足够的动力加入利益集团或采取其他政治行动。当某些事情威胁或似乎威胁到人们的生计来源或生活方式时,例如当商业发展打破了传统的邻里关系,或者政府对当地的教育或公共安全需求没有及时回应时,人们通常会采取行动。有些人会组织起来试图让政府对某个问题采取措施,有些人会组织起来建议政府不做某事——禁止新的废物堆放,禁止互联网上的淫秽物品的传播,禁止不道德的政治竞选活动的发生。不批准某项议案或不做某事的决定与采取行动做某事的决定同样可以是一项政策,只是与实际推进政策的构想相比,阻止行动更容易实现。

利益集团

利益集团由许多有着共同利益和目标的人组成。当利益集团聚集在一起并产生更广泛的变革需求时,就会产生社会运动。社会运动涉及的人数要足够多——尽管并非所有人参与活动的热情一样高。社会运动通常涉及具有相似目标的团体联盟,而其他人则支持没有正式团体联盟的运动。有很多方式可以对利益集团进行分类。特定机构的利益集团的成员也可以同时属于不同的特定的小组成员。如果你是大学生,你可以是不同兴趣小组的成员,你与你的同学可能有一些共同的关注点,例如对可负担的学费和优质教育的提供的关注。利益集团也可以分为经济的或私人利益集团与公共利益集团。私人利益集团,主要是为自己的会员追求利益,如各国的农业利益集团、劳工组织和工商业利益集团等。公共利益集团如环保团体，寻求为社会创造更广泛的利益，而不仅仅是为自己的成员创造利益。

政党

政党在政策过程中发挥重要作用。首先，政党派别为选民提供投票线索。其次，政党为选民提供了一种途径，将大致的政治偏好传递给民选的政府部门。再次，政党帮助民选官员及其支持者制定一揽子政策理念，用以拉拢选民，最终形成立法。最后，政党对组织立法部门至关重要。

智库和其他研究团体

更复杂的政府问题和对更高分析能力的需求带来了独立的研究组织或通常被称为智库的增加。研究团体和智库可以为政策过程提供有价值的信息。

媒体

新闻媒体是政策过程的重要参与者。实际上，作为政府的"监督者"，新闻自由（包括广播、电视、互联网和其他新媒体）为其提供了一个充满活力的新闻媒体环境。记者和学者们坚信这样一种信念，即新闻媒体在向公民提供有关问题的信息以及政府正在采取的措施方面发挥着重要作用。大众传媒通过影响和引导社会舆论，从而影响政府的公共政策议程的设置。

报纸对政策精英和一些大众也很重要。政策制定过程中许多人通过报纸的阅读获取相关信息。此外，网络受众也在成倍增加。在地铁中分发的免费报纸是另一个新的媒介方式。电视也仍是很多人获取新闻的主要来源。媒体的特殊重要性在于其议程设定功能，它们会提出一些问题以引起公众的注意。

思考问题

1. 官方决策者和非官方参与者之间有什么区别？举几个例子。
2. 在我国，官方决策者主要有哪些？它们具体的权力是什么？
3. 公民可以通过哪些方式参与政策议程？
5. 哪些官方决策者和非官方参与者最有权力制定政策议程？
6. 政党有哪些优势？
7. 不同的非官方参与者其影响力存在哪些问题？

词汇

官方决策者
非官方参与者
立法机构

行政机构

司法机构

国民议会

公民

利益集团

政党

智库

研究团体

媒介

参考文献

Birkland，Thomas A. 2001. An Introduction to the Policy Process：Theories, Concepts, and Models of Public Policy Making. New York：M. E. Sharpe.

"Constitution of the Republic of South Korea" from http：//South Korea. na. go. kr/-res/low_01_read. jsp

Kingdon，John W. 1995. Agendas，Alternatives and Public Policies. 2nd ed. New York：Harper Collins.

Kraft，Michael E. and Furlong，Scott R. 2004. Public Policy：Politics, Analysis, and Alternatives. Washington，D. C.：CQ Press.

Levi，Edward. 1949. An Introduction to Legal Reasoning. Chicago：University of Chicago Press.

Olson，Mancur. 1971. The Logic of Collective Action. Cambridge：Harvard University Press.

"Powers of the National Assembly" from http：//South Korea. na. go. kr/ int/aut_01. jsp？leftid＝CA

Ripley，Randall and Franklin，Grace. 1991. Congress，the Bureaucracy and Public Policy. 5th ed. Pacific Grove, California：Brooks-Cole.

Wilson，Woodrow. 1887. "The Study of Administration," pp. 22-37, in Shafritz, Jay, Hyde, Alan, and Parkes, Sandra (eds). 2004. Classics of Public Administration, 5th ed. Belmont, California：Wadsworth.

Wood，B. Dan. 1991. "Federalism and Policy Responsiveness：The Clean Air Case." Journal of Politics, 53(3)：851-859.

陈庆云. 公共政策分析. 北京：北京大学出版社，2006.

陈振明. 政策科学——公共政策分析导论. 2版. 北京：中国人民大学出版社，2003.

宁骚. 公共政策. 北京：高等教育出版社，2000.

谢明. 公共政策分析导论. 5版. 北京：中国人民大学出版社，2022.

张金马. 公共政策分析:概念·过程·方法. 北京:人民出版社,2004.

张国庆. 公共政策分析. 上海:复旦大学出版社,2004.

詹姆斯·E.安德森. 公共政策制定. 5版. 谢明,等,译. 北京:中国人民大学出版社,2009.

托马斯·R.戴伊. 理解公共政策. 12版,谢明,等,译. 北京中国人民大学出版社,2011.

保罗·A.萨巴蒂尔. 政策过程理论. 胡总超,钟开斌,等,译. 北京:生活·读书·新知三联书店,2004.

戴博拉·斯通. 政策悖论. 顾建光,译. 北京:中国人民大学出版社,2006.

Chapter 4
Models and Theories

Summary

Social scientists use models that are abstract representation of how things work. Elite theory says that there is a divide between the few with power and the many without. The few are not typical, have a consensus, and their values are reflected in public policy. Active elites are not greatly influenced by the masses, although there are different elites and different elites' actors. Group theory is associated with pluralism. It says that policy is the product of continuous struggle among organized groups. institutional theory emphasizes the formal, legal aspects of government structure. Rational choice, also known as public choice, uses economics, and mathematical modeling. Public choice is the consideration of individual valuation in pursuit of self-interest. Political systems theory looks at the operation of the political system in term of inputs, environmental demands, policy outputs and outcomes, and feedback. The policy process model looks at the logical sequence of activities affecting policy development, through the stream metaphor, advocacy coalition framework, and punctuated equilibrium.

4.1 Policy Theories

Social scientists use models and theories that are abstract representations of the real world, to understand the way things work. Policy scientists use several different models and theories for policy making. The most common theories are:
— elite theory
— group theory
— institutional theory
— rational choice theory
— political system theory

Elite Theory

Elite theory suggests that a relatively few people in key positions in government, industry, academia, the media, and other institutions control a disproportionate share of the nation's economic and political resources. Policy is dominated by the best educated, wealthiest, and most powerful elites. This is the principal belief of elite theory.

Elite theory emphasizes how the values and preferences of governing elites, which may differ from those of the public at large, affect public policy development. The primary assumption of this theory is that the values and preferences of the general public are less influential in shaping public policy than those of a smaller unrepresentative group of people, or elites. Elite theory suggests that the people are apathetic and ill-informed about public policy, that elites actually shape mass opinion on policy questions more than masses shape elite opinion.

The Elite Model can be summarized briefly as follows:

— Society is divided into the few who have power and the many who do not. Only a small number of people allocate values for society. The masses do not decide public policy.

— The few who govern are not typical of the masses who are governed. Elites are drawn disproportionately from the upper socioeconomic strata of society.

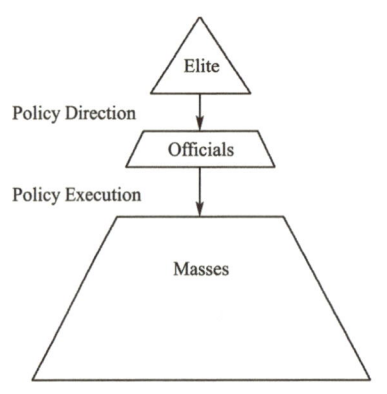

Figure 4-1　The Elite Model

— The movement of non-elites to elite positions must be slow and continuous to maintain stability and avoid revolution. Only non-elites who have accepted the basic elite consensus can be admitted to governing circles.

— Elites share a consensus on behalf of the basic values of the social system and the preservation of the system.

— Public policy does not reflect the demands of masses but rather the prevailing values of the elite. Changes in public policy will be incremental rather than revolutionary.

— Active elites are subject to relatively little direct influence from apathetic masses. Elites influence masses more than masses influence elites.

Policy actors according to elite theory. Policy actors may be economic elites-chaebols, wealthy people, corporate executives, and professionals such as physicians and attorneys. They may be cultural elites, such as actors, filmmakers, recording artists, and media stars. Elected officials constitute an elite, as do other influential policy actors, such as scientists and policy analysts. Elite theory, then, focuses on the role of leaders and leadership in the development of public policy.

A single power elite or establishment is seldom at the center of policy decisions because different policy elites tend to dominate in different policy areas. The role of different elites is particularly evident in sub-governments or issue networks. Elites can sometimes exert their influence through a process of symbolic politics. Policy makers often formulate public policies that appear to meet public needs but serve the material needs of narrow elites. The benefits conveyed to the public are largely symbolic.

A major shortcoming of elite theory is that elite theory has more emphasized the interests of elites, and to some extent deviated from the "public" principle of public policy, and ignored the public interest of the public.

Group Theory

Group theory, closely associated with pluralism, sees public policy as the product of a continuous struggle among organized interest groups. Pluralists believe that power in the political system is widely shared among interest groups, each of which seeks access to the policy making process. Some groups provide countervailing power to others as they lobby legislators and executive officials and appeal to the broader public through issue-advocacy campaigns.

This is one kind of balance that helps to ensure that no single group dominates the policy process. Even so, it is logical to assume that groups with greater financial resources, recognition, prestige, and access to policy makers are likely to have more influence than others. The poor and homeless are not well organized, lack significant political resources, and are poorly represented in the policy process. When people speak of "special interests" influencing government decisions, they are using the concept of group theory.

Group theory tends to exaggerate the role and influence of organized interest groups over policy and to underestimate the leadership of public officials and the considerable discretion they have in making policy choices. Hiding behind every policy decision is a special interest group eager to have its way, but assigning too much power to organized groups over simplifies a more complex policy dynamic. Public officials also frequently use organized interest groups to promote their own political agendas and build support for policy initiatives. The relationship between groups and policy makers is often a subtle, two-way exercise of influence.

According to group theorists, public policy at any given time is the equilibrium reached in a group struggle. This equilibrium is determined by the relative influence of any interest group. Changes in the relative influence of interest groups can be expected to result in changes in public policy. Policy will move in the direction desired by the groups gaining influence and away from the desires of groups losing influence. The influence of groups is determined by their numbers, wealth, organizational strength, leadership, access to decision makers, and internal cohesion.

The whole interest group system is held together as part of the political system in equilibrium by several forces. First, there is a large group that supports the constitutional system and the prevailing rules of the game. This group is not always visible but can be activated to administer overwhelming rebuke to any group that attacks the system and threatens to destroy the equilibrium.

Second, overlapping group membership helps to maintain the equilibrium by preventing any one group from moving too far from prevailing values. Individuals who belong to any one group also belong to other groups, and this fact moderates the demands of groups who must avoid offending their members who have other group affiliations.

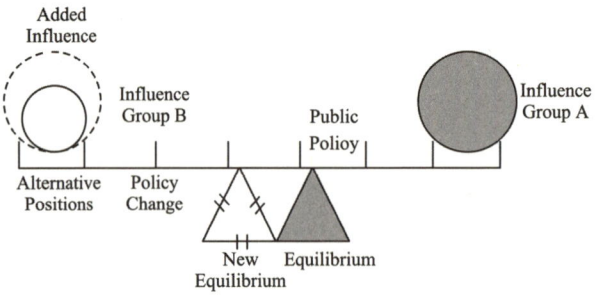

Figure 4-2 The Group Model

Finally, the balance resulting from group competition also helps to maintain equilibrium in the system. No single group constitutes an absolute majority on all questions. The power of each group is checked by the power of competing groups. Countervailing centers of power function to check the influence of any single group and protect individuals from exploitation.

Institutional Theory

Institutional theory emphasizes the formal and legal aspects of government structure. Institutional models look at the way governments are arranged, their legal powers, and their rules and procedures. Those rules include basic characteristics such as the degree of access to decision making provided to the public, the availability of information from government agencies, and the sharing of authority between national and local governments. The term institution refers to both the organizations and the rules used to structure patterns of interaction within and across organizations. Many kinds of institutions can influence public policy: markets, individual firms/corporations/-chaebol,-national and local governments, voluntary associations such as political parties and interest groups.

Rational Choice Theory

Rational choice theory, also called public choice, draws heavily on economics, especially microeconomic theory, and often uses elaborate mathematical modeling. Rational choice theory has been widely applied to questions of public policy. Analysts have used this theory to explain actions as diverse as individual voter decisions and the calculations of public officials as they face national security threats. It assumes that individuals are rational actors when making decisions.

Rational choice theory suggests that analysts consider what individuals' value, how they perceive a given situation, the information they have about it, various uncertainties that might affect the outcome, and how a particular context or the expectations of others (rules and norms) might affect their actions. This theory tries to explain public policy in terms of the actions of individual self-interested policy actors, whether they are voters, corporate lobbyists, agency officials, or legislators. Public choice theory forces people to think about the core motivation of individual political actors and the consequences of such motivations for public policy and the larger political system.

This provides useful insights into political behavior that can affect the design of public policies. It is especially useful to formulate predictions of how agency officials and those who are the objects or targets of the policy are likely to respond to policy initiatives.

In order to select a rational policy, policy makers must: (1) know society's value preferences and their relative weights; (2) know all the policy alternatives available; (3) know all the consequences of each policy alternative; (4) calculate the ratio of benefits to costs for each policy alternative; and (5) select the most efficient policy alternative. This rationality assumes that the value preferences of society as a whole can be known and weighed. It is not enough to know and weigh the values of some groups and not others. There must be a complete understanding of societal values.

Rational policy making also requires information about alternate policies. It also requires the intelligence to calculate the ratio of costs to benefits accurately. Finally, rational policy making requires a decision-making system that facilitates rationality in policy formation. Critics of public choice theory argue that individuals do not always pursue their own self-interest. The critics also question the narrow and rigid assumptions that underlie the theory. In addition, there are many barriers to rational decision making. Several important obstacles to rational policy making can be identified:

— No societal benefits are really agreed on-just benefits to specific groups and individuals, many of which are conflicting.

— Many conflicting benefits and costs cannot be compared or weighted. For example, it is impossible to compare or weight the value of individual dignity against a tax increase.

— Policy makers are not motivated to make decisions on the basis of societal goals but instead try to maximize their own rewards, such as power, status, and money.

— Policy makers are not motivated to maximize net social gain but merely to satisfy demands for progress. They do not search until they find "theone best way." Instead, they halt their search when they find an alternative that will work.

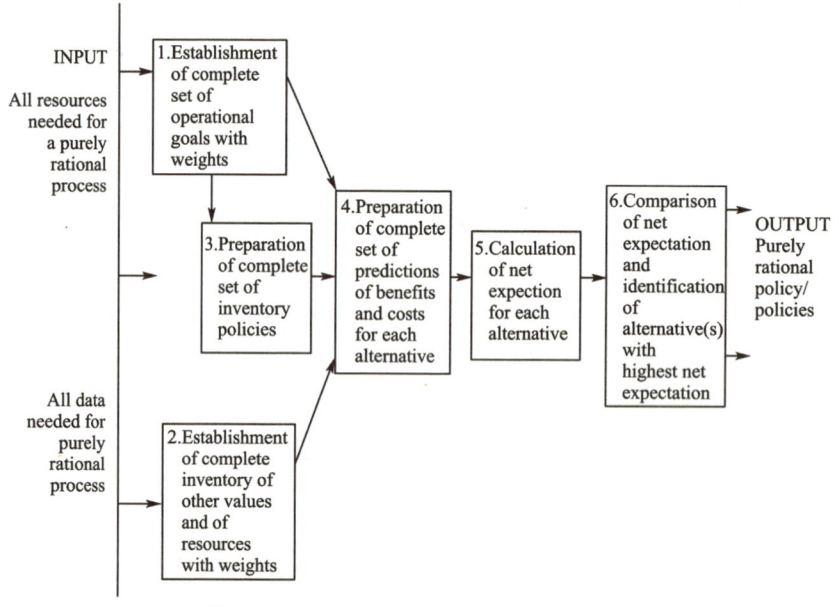

Figure 4-3 A Rational Decision Model System

— Large investments in existing programs and policies (sunk costs) prevent policy makers from reconsidering alternatives now closed by previous decisions.

— There are innumerable barriers to collecting of the all information required to know all possible policy alternatives and the consequences of each. These include the cost of gathering information, the availability of information, and the time involved in data collection.

— Neither the predictive capacities of the social and behavioral sciences nor those of the physical and biological sciences are sufficiently advanced to enable policy makers to understand the full benefits or costs of each pol icy alternative.

— Policy makers do not have sufficient intelligence to calculate costs and benefits accurately even with the most advanced computerized analytical techniques. This is especially true when a large number of diverse political, social, economic, and cultural values are at stake.

— Uncertainty about the consequences of various policy alternatives compels policy makers to stick as closely as possible to previous policies to reduce the likelihood of unanticipated or disturbing consequences.

— The segmented nature of policy in large bureaucracies makes it difficult to coordinate decisions so that the input of all the various specialists is brought to bear at the point of making the final decision.

Political System Theory

Political system theory stresses the way the political system (the institutions and activities of government) responds to demands that arise from its environment, such as public opinion and interest group pressures. This theory emphasizes the larger social, economic, and cultural context in which political decisions and policy choices are made. Political system theory is a more formal way of thinking about the interrelationships between institutions and policy actors as well as the role of the larger environment. System theory also supplies some useful terms, such as *input*, *demands*, *support*, *policy outputs*, *policy outcomes*, and *feedback*.

Input into the political system comes from demands and support. Demands are the claims individuals and groups seeking to further their interests and values make on the political system. System theory is a simple way of portraying how governments respond to societal demands. It proposes an almost biological model of politics. It also suggests that governments and public officials react to the political climate like organisms respond to environmental stimuli (Katz and Kahn, 1966).

System theory portrays public policy as an output of the political system. The concept of "system" implies an identifiable set of institutions and activities in society that function to transform demands into authoritative decisions requiring the support of the whole society. The concept of system also implies that elements of the system are interrelated, that the system can respond to forces in its environment, and that it will do so to preserve itself. Inputs are received into the political system in the form of both demands and support. Support is when individuals or groups accept the outcome of elections, obey the laws, pay their taxes, and generally conform to policy decisions. Any system also absorbs a variety of demands, some of which conflict with each another.

The system must arrange and enforce settlements on the parties concerned to transform these demands into outputs (public policies). It is recognized that outputs (public policies) may have a modifying effect on the environment and the demands arising from it, and they may also have an effect on the character of the political system. The system preserves itself by: (1) producing reasonably satisfying outputs; (2) relying on deeply-rooted attachments to the system itself; and (3) using or threatening to use force.

The value of the systems model to policy analysis lies in the questions that it poses:

— What are the significant dimensions of the environment that generate demands on the political system?

— What are the characteristics of the political system that enable it to change demands into policy to preserve itself over time?

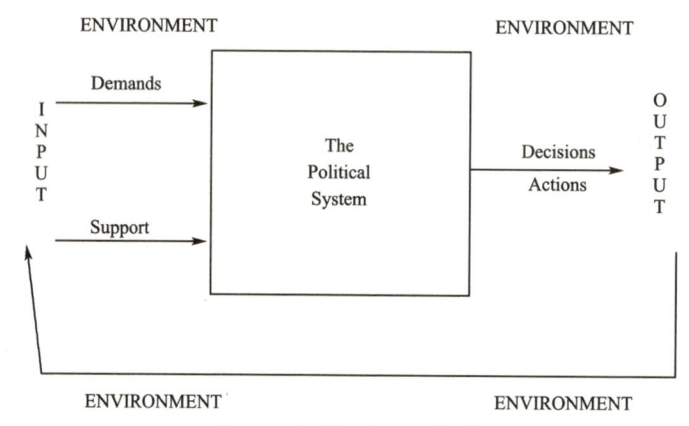

Figure 4-4 The System Model

Each theory offers a different perspective on the principle determinants of decision making within government. Every theory suggests a distinct conceptual framework through which to view politics and public policy, highlighting particular features of the political and institutional landscape, though none is completely satisfactory by itself.

4.2 The Policy Process Model

A policy process model posits a logical sequence of activities affecting the development of public policies. It can also be helpful for understanding the flow of events and decisions in different cultures and institutional settings. The language and concepts are general enough to fit any political system and its policy process. Sometimes the phrase policy cycle is used to make clear that the process is cyclical or continuous rather than a one-time set of actions.

Any policy process model captures important aspects of policy making that correspond to political reality. Here are three prominent recent models of the policy process:

— John Kingdon's "Streams metaphor"

— Paul Sabatier's "Advocacy coalition framework"

— Frank Baumgartner and Bryan Jones's "Punctuated equilibrium"

Streams Metaphor

Kingdon (1995) argues that issues gain agenda status and alternative solutions are selected when elements of three "streams" come together. Each of these three streams is associated with various individuals, groups, agencies, and institutions that are involved in the policy-making process. These three steams are (1) the **politics stream** that encompasses the state of politics and public opinion as well as (2) **the policy stream**, containing the potential solutions to a problem and (3) the **problem stream**, encompassing the attributes of a problem (Is it getting better or worse? Does it have a focusing event? Can it be solved with the alternatives available in the policy stream?).

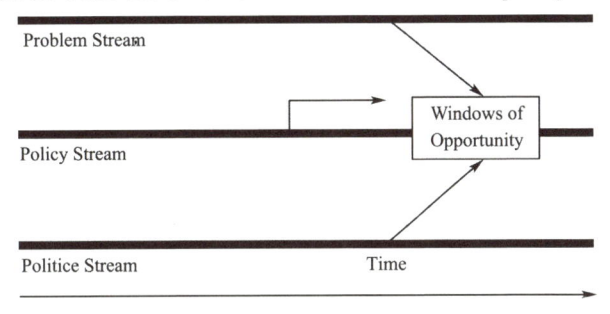

Figure 4-5 The Streams Metaphor

The Advocacy Coalition Framework (ACF)

Sabatier's Advocacy Coalition Framework(ACF) (Sabatier, 1988) is an important model of the policy process, based on the idea that interest groups are organized into policy communities within a policy domain. The most recent version of this framework is depicted in Figure 4-8. In the ACF two to four advocacy coalitions typically form in a particular policy domain when groups come together around a shared set of core values and beliefs. These groups engage in policy debates, competing and compromising over solutions based on their core values and beliefs. Competition between coalitions is mediated by policy brokers who have a stake in resolving the problem, either on substantive grounds or because of their interest in maintaining political harmony in the system. These brokers are more likely to succeed when they can develop compromises that do not threaten either an advocacy coalition's core beliefs or values. Policy change is much less likely if polarization of advocacy coalitions is so great that there is no room on the periphery of the groups' belief systems where a compromise can be found.

Punctuated Equilibrium

Baumgartner and Jones (1993) argue that the balance of political power between groups of interests remains relatively stable over long periods of time punctuated by relatively sudden shifts in public understanding of problems and in the balance of power between the groups seeking to fight entrenched interests.

Key to their theory of equilibrium is the idea of the policy monopoly. This corresponds with the idea of policy subsystems. A policy monopoly is a fairly concentrated, closed system of the most important policy making actors. Such a monopoly has an interest in keeping policy making closed, because a closed system benefits the interests of those in the monopoly and keeps policymaking under some measure of control. Under the iron triangle notion of policy making, this system remains closed and stable for a long time.

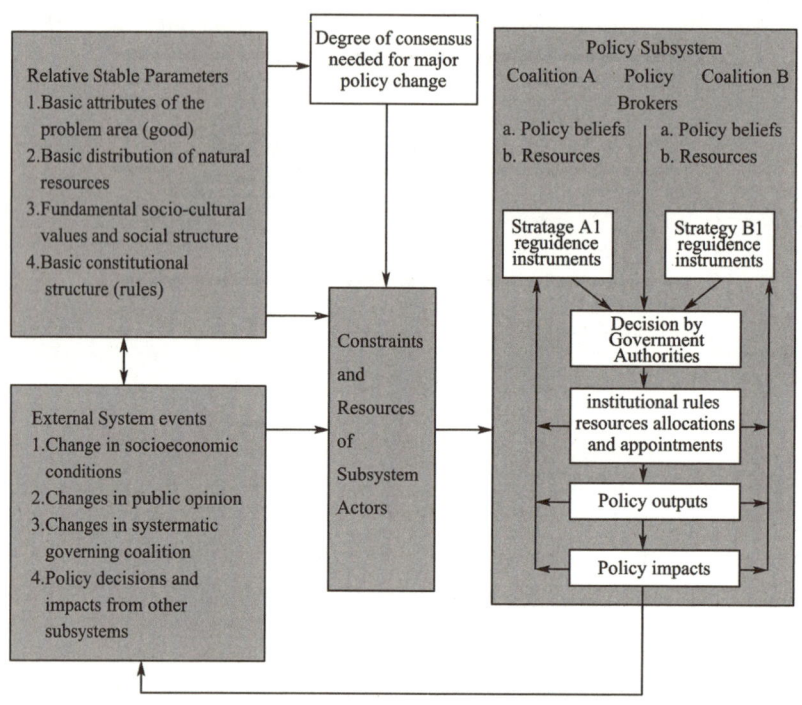

Figure 4-6 Advocacy Coalition Framework(ACF)

Baumgartner and Jones argue that there are instances when the "equilibrium" maintained by policy monopolies breaks down. At such times greater and more critical attention to issues follows and rapid policy change is the result. Policy monopolies themselves can then break down or at least become more open issue networks.

Discussion Questions

1. What are the five policy theories?
2. Who are the main actors in the different theories? Who plays those roles in South Korea?
3. Which theory do you think best describes the policy process in China? Why do you think so?
4. What are the three policy streams? Give an example of a window of opportunity.
5. What is an example of an advocacy coalition framework?
6. Give an example of a breakdown of a policy equilibrium in South Korea. What happened to the policy monopoly?

Chapter 4 Models and Theories

Vocabularies

elite theory
group theory
institutional theory
rational choice theory
political system theory
cost/benefit analysis
sunk costs
input
demands
support
policy outputs
policy outcomes
feedback
streams metaphor
politics stream
policy stream
problem stream
window of opportunity
advocacy coalition
framework
punctuated equilibrium
policy monopoly

References

Baumgartner, Frank, and Jones, Bryan D. 1993. Agendas and Instability in American Politics. Chicago: University of Chicago Press.

Birkland, Thomas A. 2001. An Introduction to the Policy Process. New York: M. E. Sharpe.

Cochran, Clarke E., Mayer, Lawrence C., Carr, T. R., Cayer, N. Joseph, McKenzie, Mark J., and Peck, Laura R. 1999. American Public Policy: An Introduction. 6th ed. New York: St. Martin's Press.

Dye, R. Thomas. 1995. Understanding Public Policy. 8th ed. Englewood Cliffs, New Jersey: Prentice Hall.

Katz, Daniel and Kahn, Robert L. 1966. "Organizations and the System Concept." pp. 206-216, in Shafritz, Jay, Hyde, Alan, and Parkes, Sandra (eds). 2004. Classics of Public Administration, 5th ed. Belmont, California: Wadsworth.

Kingdon, John W. 1995. Agendas, Alternatives and Public Policies. 2nd ed. New York: Harper Collins.

Kraft, Michael E. and Furlong, Scott R. 2004. Public Policy: Politics, Analysis, and Alternatives. Washington, D.C. CQ Press.

Lindblom, E. Charles. 1959. "The Science of Muddling Through." Public Administration Review, 19 (Spring): 79-88.

Sabatier, Paul A. 1988. "An Advocacy Coalition Framework of Policy Change and the Role of Policy-Oriented Learning Therein." Policy Sciences, 21: 129-168.

Wildavsky, Aaron. 1964. The Politics of the Budgetary Process. Boston: Little, Brown.

第 4 章

政策执行理论与模型

社会学家习惯用作为现实世界抽象表征的模型理解事务如何运作。精英理论认为，在有权的少数人和无权的多数人之间存在着意见分歧。少数非典型的达成共识的人，其价值观可以反映在公共政策中。虽然有不同的精英和不同的精英群体，但活跃的精英们很大程度上不受大众的影响。集团理论与多元主义相关，都认为政策是有组织的集团之间持续斗争的产物。制度理论强调政府机构的正式性和法律因素。理性决策理论（也被称为公共选择理论）使用经济和数学模型规划政策。公共选择是为追求自身利益而对个人价值的评估。政治系统理论从投入、环境需求、政策产出和结果以及反馈的角度来看待政治系统的运作。政策过程模型通过多源流模型，倡导联盟框架和间断性均衡框架着眼于影响政策发展活动的逻辑顺序。

4.1 政策执行理论

社会学家使用作为现实世界抽象表征的模型和理论来理解事物的运作方式。政策学者使用几种不同的模型和理论来制定政策。最常见的理论是：
——精英理论
——集团理论
——制度理论
——理性决策理论
——政治系统理论

精英理论

精英理论认为,在政府、商界、学界、媒体和其他机构中担任重要职位的人虽然相对较少,却控制着国民经济和政治资源。精英理论的主要观点在于公共政策由少数受过良好教育的、富有的、强大的精英人物决定。

由于精英可能与大众的价值观和偏好不同,故而精英理论强调对精英的价值观和偏好的管理如何影响公共政策的发展。其主要假设为,大众的价值观和偏好在塑造公共政策方面的影响力要小于少部分不具代表性的人群或精英阶层。精英理论认为,大众对公共政策态度冷漠和缺乏了解,精英实际上在政治问题上塑造大众的意见,而不是大众塑造精英的意见。

精英模型(图4-1)可简要归纳如下:

——社会分为有权的少数和无权的多数。掌握社会收益分配的只是少数人,国家政策不是由大众决定的。

——少数的统治者并不代表多数的被统治者。精英大多来自社会经济的上等阶层。

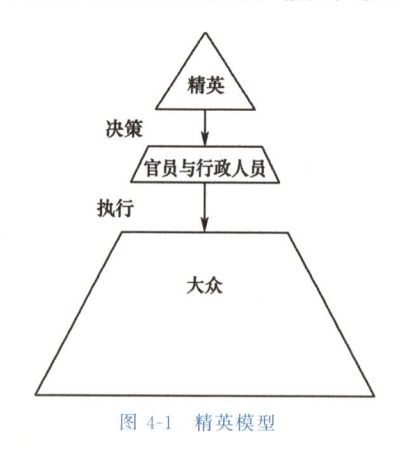

图 4-1 精英模型

——为了确保社会稳定并避免发生革命,非精英阶层上升到精英阶层的过程必须是缓慢而又不间断的。非精英只有接受精英阶层的价值观,才能进入统治精英的行列。

——精英们在维护社会制度的基本准则和现有社会制度等方面意见一致。

——国家的政策并不反映大众的要求,而只反映盛行于精英中的价值观。公共政策的变化是渐进性的,而不是革命性的。

——相对说来,行动积极的精英不会受态度冷漠的大众的直接影响,精英对大众的影响多于民众对精英的影响。

精英理论的政策主体

政策主体可能是经济精英——财阀、富人、企业高管以及医生和律师等专业人士。也可能是文化精英,如演员、电影制作人、录音艺术家和媒体明星。选举产生的官员和其他有影响力的政策参与者如科学家和政策分析家都是精英。因此,精英理论关注领导者和领导力在公共政策制定中的作用。

单一的权力精英很少处于政策决策的中心,因为不同的政策精英往往在不同的政策领域占主导地位,不同精英的作用在地方政府或问题网络中尤为明显。精英有时可以通过象征性的政治议程施加自己的影响。政策制定者制定公共政策看似满足公众需求,但实际上仅服务于狭隘的精英的物质需求,传递给公众的利益在很大程度上只是象征性的。

精英理论的一个主要缺陷在于,过多地强调了少数的精英阶层的利益,一定程度上偏离了公共政策的"公共"原则,漠视了公众的公共利益。

集团理论

与多元主义密切相关的集团理论认为公共政策是有组织的利益集团之间持续斗争的产物。多元主义者认为,政治体系中的权力在利益集团中被广泛分享,每个利益集团都在寻求政策制定过程的路径。当游说立法者和行政官员的时候,一些团体向其他人提供补偿,并通过对问题的宣传吸引更广泛的公众。

这是一种致力于追求没有任何一个群体可以支配政策流程的平衡。即便如此,合乎逻辑的假设是拥有更多财政资源、认可、声望和路径的政策制定者很可能比其他群体拥有更大的影响力。穷人和无家可归者没有良好的组织,缺乏重要的政治资源,在政策过程中无足轻重。当人们谈到影响政府决策的"特殊利益"时,他们就是在使用集团理论的概念。

集团理论倾向于夸大有组织的利益集团对政策的作用和影响,并低估公职人员的领导力以及他们在做出政策选择方面的相当大的自由裁量权。隐藏在每个政策决策背后的是一个渴望走上正轨的特殊利益集团,但为有组织的集团分配过多的权力则会过度简化复杂的政策动态。政府官员经常会利用有组织的利益集团来宣传自己的政治议程,并为其政策举措寻求支持。集团和政策制定者之间的关系往往是微妙的和双向影响的。

根据集团理论家的观点,任何时候的公共政策都是群体斗争中实现的一种均衡(图4-2)。这种均衡取决于任何利益集团间的相互影响。利益集团间相互影响力的变化可能会导致公共政策的变化。政策将朝着获得更多影响力的集团所希望的方向发展,并远离失去影响力的集团。集团的影响力取决于成员的数量、财富、组织性、领导力以及决策者的路径和内部的凝聚力。

整个利益集团系统(政治系统本身)由力量维持着均衡。第一种力量是存在一个巨大的维护宪政体制和占主导地位的游戏规则的团体。这个团体并不总是显现的,但是一旦有任何集团破坏游戏规则,威胁集团间的平衡,这个潜在的团体就会被激活,以维持系统的平衡。

第二种力量是集团间成员资格的相互重叠,可以防止任何团体都不会偏离社会的主流价值观,从而维持系统的平衡。个体既属于这个集团,同时又属于其他集团,这种力量可以缓和不同集团之间的冲突,从而避免侵犯集团中的那些与其他集团有联系的成员。

最后,集团竞争形成的制约也有助于维持系统的平衡。在所有问题上,没有任何一个集团构成压倒性多数。每一个集团的权力都受到竞争团体的制约。"相互制衡"的圆圈里能够制约任何单一集团的影响,并保护个体权利不受剥夺。

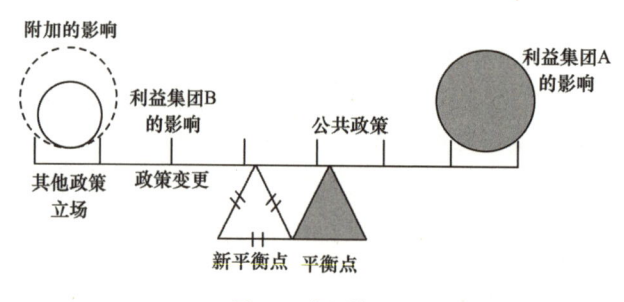

图 4-2 集团模型

制度理论

制度理论强调政府结构的正式和法律因素，着眼于政府的安排方式、法律权力以及规则和程序。这些规则包括一些共同的特征，例如向公众提供决策的机会，政府机构提供的信息以及中央和地方政府之间的权力共享。制度一词指用于组织内部和跨组织交互模式的组织和规则。许多机构可以影响公共政策：市场、私人公司、财阀、中央和地方政府、政党和利益集团等。

理性决策理论

理性决策理论也称为公共选择理论，在很大程度上依赖于经济学，特别是微观经济理论，并且经常使用精细的数学建模。理性决策理论已广泛应用于公共政策分析领域，分析人员利用这一理论来解释各种行为，如个体的选举决策和政府官员在面临国家安全威胁时的权衡，它假设个人在做决定时是理性的行动者。

理性决策理论认为，分析人员会考虑个人的价值，个体如何看待给定的特定情形，个体已有的信息可能影响结果的各种不确定性，以及特定背景或他人的期望（规则和规范）如何影响个体的行为。该理论试图从个体（政策主体）自利的行为来解释公共政策，无论他们是选民、集团游说者、政府官员还是立法者。公共选择理论迫使人们思考个体政治主体的核心动机以及这种动机对公共政策和政治制度的影响，这为可能影响公共政策设计的政治行为提供了有用的见解，尤其是对政府官员以及作为政策对象或目标的人员如何应对政策举措进行预测。

为了选择合理的政策，政策制定者必须：(1)了解社会的价值偏好及其相对权重；(2)了解所有可用的政策选择；(3)了解每种政策选择的所有可能后果；(4)计算每种政策选择的收益与成本的比率；(5)选择最有效的政策选择。这种理性假定整个社会的价值偏好可以被了解和权衡。即仅仅了解和权衡某些群体的价值观是不够的，必须完全理解整个社会的价值观。

理性的政策制定还需要相关备选政策方案的信息。它还需要准确地计算成本与收益的比率的智慧。最后，理性的政策制定需要一个促进政策形成合理性的决策系统。如图 4-3 所示。

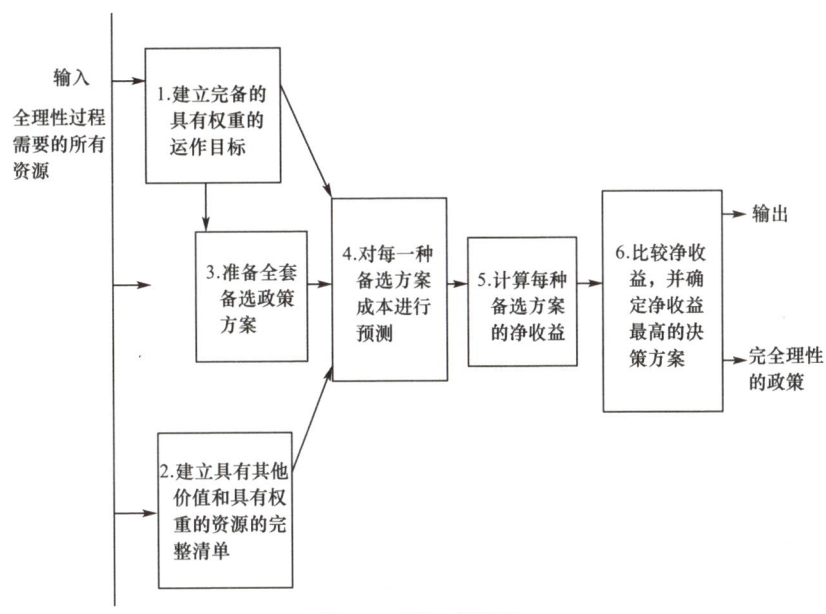

图 4-3　理性决策模型

公共选择理论的批评者认为，个人并不总是追求自己的私利，还质疑该理论背后的狭隘和僵化的假设。此外，理性决策存在许多局限性：

——没有对社会利益达成共识——仅仅对特定群体和个人有益，其中许多是相互矛盾的。

——许多相互冲突的利益和成本无法进行比较或加权。例如，不可能将个人尊严的价值与税收增加进行比较或加权。

——政策制定者没有动力根据社会目标做出决策，而是试图最大化自己的回报，例如权力、地位、连任和金钱。

——一些政策制定者没有动力使社会收益最大化，而只是为了满足进展的需求。他们会一直寻找，直到发现"最好的方法"，相反，当他们找到可行的替代方案时，他们会停止寻找。

——对现有方案和政策的大量投资（沉没成本）使政策制定者无法重新考虑因先前决定而放弃的替代方案。

——收集并了解所有可能的政策选择所需的全部信息以及每种政策选择的后果都存在无数障碍，其中包括收集信息的成本、信息的可用性以及数据收集所需要的时间。

——社会和行为科学的预测能力以及物理和生物科学的预测能力都不够先进，以使决策者能够评估每种政策选择的全部利益或成本。

——即使使用最先进的计算机分析技术，政策制定者也没有足够的智慧来准确计算成本和收益，尤其涉及大量不同的政治、社会、经济和文化价值时更是如此。

——关于各种政策选择的后果的不确定性迫使政策制定者尽可能地密切关注以前的政策，以减少意外或令人不安的后果的可能性。

——在大型官僚机构中，政策的阶段性使得决策难以协调，所以在做出最终决策时需要考虑所有专家的意见。

政治系统理论

政治系统理论强调政治系统(制度和政府的活动)对其环境所产生的需求(例如公众舆论和来自利益集团的压力)做出的反应，该理论强调制定政治决策和政策选择更大的社会、经济和文化背景。政治系统理论是一种更为正规的思考制度与政策参与者之间的相互关系以及大环境的作用思维方式。系统理论还提供了一些有用的术语，例如输入、需求、支持、政策输出、政策结果和反馈。

对政治制度的输入来自需求和支持。需求是个人和团体在政治制度上寻求进一步发展其利益和价值观的主张。系统理论是描述政府如何应对社会需求的简单方法，它提出了一种近乎生物学的政治模型，表明政府和政府官员对政治气候作出反应，就像有机体对自然环境刺激的反应一样(卡茨和卡恩，1966)。

系统理论将公共政策描述为政治系统的输出。"系统"的概念意味着一系列可识别的社会制度和活动，其功能是将需求转化为需要整个社会支持的权威决策。系统的概念也意味着系统的要素间是相互关联的，系统可以对环境中的力量做出反应，并且这样也可以保护自己。输入以需求和支持的形式被纳入到政治系统中。支持是指个人或团体接受选举结果，遵守法律，缴纳税款，并且通常符合政策决定。任何系统都会输入各种需求，但其中也有一些需求是相互冲突的。

该系统必须安排并执行相关方可接受的解决方案，将这些要求转化为输出(公共政策)。人们认识到，输出(公共政策)可能改变环境及其产生的需求，也可能对政治系统的性质产生影响。该系统通过以下方式保持自身稳定：(1)产生合理满意的输出；(2)依靠对系统本身的根深蒂固的依附；(3)使用或威胁使用武力。

系统模型对政策分析的价值在于它所带来的思考：

——对政治系统产生需求的环境的重要维度是什么？

——政治系统的哪些特点让它能够将需求转变为政策并随着时间的推移而保持自身？

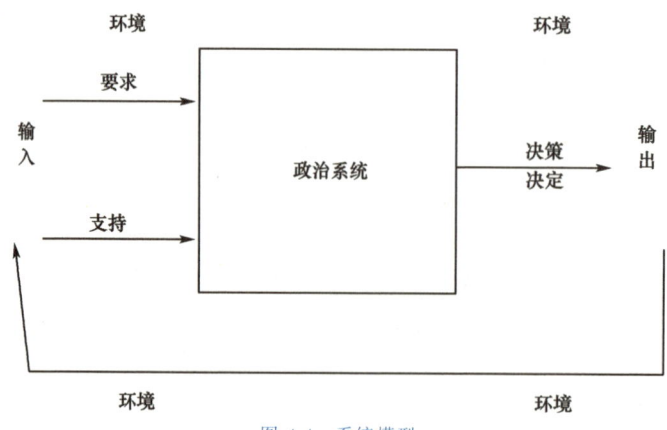

图 4-4 系统模型

每种理论都为政府内部决策的主要决定因素提供了不同的视角,都提出了一个独特的概念框架,尽管没有一个是完全令人满意的,但是通过它们可以观察政治和公共政策,突出政治和制度领域的特征。

4.2 政策执行的模型

政策过程模型是指对政策执行过程中牵涉的重大因素分析政策执行的模型。政策过程模型假定了影响公共政策制定的活动的逻辑顺序,有助于理解不同文化和制度中的事件和决策流程。语言和概念是通用的并足以适应任何政治制度及其政策过程。有时,"政策周期"用于表明流程是周期性的或连续的,而不是一次性的行动。

任何政策过程模型都可以捕捉与政治现实相对应的政策制定的重要方面。以下是政策过程的三个主要模型:
——约翰·W.金登的多源流模型(溪流隐喻)
——保罗·A.萨巴蒂尔的"倡导联盟框架"
——弗兰克·鲍姆加特纳和布赖恩·琼斯的"间断-均衡"框架

多源流模型

Kingdon(1995)认为,当三个"流"的元素汇集在一起时,问题会进入议程状态,并且会选择替代的解决方案。这三个流中的每一个都与参与决策过程的个人、团体、机构和制度相关联。这三个流是:(1)包含政治和公众舆论状况的政治流;(2)包含问题的潜在解决方案的政策流;(3)包含问题属性的问题流(它变得越来越好吗?它是否有焦点事件?是否可以使用政策流中可用的替代方案来解决?)图4-5表明了流的隐喻。

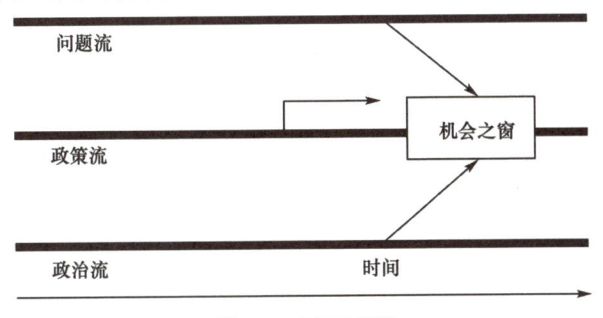

图 4-5 多源流模型

倡导联盟框架(ACF)

萨巴蒂尔的"倡导联盟框架"(萨巴蒂尔,1988)是政策过程的一个重要模型,基于利益集团在政策领域内构建政策社区的理念。该框架的最新版本如图4-6所示。在ACF中,当群体围绕一组共同的核心价值观和信念聚集在一起时,通常会在特定的政策领域形成两到四个支持联盟。这些联盟参与政策辩论,基于其核心价值观和信仰在解决方案上进行竞争和妥协。联盟之间的竞争由与解决问题有利害关系的政策中间人进行调解,无论是出于实质性原因,还是出于维护体制内政治和谐的利益的需求。当这些中间人能够制定出既不威胁倡导联盟核心信念也不威胁其价值观的妥协方案时,他们更有可能取得成功。如果倡导联盟中的两极分化非常大,以至于在这些团体的信仰体系边缘没有任何妥协的空间,政策变迁的可能性就大大降低。

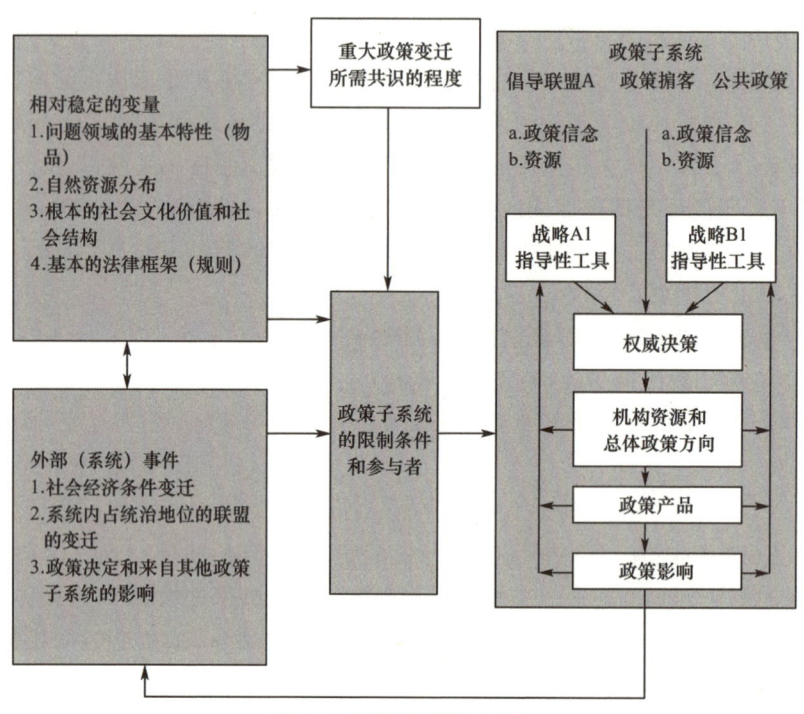

图 4-6　倡导联盟框架(ACF)

间断性均衡框架

鲍姆加特纳和琼斯(1993)认为,从长期来看,利益集团政治权力的平衡相对稳定。而一旦公众对公共性的理解突然有了变化,或者集团寻求打破已有的利益格局,这种平衡就会被打破。

理解间断均衡的关键在于理解政策垄断的作用。政策垄断是指在政策制定中,由最重要的行动者(统治集团或联盟)所组成的集中的、封闭的体系。他们倾向于将政策制定封闭起来,因为封闭的系统有利于垄断者的利益,并在一定程度上保持政策制定的可控性。在政策制定的铁三角概念下,该系统长期保持封闭和稳定。

鲍姆加特纳和琼斯认为,政策垄断所维持的"均衡"有时会被打破。在这种情况下,随之而来的是对问题的更多和更关键的关注,结果带来快速的政策变迁。政策垄断本身可以被打破或至少成为更开放的问题网络。

思考问题

1. 五种政策理论是什么？
2. 不同理论中主要的政策主体都包括什么？在我国由谁充当这些主体？
3. 你认为哪种理论最能描述我国的政策过程？为什么？
4. 什么是三个政策流？举一个机会之窗的例子。
5. 请列举一个支持联盟框架的例子。
6. 请列举一个间断性均衡框架的例子。政策垄断会带来什么？

词 汇

精英理论
集团理论
制度理论
理性决策理论
政治制度理论
成本效益分析
沉没成本
政策输入
需求
支持
政策输出
政策成效
反馈
溪流隐喻
政治流
政策流
问题流
机会之窗
倡导联盟
架构
间断性均衡框架
政策垄断

参考文献

Baumgartner，Frank，and Jones，Bryan D. 1993．Agendas and Instability in American Politics．Chicago：University of Chicago Press．

Birkland，Thomas A. 2001．An Introduction to the Policy Process．New York：M.

E. Sharpe.

Cochran, Clarke E., Mayer, Lawrence C., Carr, T. R., Cayer, N. Joseph, McKenzie, Mark J., and Peck, Laura R. 1999. American Public Policy: An Introduction. 6th ed. New York: St. Martin's Press.

"Consumer Groups Urge Lotte Boycott." 2015. English Chosun, August 5, 2015 from http://english.chosun.com/site/data/html_dir/2015/08/05/2015080501247.html

Dye, R. Thomas. 1995. Understanding Public Policy. 8th ed. Englewood Cliffs, New Jersey: Prentice Hall.

Katz, Daniel and Kahn, Robert L. 1966. "Organizations and the System Concept." pp. 206-216, in Shafritz, Jay, Hyde, Alan, and Parkes, Sandra (eds). 2004. Classics of Public Administration, 5th ed. Belmont, California: Wadsworth.

Kingdon, John W. 1995. Agendas, Alternatives and Public Policies. 2nd ed. New York: Harper Collins.

Kraft, Michael E. and Furlong, Scott R. 2004. Public Policy: Politics, Analysis, and Alternatives. Washington, D.C. CQ Press.

Lindblom, E. Charles. 1959. "The Science of Muddling Through." Public Administration Review, 19 (Spring): 79-88.

Sabatier, Paul A. 1988. "An Advocacy Coalition Framework of Policy Change and the Role of Policy-Oriented Learning Therein." Policy Sciences, 21: 129-168.

Wildavsky, Aaron. 1964. The Politics of the Budgetary Process. Boston: Little, Brown.

陈庆云. 公共政策分析. 北京:北京大学出版社,2006.

陈振明. 政策科学——公共政策分析导论. 2版. 北京:中国人民大学出版社,2003.

宁骚. 公共政策. 北京:高等教育出版社,2000.

谢明. 公共政策分析导论. 5版. 北京:中国人民大学出版社,2022.

张金马. 公共政策分析:概念·过程·方法. 北京:人民出版社,2004.

张国庆. 公共政策分析. 上海:复旦大学出版社,2004.

詹姆斯·E.安德森. 公共政策制定. 5版. 谢明,等,译. 北京:中国人民大学出版社,2009.

托马斯·R.戴伊. 理解公共政策. 12版. 谢明,等,译. 北京中国人民大学出版社,2011.

保罗·A.萨巴蒂尔. 政策过程理论. 胡总超,钟开斌,等,译. 北京:生活·读书·新知三联书店,2004.

戴博拉·斯通. 政策悖论. 顾建光,译. 北京:中国人民大学出版社,2006.

Chapter 5

Policy Instruments

Summary

> Policy instruments are the means and approaches of government governance and the bridge between policy objectives and results. When implementing a policy, the choice of policy instruments and the criteria used to evaluate the effect of the policy instruments have a decisive impact on whether the government can achieve the immediate policy goals. In this sense, it is necessary to study policy instruments. This chapter will discuss several basic issues of policy tools.

5.1 Definition of Policy Instrument

As for definition of policy instrument, researchers give different views based on various perspectives. The widely accepted view is that policy instruments are regarded as "objects". For example, Hood believed that the concept of "instrument" could be more clearly understood by distinguishing it into "object" and "activity". In his book Introduction to Public Management, Owen E. Hughes defined policy instruments as "the way of government's behavior and the mechanism used to regulate government's behavior in some way". We define policy instruments as specific means and ways that people use to solve a certain social problem.

To understand the policy instruments, the following points should be clarified:

— First of all, policy instruments are concrete, which are the way to achieve specific goals, and their role is to achieve existing policy goals;

— Secondly, the use of policy instruments will change the policy process, so it has the nature of a certain institutional arrangement;

— Finally, the actual application of policy instruments will be affected by the specific policy environment. The same policy instrument may play a completely different role in different policy environments.

5.2 Policy Typologies (tools)

For a long time, the typology of policy instruments was mainly based on their characteristics. In order to form a clear classification, people have involved a lot of time and energy. However, the existing classifications are not very satisfactory, and none of them can give a comprehensive and exhaustive introduction to policy instruments. Because the classification standards are not uniform, scholars have their own views on the classification of tools.

5.2.1 Typology of Schneider and Ingram

Schneider and Ingram (1993) distinguished five kinds of policy instruments:
— authority instrument
— inducements and sanctions
— capacity-building instruments
— hortatory instruments
— learning instruments

Authority Instrument

These are pronouncements of policy that carry the force of law. They compel particular behaviors and compliance. People do things because someone in authority asks them to do so. The use such of tools, not always effective or democratic, depends on the perceived legitimacy of government. These tools may be particularly suitable during times of crisis when favorable responses by the public are more likely. Examples include criminal law and environmental regulations. Authority tools are also known as law (Peters, 1999), law and regulation (Levine et al., 1990), and directive power (Anderson, 2000).

Inducements and Sanctions

These are tools that induce voluntary or coerced actions based on tangible payoffs. The assumption is here that people are rational actors who seek to maximize their self interest. Inducements encourage people to act in a certain way because they will gain from doing so. Sanctions are negative incentives or penalties that are thought to discourage behavior that is inconsistent with policy goals. Examples include fines for violating regulations and bonus payments for timely completion of contracts.

Capacity-Building Instrument

These instruments involve training, technical assistance, education, and information needed for taking policy actions and empowering other agencies. They provide training, education, information, and technical assistance, and they aim to inform or enlighten and thus empower people, either those in the target population or policy agents. Examples include training, technology transfer, the provision of information to local government as well as cash transfers to hire more staff.

Hortatory Instrument

These are attempts to persuade people to engage in desirable behaviors or to avoid engaging in undesirable behaviors. Governments invoke images and values through speeches, proclamations, and other communication to exhort people to behave in a certain way. Examples include public campaigns to change the birth rate, encourage voting, and discourage smoking. Hortatory instruments are also known as suasion (Peters, 1999).

Learning Instrument

These are tools to help understand the relevant aspects of policy problems. Policy agents and target populations are encouraged to participate and learn, for example, through citizen advisory panels and collaborative processes. Examples include focus groups, opinion polls, censuses, basic and applied research.

5.2.2 Other Typologies

American political scientists Rowe, Dahl and Lindblom (1981) have also done similar research, but they tend to put these instruments into a broad classification framework, such as dividing them into regulatory tools and non-regulatory tools.

In his book Introduction to Public Management, Owen E. Hughes believed that the vast majority of government intervention can be achieved through four economic means:

—Supply. That is, the government provides goods and services through the financial budget.

—Subsidy. In fact, it is a supplementary means of supply. The government subsidizes some individuals in the private economic field to produce goods and services that the government needs in this way.

—Production. Only the government produces goods and services sold on the market.

—Regulation. It refers to the government's use of national coercive force to approve or prohibit certain activities in the private economic field.

In Public Policy Research, Canadian public policy scholars M. Howlett and M. Ramesh (1995) classified according to the degree of enforceability of policy instrument. They divided policy instruments into voluntary tools (non-mandatory instruments), compulsoryinstruments and mixed instruments.

Hood (1983,1986) proposed a systematic classification framework. In his view, all policy instruments use one of the following four broad "government resources", that is, the government deals with public issues by using its information, authority, financial resources and available formal organizations. See table 5-1.

Table 5-1   Framework of Policy Instruments Classification (Hood's)

Nodality	Authority	Treasure	Organization
Information Monitoring and Release	Command and Control Regulation	Grant and Loans	Direct Provision of Goods and Services and Public Enterprises
Advice and Exhortation	Self-regulation	User Charges	Use of Family, Community, and Voluntary Organizations
Advertising	Standard-setting and Delegated Regulation	Taxes and Tax Expenditures	Market Creation
Commissions and Research Inquiries	Advisory Committees and Consultations	Interest Group Creation and Funding	Government Reorganization

SOURCE: Adapted from Lester M. Salamon, The Tools of Government: A Guide to the New Governance. (Peking University Press, 2016).

5.3 Elements for Selecting Policy Instruments

Consistent with the stage change characteristics of the research on policy instruments, the research on the selection of policy instruments also needs to consider the nature, category, use, and subsequent factors such as policy resources, policy issues, policy objectives, policy environment, and policy instruments. For the question of choice, Hood gave four principles: fully consider the alternatives; the instruments should match the work; the selection of instruments should conform to certain ethics; Focus on effectiveness and other goals, the ideal situation should be obtained at the minimum cost. Salamon refined four key dimensions: mandatory, directness, autonomy and visibility.

Of course, there are many factors that affect the choice of policy instruments, such as the characteristics of policy instruments, the nature of problems to be solved, the past experience of the government, the subjective preferences of decision-makers, and the possible reactions of affected social groups. At this time, the policy instrument is not a simple economic problem, but also involves political factors.

We can divide the coordinates according to the complexity of the national capacity policy subsystem, and fill the voluntary tools, mandatory tools and hybrid tools into different quadrants, it can also be constructed according to the two axes of government capacity and social capacity, and more detailed spectral analysis methods can be used. In addition, when selecting policy tools, policy designers also need to consider the following factors:

— political feasibility
— availability of resources

— behavioral assumptions

Political Feasibility

Policy making is at least as much a political process as it is a technical process. Even technically superior policy tools may not be adopted because they are politically unpopular. For example, the United States has no equivalent of South Korean National Health Insurance. Americans must get private health insurance, receive assistance from a public program, or go without, even though this leads to much higher costs than in systems with national health insurance or national healthcare.

In the face of a major youth unemployment problem, the government could directly provide a large number of jobs, but this solution would require a major expansion in the size of government and big tax increases. There is strong enough resistance to both that creating enough government jobs to solve the youth unemployment issue is not raised as a serious option.

Availability of Resources

A second factor in policy tool choice is the availability of resources for implementing policy. For example, there may be two ways to battle the problem of forest fires: posting thousands of lookouts in forests or employing a public education program to tell people that "only you can prevent forest fires," making a bear cub the symbol of that campaign. The US Forest Service chose the latter hortatory tool because it is much less expensive than more aggressive efforts to detect and prevent fires caused by carelessness. As another example, South Korea could use hortatory tools to discourage littering, but it does not have strict enforcement of anti-littering laws because there are many people available to pick up litter off the streets at a low labor cost.

Behavioral Assumptions

The final element for selecting policy tools depends on the policy theory. That is, what causes the problem and how can a particular policy change people's behavior to produce the desired result? For example, monetary policy is based on behavioral assumptions about the market. One assumption is that a lower exchange rate with the US dollar will increase exports. Another assumption is that increased exports would increase employment and other desired outcomes.

Discussion Questions

1. What are the strengths and weaknesses of the various policy instruments?
2. What are the factors that determine the choice of a policy instrument?
3. What is the advantage of dividing policies into Lowi's typologies instead of dividing them into policy domains?

Vocabularies

regulation

government management

taxing and spending

market mechanisms

exhortation

hortatory appeal

capacity building tool

policy typologies

distributive policy

redistributive policy

regulatory policy

pork-barrel spending

logrolling

protective regulation

competitive regulation

References

Affholter, Dennis P. 1994. "Outcome Monitoring." In Handbook of Practical Program Evaluation. Ed. Joseph S. Wholey, Harry P. Harty, and Kathryn E. Newcomer. San Francisco: Josse Bass.

Anderson, James E. 2000. Public Policymaking. 4th ed. Boston: Houghton Mifflin.

Birkland, Thomas A. 2001. An Introduction to the Policy Process: Theories, Concepts, and Models of Public Policy Making. New York: M. E. Sharpe.

Ingram, Helen and Mann, Dean. 1980. "Policy Failure: An Issue Deserving Attention." In Why Policies Succeed or Fail. Ed. Helen Ingram and Dean Mann. Beverly Hills: Sage.

Kraft, Michael E. and Furlong, Scott R. 2004. Public Policy: Politics, Analysis, and Alternatives. Washington, D. C. CQ Press.

Laumann, Edward O. , and Knoke, David. 1987. The Organizational State: Social Choice in National Policy Domains. Madison: University of Wisconsin Press.

Levine, Charles H. , Peters, B. Guy, and Thompson, Frank J. 1990. Public Administration: Challenges, Choices, Consequences. Glenview, Illinois: Scott, Foresman/Little Brown.

Michael Howlett and M. Ramesh, Studying Public Policy: Policy Cycles and Policy

Subsystems. 1995. London: Oxford University Press.

Owen E. Hughes. 2022. Public Management and Administration: An Introduction. 5thed. Beijing: China Renmin University Press.

Peters, B. Guy. 1999. American Public Policy: Promise and Performance. Chappaqua, New York: Chatham House/Seven Rivers.

Schneider, Anne and Ingram, Helen. 1993. "The Social Con-struction of Target Populations: Implications for Politics and Policy."American Political Science Review, 87(22): 334-348.

Stone, Deborah. 1997. Policy Paradox: The Art of Political Decision Making. New York: W. W. Norton.

第5章

政策工具

政策工具是政府治理的手段和途径，是政策目标与结果之间的桥梁。在执行政策时，选用何种政策工具以及用哪一种标准来评价该政策工具的效果等问题对政府能否达成既定政策目标具有决定性影响。从这个意义上来说，政策工具研究是十分有必要的。本章将对政策工具的几个基本问题加以探讨。

5.1 政策工具的内涵

对于什么是政策工具，由于研究者们的理解角度不同，给出的定义也是各不相同。得到广泛认同的观点是把政策工具看成是一种"客体"，如胡德认为，通过将"工具"区分为"对象"和"活动"，可以更清楚地理解"工具"的概念。欧文·E. 休斯在《公共管理导论》一书中将政策工具定义为："政府的行为方式，以及通过某种途径调节政府行为的机制"。我们将政策工具定义为：人们用来解决某个社会问题的具体手段和方式。理解政策工具需要明确以下几点：

——首先，政策工具是具体的，是实现特定目标的途径，其作用是实现既有的政策目标；

——其次，政策工具的运用会改变政策过程，因而具有某种制度安排的性质；

——最后，政策工具的实际运用会受到具体政策环境的影响，同一种政策工具在不同的政策环境中可能发挥完全不同的作用。

5.2 政策工具的分类

在很长一段时间里,政策工具的分类主要依据工具特性来进行。为了形成一种明确的分类,人们投入了不少的时间和精力。然而,现有的分类都不怎么让人满意,没有一个能够对政策工具做全面的介绍。由于分类标准不统一,学者们对于政策工具分类也都各持己见。

5.2.1 施耐德和英格拉姆的分类方法

施耐德和英格拉姆(1993)区分了五种政策工具:
——权威型工具
——诱导和制裁型工具
——能力建设型工具
——规劝型工具
——学习型工具

权威型工具

以正当性权威为基础,再限定的情况下要求、允许、禁止某些行为,通常是具有法律效力的政策声明,迫使人们某种特定的行为如遵守。人们这样做是因为有权威人士要求他们这样做。这种工具的使用并不总是有效或民主的,它取决于政府的合法性。这些工具在危机时期可能更适合,更可能获得公众有效的应急反应。例如,刑法和环境法。权威工具也被称为法律(彼得斯,1999),法律和规定(莱文等,1990)和指令权(安德森,2000)。

诱因和制裁型工具

诱因和制裁型工具是基于有形收益诱导自愿或强制行为的工具。假设人是寻求最大化自身利益的理性行为者,诱因会鼓励人们以某种方式行事,因为他们会从中获益。制裁是负面的激励或惩罚,被认为会阻止与政策目标不一致的行为。例如,违反规定的罚款和及时完成合同的奖金。

能力建设型工具

能力建设型工具涉及采取政策行动和赋予其他机构权力所需的培训、技术援助、教育和信息。他们提供培训、教育、信息和技术援助,旨在为人们提供信息或启发,从而赋予他们权力,无论是目标人群还是政策制定者。例如培训,技术转让,向当地政府提供信息以及现金货币支付等。

象征及劝说工具

象征及劝说工具认为人们是根据自己的价值和信仰体系而做决定,于是利用此类工具使得政策目标群体的价值与政策目标趋于一致。政府通过演讲,宣言和其他交流方式来影响公众的价值观,以劝告其以某种方式行事。例如改变出生率,鼓励投票和禁止吸烟等公共运动。劝说工具也被称为劝告(彼得斯,1999)。

学习型工具

学习型工具是帮助理解政策问题的工具。当人们对问题缺乏了解,或者缺乏共识时,可以通过一些学习所得的经验,增进相关人员对问题以及解决方案的理解。例如民意调查,人口普查,基础研究和应用研究。

5.2.2 其他分类方法

美国政治学家罗威、达尔和林德布洛姆(1981)等人也做过类似的研究,但他们倾向于将这些工具归入一个宽泛的分类框架中,如将工具分为规制性工具和非规制性工具两类。萨尔蒙推进了他们的讨论,增加了开支性工具和非开支性工具两种类型。

麦克唐纳尔和艾莫尔根据工具所要获得的目标将政策工具分为四类,即命令性工具、激励性工具、能力建设工具和系统变化工具。英格拉姆(1990)等人也做出了一个类似的分类,将政策工具分为激励、能力建设、符号和规劝、学习四类。

欧文·E. 休斯(2022)在《公共管理导论》一书中认为绝大多数的政府干预往往可以通过四种的经济手段得以实现,它们是:(1)供应,即政府通过财政预算提供商品和服务;(2)补贴,它事实上是供应的一种补充手段,政府正是通过这种方式来资助私人经济领域的某些个人去生产政府需要的商品和服务;(3)生产,指政府生产在市场上出售的商品和服务;(4)管制,指政府运用国家强制力批准或禁止私人经济领域的某种活动。

加拿大公共政策学者霍莱特和拉梅什(1995)在《公共政策研究》一书中根据政策工具的强制性程度来分类。他们将政策工具分为自愿性工具(非强制性工具)、强制性工具和混合性工具三类。与其他分类方法相比,他们的分类框架更具解释力、更合理。

胡德(1983,1986)提出了一种系统化的分类框架。他认为,所有政策工具都使用下列四种广泛的"政府资源"之一,即政府通过使用其所拥有的信息、权威、财力和可利用的正式组织来处理公共问题。见表 5-1。

表 5-1　　　　　　　　胡德的政策工具分类框架

节点	权威	财政	组织
信息监控和发布	命令与控制性管制	补助和借贷	直接提供产品和服务,设立公共企业
忠告和劝诫	自我调节	使用者付费	家庭、社区和志愿组织的使用
广告	标准制定和授权监管	税收和税收支出	创造市场
委员会和研究调查	咨询委员会和协商	利益集团创建和融资	改革政府

来源:根据(美)莱斯特·M. 萨拉蒙《政府工具:新治理指南》(北京大学出版社 2016)整理

5.3　政策工具的选择

同政策工具的研究的阶段变化特征相适应,政策工具的选择研究也需要考虑到性质、类别、用途,以及后续的政策资源、政策问题、政策目标、政策环境、政策工具等因素。对于选择问题,胡德给出了四项原则:充分考虑可替代方案;工具与问题相匹配;工具选择需符合一定伦理道德;关注有效性以及其他目标,理想状况应该以最小代价取得。而萨拉蒙则提炼出四个关键维度:强制性、直接性、自治性与可见性。

当然,影响政策工具选择的因素有很多,比如政策工具的特性、待解决问题的性质、政府过去的经验、决策者的主观偏好、受影响的社会群体的可能反应等。此时政策工具并非是简单的经济学问题,也牵扯到了政治因素。

我们可以按照国家能力－政策子系统复杂程度进行坐标分割,将自愿性工具、强制性工具和混合型工具填入不同的象限内,也可以按照政府能力与社会能力两个坐标轴进行构建,并且采用更加精细的光谱分析法。此外,在选择政策工具时,政策设计者也需要考虑如下因素:

——政治可行性
——资源可用性
——行为假设

政治可行性

政策制定至少既是一个政治过程,也是一个技术过程。即使是技术上优越的政策工具也可能因为它们在政治上不受欢迎而不被采用。例如,美国没有相当于韩国的国民健康保险。美国人必须获得私人医疗保险,接受公共计划的援助,也可以不参加,但这会导致成本远高于拥有国家医疗保险或国家医疗保健的系统。

面对严重的青年失业问题,政府可以直接提供大量就业机会,但这种解决方案需要扩大政府规模和大幅增加税收。这两种方案都会遇到不同程度的阻力,因此创造足够多的政府工作来解决青年失业问题并不是一个明智的选择。

资源可用性

政策工具选择的第二个考量因素是政策资源的可用性。例如,可能有两种方法可以解决森林火灾问题:在森林中安排数千名瞭望员或采用公共教育计划告诉人们"只有你能防止森林火灾",并让小熊成为该计划的象征物。美国林业局选择了后者作为规劝工具,因为它比检测和防止粗心造成的火灾的努力要容易得多。另一个例子是,韩国使用规劝工具来阻止乱扔垃圾,而不是实施严格的处罚乱丢垃圾的法律。

行为假设

选择政策工具的最后一个要素取决于政策理论。也就是说,导致问题的原因是什么,特定政策如何改变人们的行为以产生预期的效果呢?例如,货币政策是基于对市场的行为假设。一个假设是,美元汇率较低将增加出口,另一个假设是增加出口会增加就业和其他预期效果。

思考问题

1. 各种政策工具的优点和缺点是什么？
2. 决定政策工具选择的因素有哪些？
3. 将政策划分为 Lowi 的类型而不是将其划分为政策领域的优势是什么？

词　汇

管制
政府管理
税收和支出
市场机制
号召
呼吁
能力建设工具
政策类型
监管政策

参考文献

Affholter, Dennis P. 1994. "Outcome Monitoring." In Handbook of Practical Program Evaluation. Ed. Joseph S. Wholey, Harry P. Harty, and Kathryn E. Newcomer. San Francisco: Josse Bass.

Anderson, James E. 2000. Public Policymaking. 4th ed. Boston: Houghton Mifflin.

Birkland, Thomas A. 2001. An Introduction to the Policy Process: Theories, Concepts, and Models of Public Policy Making. New York: M. E. Sharpe.

Ingram, Helen and Mann, Dean. 1980. "Policy Failure: An Issue Deserving Attention." In Why Policies Succeed or Fail. Ed. Helen Ingram and Dean Mann. Beverly Hills: Sage.

Kraft, Michael E. and Furlong, Scott R. 2004. Public Policy: Politics, Analysis, and Alternatives. Washington, D. C. CQ Press.

Laumann, Edward O., and Knoke, David. 1987. The Organizational State: Social Choice in National Policy Domains. Madison: University of Wisconsin Press.

Levine, Charles H., Peters, B. Guy, and Thompson, Frank J. 1990. Public Administration: Challenges, Choices, Consequences. Glenview, Illinois: Scott, Foresman/Little Brown.

Michael Howlett and M. Ramesh, Studying Public Policy: Policy Cycles and Policy Subsystems. 1995. London: Oxford University Press.

Owen E. Hughes. 2022. Public Management and Administration: An Introduction. 5thed. Beijing: China Renmin University Press.

Peters, B. Guy. 1999. American Public Policy: Promise and Performance. Chappaqua, New York: Chatham House/Seven Rivers.

Schneider, Anne and Ingram, Helen. 1993. "The Social Con-struction of Target Populations: Implications for Politics and Policy." American Political Science Review, 87(22): 334-348.

Stone, Deborah. 1997. Policy Paradox: The Art of Political Decision Making. New York: W. W. Norton.

陈庆云. 公共政策分析. 北京:北京大学出版社,2006.

陈振明. 政策科学——公共政策分析导论. 2版. 北京:中国人民大学出版社,2003.

宁骚. 公共政策. 北京:高等教育出版社,2000.

谢明. 公共政策分析导论. 5版. 北京:中国人民大学出版社,2022.

张金马. 公共政策分析:概念·过程·方法. 北京:人民出版社,2004.

张国庆. 公共政策分析. 上海:复旦大学出版社,2004.

詹姆斯·E.安德森. 公共政策制定. 5版. 谢明,等,译. 北京:中国人民大学出版社,2009.

托马斯·R.戴伊. 理解公共政策. 12版,谢明,等,译. 北京中国人民大学出版社,2011.

保罗·A.萨巴蒂尔. 政策过程理论. 胡总超,钟开斌,等,译. 北京:生活·读书·新知三联书店,2004.

戴博拉·斯通. 政策悖论. 顾建光,译. 北京:中国人民大学出版社,2006.

莱斯特·M.萨拉蒙. 政府工具:新治理指南. 北京:北京大学出版社,2016.

Chapter 6 Analyzing Public Policy

Summary

> Policy analysis is a systematic way of evaluating public policy alternatives as well as existing government programs. It is especially important in policy formulation. The nature of policy analysis is that it refers to the assessment of policy alternatives. The type of analysis includes scientific, professional, and political. The steps in policy analysis are defining and analyzing the problem, constructing alternatives, developing evaluative criteria, assessing the alternatives, and drawing conclusions.

6.1　Defination and Nature of Policy Analysis

Policy analysis is usually described as a systematic and organized way of evaluating public policy alternatives or existing government programs. It often involves applying economic tools and other quantitative methods or measures. Policy analysis may therefore seem to some students of public policy to hold little relevance to anyone except policy specialists, but in reality everyone uses policy analysis in many day-to-day activities. Buying a car, selecting a particular college course, and choosing a restaurant for dinner all require thinking about the pluses and minuses of the available choices. This includes any decision about how to spend money.

Policy analysis can be used throughout the policy process, but it becomes especially important in the formulation of policies and evaluation of programs after they are implemented. In assessing a public problem, policy analysis may assist in describing its scope, such as the percentage of people in poverty. When developing alternatives and choosing a direction, a decision maker can use analysis to assess the feasibility of the choices based on economic, administrative, political, and ethical criteria. The same methods can be used to evaluate a program to determine its effectiveness, or whether it has achieved its expected results.

Chapter 6　Analyzing Public Policy

What Is Policy Analysis?

Analysis means deconstructing an object of study. That means breaking it down into its basic elements to understand it better. Policy analysis is the examination of components of public policy, the policy process, or both. In another way, it is the study of the causes and consequences of policy decisions. MacRae and Wilde (1979) called policy analysis the use of reason and evidence to choose the best policy among a number of alternatives.

Policy analysis may mean examining the components of the policy-making process, such as policy formulation and implementation, or substantive public policy issues, or both. The process usually involves collecting and interpreting information that clarifies the causes and effects of public problems and the likely consequences of using one policy option or another to address them.

Theoretically, a complete policy analysis process includes six steps: first of all, initially define the policy issues through the analysis of the problem situation; Secondly, to clarify the policy issues and establish the policy objectives; thirdly, in view of the policy objectives, search for alternatives as well as design and screen them; fourth, predict the prospects and consequences of each alternative; fifth, evaluate the advantages and disadvantages of each alternative according to the prediction results; finally, it need evaluate the effect of the policy implementation and draw a conclusion. Policy analysis is a process of using various science and technology to analyze problem situations and solve policy problems. Therefore, whether the policy analysis method is applicable or not plays an important role in effectively solving policy problems. The research on methodology is helpful to the implementation of scientific decision-making and avoid major mistakes.

The Nature of Policy Analysis

Policy analysis most often refers to assessment of policy alternatives. It is the systematic investigation of alternative policy options and the assembly and integration of the evidence for and against each option. Policy analysis is not intended to make policy decisions but to inform the process of public debate and deliberation.

The study of public policy and the conduct of policy analysis are rarely simple matters. Public problems are usually complex and multifaceted, and people are bound to disagree intensely over how serious they are, what might be done about them, and the role of government in relation to the private sector. Some problems, such as global climate change or the challenge of international terrorism, are monumental. Some, such as how best to provide for a high-quality public-school system or limit urban sprawl, may be a bit easier to grasp. However, none are simple. If they were, the course of action would be clear and not very controversial-removing snow and collecting trash, for example. Unfortunately, dealing with most problems is not so straight forward.

One of the primary functions of policy analysis is to satisfy the need for pertinent information and thoughtful and impartial assessments in the policy process. The information may not be widely available, or citizens and policy makers may not be able to understand it sufficiently, particularly when decisions must be made quickly because of impending deadlines or when the issues are politically controversial.

Under these conditions, policy analysis can clarify the issues, the available alternatives, and the effects of decisions that citizens and policy makers might choose to make. Policy analysis essentially involves looking ahead to anticipate the consequences of decisions and thinking seriously and critically about them. It is an alternative to "shooting from the hip" or making snap decisions based on ideology, personal experience, or limited or biased analysis of what should be done.

The solution to any controversial public problem is rarely achieved by relying solely on government agency officials, policy analysts, or other experts. The "best" solution will always be a matter of judgment and political choice because questions inevitably arise about the likely effectiveness of the policies chosen, their costs, who gains and who loses as a result, or whether the action can be justified on ethical or moral grounds. Policy analysis has been called an intellectual activity that takes place within a political setting. Its character and impact reflect that reality.

The politics are readily apparent in policy areas such as rights to privacy, or the use of public funds to support private school education where issues touch on basic questions of values. These kinds of policy choices reflect a combination of political preferences and an impartial assessment of the problem and possible solutions. In this context, policy analysis can pinpoint the nature of the problem, the policy choices available, and how each choice stands up against the different standards of judgment that might be used. People discuss government and public policy issues in many different settings: at home, in school, at work, and in bars and restaurants. In many cases the commentary is informal and can tend toward simplistic statement about, for instance, government proposals for some kind of policy change, from reducing crime rates to providing better health care services.

Citizens often air their views about government, politics, and public policy. Indeed, they hold strong opinions about what should be done about various problems. Even so, they may not think systematically about why the problems exist in the first place or what kind of policy action is most appropriate. Policy analysts hope to raise the level of such discussions, even if it remains unlikely that general conversations will be anchored in data analysis.

6.2 Types of Policy Analysis

The abundance of policy studies reflects not only the dramatic rise in the number of think tanks but also the increase in the number of interest groups that seek to shape

Chapter 6　Analyzing Public Policy

opinion on the issues and affect policy process. Prominent think tanks, interest groups, and policy-oriented law firms and consulting companies tend to establish their offices in the capitol, or in the main city of a province, but organized interest groups are found all over most countries. Whether they are unions, environmental activists, corporate trade associations, or professional organizations, they all have a stake in policy decisions made by government, and most set up a public or governmental affairs office to monitor pending legislation or agency acts.

Policy analysis organizations often continue to thrive in a country because of the character of government institutions and the political process. Fragmentation of government authority creates many opportunities for both interest group lobbying and policy analysis conducted outside of government. As political parties have weakened, interest group and think tank activity has increased.

The large number of think tanks and active interest groups almost guarantees that the public and policy makers will suffer from information overload as they try to make sense of the excess of reports and studies available on any public policy topic. Wilson (1998) observed that people are "drowning in information, while starving for wisdom." The future will belong to those capable of synthesizing information to make it usable.

This synthesizer is the policy analyst who is able to put together the right information at the right time, think critically about it, and make important choices wisely. Analysis, however, comes in many varieties, and policy makers and the public need to be able to differentiate the worthier from the less worthy.

Policy analysis falls into three broad categories: scientific, professional, and political. All serve valid purposes but have varying goals and objectives and use different methods. Table 6-1 offers a summary of the distinctions among the three perspectives.

Table 6-1　　　　　　　　　　Types of Policy Analysis

Types of Analysis	Objectives	Approaches	Limitations	Examples
Scientific	Search for "truth" and build theory about policy actions and effects	Use the scientific method to test hypotheses and theories; aim for objective and rigorous analysis; policy relevance less important than advancing knowledge	May be too theoretical and not adequately address information needs of decision makers	Academics and natural scientists, National Academy of Sciences, Intergovernmental Panel on Climate Change

(续表)

Types of Analysis	Objectives	Approaches	Limitations	Examples
Professional	Analyze policy alternatives for solving public problems	Synthesize research and theory to understand consequences of policy alternatives; evaluate current programs and their effects; aim for objectivity, but with goal of practical in policy debate	Research and analysis may be too narrow due to time and resource constraints; may neglect fundamental causes of public problems	South Korea Institute for International Economic Policy, South Korea Institute for Public Administration, National Assembly Budget Office
Political	Advocate and support preferred policies	Use legal, economic, and political arguments consistent with value positions; level of objectivity and rigor varies; aim to influence policy debate to realize organizational goals and values	Often ideological or partisan and may not be credible; may lack analytic depth	New Frontier Party, New Politics Alliance for Democracy, FKTU, KLUC, KCTU

For example, social science studies in the scientific category are not typically intended to influence public policy directly. Their purpose is to deepen, broaden, and extend policy makers' capacity for judgment, not to provide them with answers. In contrast, work that falls into the professional category, such as policy analysis from think tanks, is nearly always directed at policy makers with the clear intent of providing answers to policy questions.

Some think tanks should be placed in the political category because they have explicit ideological missions. All think tanks conduct analysis and advocate positions on public policy issues, but some of these groups are committed to political or ideological positions that affect their analyses and recommendations.

6.3 Framwork of Policy Analysis

The word analysis comes from the Greek word meaning to break down into component parts. Teachers of policy analysis usually specify the components of the analytical process as a series of steps. The most common approach to policy analysis is to picture it as a series of analytical steps or stages, which are the elements of rational problem solving. According to models of rational decision making, you define a problem, indicate the goals and objectives to be sought, consider a range of alternative solutions, evaluate each of the alternatives to clarify their consequences, and then recommend or

Chapter 6　Analyzing Public Policy

choose the alternative with the greatest potential for solving the problem. This process is similar to the way most people make everyday decisions, although they do it much more casually.

6.3.1　Steps of Policy Analysis

Table 6-2 summarizes the major steps of policy analysis and the kinds of questions analysts pose. It also illustrates how each stage of analysis might apply to a particular policy problem. Each step is considered briefly here as a description of what policy analysis aspires to do.

Table 6-2　　　　　　　　　　　Policy Analysis Steps

Steps	Types of Questions	Illustrations
Define and analyze the problem	What is the problem faced? Where does it exist? Who or what is affected? How did it develop? What are the major causes? How might the causes be affected by policy action?	How is cell phone use related to auto accidents? What is the potential to reduce accident rates through policy action? How does cell phone use compare to other distractions while driving?
Construct policy alternatives	What policy options might be considered for dealing with the problem?	Should government institute fines to reduce cell phone use while driving? Should government try to educate drivers on cell phone use? Is it technologically feasible to disable cell phones in a moving car?
Develop evaluative criteria	What criteria are most suitable for the problem and the alternatives? What are the costs of action? What is the likely effectiveness? Social and political feasibility? Equity?	What criteria are most important for regulation of cell phones? What options might be most effective in discouraging drivers from using phones? Will people find these options acceptable? Is it ethical to restrict individual behavior to achieve a social goal?
Assess the alternatives	Which alternatives are better than others? What kind of analysis might help to distinguish better and worse policy alternatives? Is the evidence available? If not, how can it be produced?	Are fines or education more likely to reduce drivers' cell phone use? How successful are the efforts of government to regulate cell phone use? What evidence is needed to answer these questions?

(续表)

Steps	Types of Questions	Illustrations
Draw Conclusions	Which policy option is the most desirable given the circumstances and the evaluative criteria? What other factors should be considered?	Should government impose stiff fines? Would fines be accepted as a legitimate action? How might the action be made more acceptable?

Define and Analyze the Problem

Defining the problem is the first step of policy analysis. Problem is different as a general term and an analytical term. For policy analysts the term specifically refers to the existence of an unsatisfactory set of conditions for which relief is sought, either through private means or by government. Analysts therefore need to describe that set of conditions, usually through the collection of pertinent facts or data on its magnitude or extent. For example, who is affected by it and how seriously? How long has the situation existed and how might it change over the next several years or decades? How amenable is it to intervention through one means or another? The goals and objectives of such intervention, whether private or governmental, may not be clear to all concerned.

It may also be necessary to clarify what is meant by the set of conditions, to define it clearly, and to develop accurate measures of it. If the problem is youth unemployment in South Korea, for example, an analyst would need to be clear about what is meant by youth unemployment, how to determine the extent of it, and who is affected by it. A great deal of information has been gathered on this problem: the Ministry of Labor reported in 2006 that 10% of youth aged 15~29 were unemployed and this had increased to 11.1% by 2015. However, "unemployment" means participating actively in the labor force but without a job. This means that most of the young people without jobs are not considered unemployed because they are studying for an employment test or preparing for work but not currently actively applying for a job. During this same period, the employment percentage gives a clearer view of the youth employment problem. Only 40.5% of youth aged 15~29 held a job in 2009, 40.3% in 2010, 40.5% in 2011, 40.4% in 2012, and 39.7% in 2013 (MOEL, 2015). Clearly, choosing a different measure frames the problem very differently. Looking at unemployment statistics makes it look like a problem of one in ten, whereas looking at employment statistics makes the problem appear to be much more urgent, affecting about six out of ten South Korean youth. Analysts will want to develop quantitative measures of this kind for most public problems.

Beyond gathering basic information about the problem, analysts want to identify its causes, which is not always an easy task. Without a good idea of how and why the problem came about, however, it is difficult to think usefully about possible solutions. This kind of diagnosis of the problem is similar to what a physician does when a patient is ill or what a mechanic does when a car is not operating.

The definition and structure of policy problems is the first important point in the process of policy analysis. It can be said that if the policy problem is not constructed correctly at the beginning of policy analysis, it is impossible to find the correct solution to the problem later. But in real life, we often solve the wrong problem, rather than find the wrong way for the right problem. For example, transport during the Spring Festival in 2003, a railway bureau sold "big tickets" to migrant workers' groups, and all passenger stations were prohibited from selling odd tickets. It is a substitute ticket for railway passenger transport. The migrant workers' groups uniformly fill in the number of people getting on the train and the station they arrive on one ticket. The original intention of the railway bureau is to crack down on scalpers through "big ticket", but the effect is not significant, instead, it saves scalpers from the trouble of hiring people to line up for tickets.

From the perspective of the policy background, the rampant illegal ticket trafficking is just an appearance, so the fight against ticket traffickers only touches on superficial policy issues at best, which is called "treating the symptoms rather than the root causes". The established interest pattern after the ticket and the system of the railway leading the industry are the deep-seated reasons for the repeated ban on scalping of Spring Festival transport tickets. The construction of policy issues makes the railway system consume a lot of manpower, material resources and financial resources every year, but with little effect.

Construct Policy Alternatives

Alternatives are choices or means used by decision-makers to achieve goals. In different occasions, they can be policies, strategies, projects or actions. The alternatives need not be obviously mutually exclusive (mutually substituted) or play the same role. Alternatives are not only those choices that the decision-maker knew from the beginning, but also those that were discovered later. Constructing policy alternatives is perhaps the most important stage in the policy analysis process. If analysts and policy makers cannot think of creative ways of solving problems, conventional approaches that may no longer be appropriate will continue. Early in the process, therefore, analysts are called upon to think imaginatively and critically about how the problem might be addressed, both within government and outside of it.

If definition is to discover the "what" of the problem and the goal establishment is to determine the "what to do", then the alternative solution is to solve the "how to do" problem. The construction of alternative plans is the first important procedure to achieve the policy objectives. It needs to be reprocessed to form the "advanced stage" of the policy plan, that is, the best plan is the policy plan that can be implemented. The design scheme must closely focus on the policy objectives and take the maximum realization of the policy objectives as the starting point. The design scheme must be predictable and predictive. The policy scheme is formulated for the coming things, so the future is both the object of policy analysis and the basis of analysis. Procedurally, prediction is the premise and basis of decision-making, and decision-making is based on the results of prediction to design the scheme.

The generation of alternatives shall follow the following principles:(1) Innovation, which is the primary principle for generating alternatives;(2) Binding;(3) diversity; (4) Time;(5) Mutual exclusion. In addition, in the process of generating alternatives, we should follow the thinking step of "scattering first and then convergence", that is, we should boldly seek out, list and imagine various options from different directions, the more the better, and then carefully design various options, strictly demonstrate and ponder over them to produce a satisfactory optimal solution.

Choose the Evaluative Criteria

When policy alternatives have been identified, the analysis shifts to assessing their potential. This task calls for selecting suitable evaluation criteria. In essence, evaluation is a kind of value judgment, and to make value judgment, we must establish the corresponding value scale, that is, evaluation criteria. It is a criterion for policy evaluators to judge the advantages and disadvantages. There are other appropriate criteria, such as ethics, feasibility (political, administrative, technical), environmental impact, and any number of political values, such as personal freedom, against which to assess policy proposals. No matter how long a list of potential evaluative criteria analysis might develop, some criteria will be more appropriate for a given problem than others. The establishment of evaluation criteria is a complex and meticulous work. The selection of evaluation criteria not only depends on the evaluation purpose and evaluator, but also is closely related to the evaluation technology and methods.

As a procedure or method, it estimates, speculates or judges the prospects of the policy (program) based on the information or knowledge about the policy issues, objectives and programs acquired at each stage of the previous policy analysis. According to the actual environment and conditions, predict the conditions that may be required during the implementation of scheme and the possible effects.

Assess the Alternatives

Analysts ask in this stage which of the several alternatives that might be considered seriously is most likely to produce the outcome sought, whether that outcome is to reduce the crime rate, improve the plight of the homeless, raise educational quality, protect the environment, or whatever. This exercise involves making judgments about how well each policy option fits in relation to the most relevant criteria. Analysts might rank the options in terms of overall desirability or consider the options in terms of each criterion, such as effectiveness, cost, and equity.

Some specialists refer to this stage of the process as projecting the outcomes or assessing impacts. A number of different methods or tools are used to do this such as cost-benefit analysis, cost-effectiveness, risk assessment, decision analysis, forecasting, impact assessment, and ethical analysis.

Analysts have many ways to present the alternatives so that policy makers and other interested parties can understand the analysis and the choices they face. For example, if three policy options are offered for consideration, the analyst might present each in terms of its likely effectiveness, economic efficiency, and equity. Tradeoffs are inevitable in this kind of decision making. Only rarely does a given policy option rank highest on all of the evaluative criteria. It is far more likely that one option is judged to be most effective, but another cheaper or more equitable in its effects. Analysts, therefore, attach weight to each criterion.

For example, is equity more important than efficiency in promoting the cleanup of hazardous waste sites? Should government clean up the most dangerous sites first or try to ameliorate the conditions at several sites at once? Or should the resources be directed to sites that have a disproportionate impact on poor and minority communities? Would doing so promote greater equity? As analysts consider more than a few conflicting bases for assessing policy options, the necessity for weighting criteria increases.

Draw Conclusions

Analysts summarize their findings and draw conclusions about the relative merits of competing policy proposals, but leave the choice of policy action to policy makers and the public. Whichever approach is taken, one must bear in mind that all analysis is necessarily partial and limited. That is, analysis can never be complete in the sense of covering every conceivable question that might be raised. It cannot be free of limitations, either, because every method or tool that might be used is subject to some constraints. Policy analysts need to develop a robust ability to deal with uncertainty, which comes with the process.

It may sometimes be difficult to draw a conclusion. In that case, students of policy analysis are advised to learn to ask critical questions about the information they collect, especially regarding its validity.

Where did the information come from, and how reliable is the source?

Is there any way to double-check the facts and their interpretation? Does the information and analysis seem believable?

Are there any signs of bias that might affect the conclusions that the study offers?

If two or more studies contradict one another, what are the reasons?

Is it because of political ideologies, differences in the preferred policy actions, or differences in the way the problem is defined?

Are the authors too selective in deciding what information should be presented and what can be left out?

By gathering information from multiple sources and comparing different interpretations, you might find it easier to determine which of the studies is the most credible.

6.3.2 Framework of Policy Analysis Process

How is policy analysis conducted? To date, there is no single, universally agreed procedure, framework or format. Many researchers and practitioners have proposed various analytical process frameworks, most of which belong to the rationalistic model of policy analysis. Let's take a look at some influential views first, and then comment and synthesize them.

(1) Quaid's Model

In his book *Public Decision Analysis*, Quaid believed that the process of policy analysis, like other systematic processes, can be seen as a process consisting of initial stage, continuous stage and final stage. What to do first and what to do later in the process of policy analysis depends on the question being studied and its context. The analysis process generally includes the following five logically related links: planning; Search; forecast; Simulation; Comprehensive.

(2) Jones's Model

In the book *Introduction to Public Policy Research*, Jones believes that the process of policy analysis includes the following functional factors: Perception/definition; Set or accumulation; Organization; Representative; Determine the agenda; Plan; Legalization; Budget; Implementation; Assessment; Adjustment/termination.

(3) Barton and Savage's Model

Barton and Savage proposed a six-step in their book *Basic Methods of Policy Analysis and Planning*: problem definition, determination of evaluation criteria, confirmation of alternatives, evaluation of alternatives, comparison of alternatives and evaluation of results.

(4) Stoke and Zackhouse's Model

In the book *Introduction to Policy Analysis*, Stoke and Zackhouse put forward a five-step process model, that is, to determine important issues and pursue goals, determine alternative action processes, predict the results of each alternative, and determine the criteria for measuring the achievements of the alternative, indicating a better choice of action. They believe that policy analysis may be carried out step by step from one step to another, and must be repeated in each step, but these basic steps are indispensable in the analysis process.

(5) Simon's Model

Herbert A. Simon analyzed the process of decision-making analysis in his book *New Science of Management and Decision Making*, and believed that any problem can be solved in three stages: information activity-looking for environmental factors that need to make decisions; design activities-exploring, developing and analyzing possible action plans; decision making activity—choose the better one from the feasible action plans.

(6) Sorensen's Model

Sorensen analyzed and studied the decision-making practice of the White House, and found the following set of analysis steps: finding out the facts, establishing goals, defining problems, making a detailed analysis of possible solutions according to the details and changes that may be involved, listing the possible consequences of each solution, recommending and choosing the final plan, communication after the decision, and preparation for implementation.

(7) Model of Urban Research Institute

The Urban Research Institute, one of the famous think tanks in the United States, has put forward an analysis process model, which includes the following steps: defining the problem, confirming the relevant purpose, selecting evaluation criteria, explaining the group of parties, identifying alternatives, estimating the cost of each alternative, determining the effect of each alternative and putting forward relevant findings.

Discussion Questions

1. What is policy analysis? What does it mean to bring scientific knowledge to the political process?
2. What is the nature of policy analysis?
3. How can policy alternatives be assessed?
4. What are the different types of analysis?
5. What are the steps of policy analysis?

Vocabularies

policy goals
causal model
policy tools
policy targets
policy implementation
authority tools
inducements and sanctions
capacity-building tools

hortatory tools
learning tools
political feasibility
availability of resources
behavioral assumptions

References

Birkland, Thomas A. 2001. An Introduction to the Policy Process: Theories, Concepts, and Models of Public Policy Making. New York: M. E. Sharpe.

Dunn, N. William. 1981. An Introduction Public Policy Analysis. Englewood Cliffs, New Jersey: Prentice-Hall, Inc.

Kingdon, John W. 1995. Agendas, Alternatives and Public Policies. 2nd ed. New York: Harper Collins.

Kraft, Michael E. and Furlong, Scott R. 2004. Public Policy: Politics, Analysis, and Alternatives. Washington, D. C. CQ Press.

MacRae, Duncan, and Wilde, James. 1979. Policy Analysis for Public Decisions. North Scituate, Massachusetts: Duxbury.

Randall R. Bovbjerg. 1985. What Is Policy Analysis? Journal of Policy Analysis and Management, 5(1), Autumn: 154-158.

Stokey, Edith and Zeckhauser, Richard. 1978. A Primer for Policy Analysis. New York: W. W. Norton & Company.

Weimer, L. David, and Vining, R. Aidan. 2005. Policy Analysis: Concepts and Practice. Pearson, New Jersey: Prentice Hall.

Wilson, Edward O. 1998. Consilience: The Unity of Knowledge. New York: Knopf.

第6章

政策分析

政策分析是评估公共政策选择以及现有政府规划的系统方法。在政策制定过程中尤为重要。政策分析的本质是对政策选择的评估,政策分析的类型包括科学的、专业的、政治的分析。政策分析的过程是指定义和分析问题,构建备选方案,制定评估标准,评估备选方案,得出结论。

6.1 政策分析的定义及本质

政策分析通常被描述为评估公共政策选择或现有政府计划的系统的和有组织的方式。它通常涉及应用经济工具和其他定量的方法或措施。因此,对于除政策专家以外的任何人而言,政策分析似乎可能与某些公共政策学生保持相关性,但实际上每个人都在许多日常活动中使用政策分析。例如购买汽车,大学课程的选择,或选择餐厅吃晚餐都需要考虑备选方案的优缺点,也包括任何有关如何花钱的决定。

政策分析存在于整个政策过程中,但在政策实施后和制定政策评估方案时尤为重要。在对公共问题进行评估时,政策分析可能有助于描述其范围,例如贫困人口的百分比。在制定替代方案和选择方向时,决策者可以使用政策分析来评估基于经济、行政、政治和道德标准的选择的可行性。同样也可以用来评估政策方案以确定其有效性,或者政策是否已达到预期效果。

什么是政策分析？

分析意味着对研究对象进行解构，将其分解为若干基本元素以便更好地理解研究对象。政策分析是对公共政策、政策过程或两者的组合进行检验，同时它也是对政策决策的原因和后果的研究。麦克雷和王尔德(1979)将政策分析称为使用理性和证据从多种替代方案中选择最佳政策方案。

政策分析意味着要审视政策制定过程的各个组成部分，例如政策的制定和实施，或实质性的公共政策问题，或两者兼而有之。该过程通常涉及信息的收集和解释，以澄清公共问题产生的原因和影响，以及使用一个或另一个政策备选方案解决问题可能带来的后果。

从理论上说，一个完整的政策分析过程包括六个步骤：首先，通过对问题情境的分析，初步界定政策问题；其次，明晰政策问题，确立政策目标；再次，针对政策目标，搜寻备选方案，并对其进行设计和筛选；第四，对各备选方案的前景和后果进行预测；第五，根据预测结果，评估各备选方案的优劣；最后，对政策实施后所产生的效果进行评估。政策分析是一个运用各种科学技术分析问题情境，解决政策问题的过程。因此，政策分析方法的适用与否对能否有效解决政策问题举足轻重，方法论的研究有助于科学决策的推行，避免重大失误。

政策分析的本质

政策分析通常是指对政策备选方案的评估，是对可替代政策选择的系统的考察，以及对每种政策选择的支持和反对的证据进行汇总和整合。政策分析的目的不是制定政策决定，而是为审议过程提供信息。

对公共政策的研究和分析的并不是一件简单的事情，公共问题通常是复杂和多方面的，人们对于问题的态度，可能采取的行动，以及政府在私营部门中的作用，都必然会产生强烈的不同意见。一些问题，例如全球气候变化或国际恐怖主义带来的挑战巨大，另一些问题，例如如何提高公立学校的质量或限制城市扩张，行动方案是明确的，那可能相对来说更容易解决。但不幸的是，大多数问题的解决不会那么简单。

政策分析的主要功能之一是满足政策过程中相关信息的获取及合理的、公正的评估的需要。公民和政策制定者不可能获取全部信息，或者可能无法充分了解这些信息，特别是在存在最后期限或问题存在争议又需要快速做出决定的时候。在这种情况下，政策分析可以厘清问题、可用的替代方案及公民和政策制定者选择做出的决策可能产生的影响。政策分析主要涉及对决策的后果的预测，并加以认真和批判性的思考。它可以避免"仔细思考以前就说话或采取行动"，或基于意识形态和个人经验，对应该做什么的有限或偏见分析做出快速决定。

在这些条件情况下，政策分析可以澄清问题，可用的替代方案以及公民和政策制定者可能选择做出的决策的影响。政策分析主要涉及对决策的后果的预测，并加以认真和批判性的思考。它可以避免"仔细思考以前就说话或采取行动"，或基于意识形态和个人经验，对应该做什么的有限或偏见分析做出快速决定。

任何有争议的公共问题的解决方案很少依赖政府官员、政策专家或其他专家来实现。

"最佳"解决方案通常涉及判断和政治选择的问题,因为所选政策的可能有效性、成本、收益和失败的问题,涉及该行为是否可以在道德层面被公正地加以判断。政策分析被称为在政治环境中发生的智力活动。它的特点和影响反映了这一现实。

在诸如隐私权或利用公共资金支持私立学校教育等政策领域,其政治性很明显,因为问题涉及价值观的基本问题。这些政策选择反映了政治偏好和对问题的公正评估和可能的解决方案的组合。在这种情况下,通过政策分析可以确定问题的性质,可用的政策选择,以及每一种选择如何面对可能使用的不同判断标准。人们在许多不同的环境中讨论政府和公共政策问题:家庭、学校、工作、酒吧和餐馆等。在许多情况下,评论是非正式的,可能仅倾向于简单的陈述,例如,从降低犯罪率到提供更好的医疗保健服务等领域对政府某种政策提出改变建议。

公民经常表达他们对政府、政治和公共政策的看法。而实际上,他们对如何解决问题也有着表达的意愿。即便如此,他们可能也不会系统地思考为什么问题存在或者哪种政策行动最合适。政策分析人员希望提高此类讨论的水平,即使一般性对话不太可能作为数据分析的基础。

6.2 政策分析的类型

丰富的政策研究不仅反映了智库数量的急剧增加,也反映了寻求就这些问题形成意见并影响政策过程的利益集团数量的增加。著名的智库、利益集团、政策导向的律师事务所和咨询公司倾向于在首都或主要城市设立办事处。无论是工会、环保活动家、行业贸易协会还是其他专业组织,他们都与政府制定的政策决策有利害关系,而且一些国家设立了公共或政府事务办公室来监督悬而未决的立法或机构行为。

由于政府机构和政治议程的特点,政策分析组织往往在一个国家持续蓬勃发展。政府权力的分散为利益集团游说和政府以外的政策分析创造了许多机会。利益集团和智库的活动也在增加。

大量的智库和活跃的利益集团使得公众和政策制定者在试图了解过多的公共政策领域的报告和研究的时候,会受到信息过载的影响。爱德华·奥斯本·威尔森(1998)观察到"虽然我们渴求智慧,但资讯多到足以把我们淹没。"未来将属于能够综合信息并加以整合利用的合成型人才。他们是能在对的时间整合对的资讯,对信息做批判性思考,并明智地做出重要决定的政策分析家。然而,分析有很多种类,政策制定者和公众需要能够对此加以区分。

政策分析分为三大类:科学分析,专业分析和政治分析。这些都是有效的方式,但目的和目标各不相同,并采用不同的方法。表6-1总结了三种观点之间的区别。

表 6-1　　　　　　　　　　　政策分析的类型

分析类型	目标	方法	局限性
科学分析	寻找"真相"并建立有关政策行动和效果的理论基础	使用科学方法对理论进行检验和假设；旨在进行客观和严格的分析；政策相关性不如提升知识重要	可能过于理论化，无法充分满足决策者的信息需求
专业分析	分析解决公共问题的政策选择	综合研究和理论以了解政策选择的后果；评估当前方案及其效果；以客观性为目标，但在政策辩论中以实用性为目标	由于时间和资源的限制，研究和分析可能过于狭隘；可能忽略了公共问题产生的根本原因
政治分析	倡导和支持首选政策	使用与价值立场一致的法律、经济和政治论点；客观性和严谨程度各不相同；旨在影响政策辩论以实现组织目标和价值观	通常基于意识形态或党派偏见，可能并不可信；可能缺乏分析深度

例如，科学范畴的社会科学研究通常不是直接地影响公共政策，他们意图加深，提高和延伸决策者的判断能力，而不是为他们提供答案。相比之下，属于专业范畴的工作，例如智库的政策分析，几乎总是针对政策制定者，其明确的意图是为政策问题提供答案。

一些智囊团应该被置于政治范畴，因为他们有明确的意识形态使命。所有的智库都在公共政策问题上进行分析和表明立场，但其中一些团体的政治或意识形态立场会影响他们的分析和建议。

6.3　政策分析过程的框架

"分析"一次来自希腊语，意思是分解为组成部分。政策分析专家通常将分析过程视为一系列的步骤。最常见的政策分析方法是将其描述为一系列分析步骤或阶段，这是理性解决问题的要素。根据理性决策模型，可以定义问题，指出要寻求的目标，考虑一系列的备选方案，评估每个备选方案并阐明其后果，然后建议或选择具有最大潜力的解决问题的备选方案。这个过程类似于大多数人做出日常决策的方式，只是日常这种决策更随意。

6.3.1　政策分析的步骤

表 6-2 归纳了政策分析的主要步骤以及分析专家提出的问题类型，说明了每个分析阶段如何适用于特定的政策问题，并对政策分析每个步骤所要做的事情进行了描述。

表 6-2 政策分析步骤

步骤	问题类型	例证
定义和分析问题	面临什么问题？存在什么地方？谁受到影响？是如何发展的？主要原因是什么？政策行动将如何影响这些原因？	手机的使用与交通事故有何关系？通过政策措施降低事故率的潜力是什么？与开车时其他干扰因素相比，手机使用情况如何？
制定政策选择	可以考虑使用哪些政策备选方案来解决该问题？	政府是否可以通过罚款以减少开车时使用手机？政府是否应该进行驾驶员规范使用手机的教育？汽车行驶过程中禁用手机在技术上是否可行？
指定评估标准	最适合该问题和方案选择的标准是什么？采取行动的代价是什么？可能带来的效果如何？社会和政治可行性如何？公平性如何？	哪些标准对规范手机使用最重要？哪些方法最可能有效地阻止驾驶员使用手机？人们会接受这些选择吗？限制个人行为以实现社会目标是否合乎道德？
评估选择方案	哪些备选方案更好？如何分析更有助于区分更好或更坏的政策方案？有依据吗？如果没有，如何生成？	罚款或教育是否更有可能减少驾驶员的手机使用情况？政府规范手机使用的努力有多成功？回答这些问题需要哪些证据？
得出结论	考虑到具体情况和评估标准，哪种政策方案最可取？还应考虑其他哪些因素吗？	政府是否应该强加罚款？罚款会被视为合法行为吗？如何使行动更容易接受？

定义和分析问题

定义问题是政策分析的第一步。问题作为一般用语和分析术语是不同的。对于政策分析人员而言，该术语具体指的是存在一系列令人不满意的，需要通过私人手段或向政府寻求救济得以解决的情况。因此，政策分析人员需要通过收集相关事实（数量或程度的数据）来描述这一系列条件。例如，谁受到了影响以及有多严重？这种情况会存在多久以及未来几年或几十年会如何变化？通过哪种方式进行干预更为合适？无论是私人还是政府干预，这种干预的目的和目标的所有方面并不都是清楚的。

有必要对这些条件进行澄清并明确加以定义，进而制定准确的衡量标准。如果问题是韩国的青年失业问题，那么分析人员就需要明确青年失业的含义，如何确定青年失业的程度以及受其影响的人。关于这个问题已经有了大量的信息收集：韩国劳工部在 2006 年的报告中说，15～29 岁的青年中有 10% 的人失业，到 2015 年这一比例增加到了 11.1%。"失业"意味着积极参与劳动力市场但没有找到工作。这意味着大多数没有工作的年轻人不会被视为失业，因为他们正在学习就业测试或准备工作但目前并没有积极寻找工作机会。在同一时期，就业百分比可以更清楚地了解青年就业问题。2009 年，15～29 岁青年中只有40.5%的人就业，2010年40.3%，2011年40.5%，2012年40.4%，2013年39.7%（MOEL，2015）。显然，选择不同的衡量标准可以以不同的方式解决问题。从失业统计数据看，不仅要看失业率，更要看到就业统计数据显示出的问题——影响了大约五分之三的韩国青年，这时候问题就变得紧迫了。分析人员希望为大多数公共问题制定此类可以量化的指标。

除了收集有关问题的基本信息之外，分析人员还希望确定问题的成因，虽然这并不容易。但是，如果不清楚问题出现的原因，那么很难对可能的解决方案进行有益的思考。这类似于医生在诊断时所做的事情，或者在汽车出现故障时维修师所做的事情。

政策问题界定及架构是政策分析过程中的第一要义，可以说如果政策分析伊始没有正确地构建政策问题，随后的为问题寻求正确的解决方法根本无从谈起。在现实生活中，我们常常是解决了错误的问题，而不是为正确的问题找到正确的解决办法。例如，2003年春运期间，某铁路局对民工团体一律发售"大票"，严禁各客运站发售零票。所谓"大票"，就是铁路客运代用票，民工团体统一在一张票面上填写上车人数和所到车站。铁路局的初衷是通过"大票"来打击票贩子，然而成效未见显著，反而省去了票贩子以往雇人排队抢票的麻烦。

从政策背景剖析，非法贩票活动猖獗只是一个表象，因此打击票贩子充其量也只触及了浅层次的政策问题，所谓"治标不治本"。车票后的既定利益格局及铁路一行独大的体制才是春运倒票屡禁不止的深层次原因。政策问题构建的舍本逐末使得铁路系统每年耗费大量的人力、物力、财力却收效甚微。

构建政策备选方案

备选方案是决策者用来达到目标的选择或手段。在不同的场合，它们可以是政策、策略、项目或行动等。备选方案之间不一定是明显地相互排斥（相互取代）或起着相同作用的。备选方案不只是那些决策者从一开始就知道的选择，也包括那些后来才被发现的选择。构建政策备选方案是政策分析过程中最重要的阶段。如果分析人员和政策制定者无法想出解决问题的创造性的方法，那么已不再适用的传统的解决问题方法可能将继续存在。因此，在政策分析过程的早期，分析人员需要以富有想象力和批判性的思维思考如何在政府内部和外部解决问题。

越来越被接受的一种方法是私有化，将某些公共服务从政府转移到私营部门。许多政策分析人员和组织推荐这种解决方案，更多时候也会得到政府的赞同，因为公共服务领域私有化更具吸引力，也更有效。许多公共服务现被移交给私营公司进行管理。例如，由私营公司提供公共汽车服务，有私立和公立学校及大学，有私人保安公司，在美国甚至有私人监狱。

如果说问题界定是为了发现问题"是什么"，明确目标是为了确定"做什么"，那么，备选方案就是解决"怎么做"的问题。搜寻备选方案是着手实现政策目标的第一道重要程序，它有待再加工，从而形成政策方案的"高级阶段"，即最优方案才是可以执行的政策方案。而设计方案则必须紧紧围绕政策目标，以最大限度地实现政策目标为出发点。设计方案必须要有预见性和预测性，政策方案是为即将到来的事物而制定的，所以未来既是政策分析的对象又是分析的依据。从程序上讲,预测是决策的前提和基础,决策是根据预测的结果来设计方案的。

备选方案的产生应遵循以下原则:(1)创新原则,这是产生备选方案的首要原则;(2)约束原则;(3)多样原则;(4)时间原则;(5)相互排斥原则。并且,在产生备选方案的过程中应当按照先发散后收敛的思维步骤,即先大胆地找寻,从不同方向上列举和设想出各种方案,数量越多越好,然后在此基础之上,对各种方案进行精心设计,严格论证和反复推敲,产生出满意的优选方案。

选择评估标准

一旦确定了政策选择,政策分析即转向政策评估。首先要求选择合适的评估标准。政策评估实质上是一种价值判断,而要进行价值判断,就必须建立相应的价值尺度,即评估标准。它是政策评估者在政策评估过程中以对政策方案和政策效果进行优劣判断的准则。有许多适当的标准用以评估政策方案,例如道德规范,可行性(政治,行政,技术),环境影响以及任何形式的政治价值观,例如个人自由。无论一个潜在的评估标准分析清单会持续多长时间,某些标准对于特定问题比其他标准更合适。作为一种程序或方法,它依据先前政策分析的各阶段所掌握的关于政策问题、目标和方案的信息或知识,对政策(方案)的未来前景做出估计、推测或判断并根据现实的环境和条件,预先推测某一方案实施过程可能需要的条件和产生的效果。建立评估标准是一项复杂而细致的工作,选择什么样的评估标准,不仅取决于评估目的和评估者,而且与评估的技术和方法密切相关。

评估选择方案

政策分析人员在这个阶段需要咨询认真考虑几种备选方案中哪一种最有可能产生所寻求的结果,无论结果是降低犯罪率,改善无家可归者的困境,还是提高教育质量,保护环境。这一步骤会涉及判断每个政策方案与相关标准的匹配程度。分析人员会根据总体满意度对方案进行排序,或者根据每个标准对方案加以考量,例如有效性、成本和收益。

一些专家将该过程的这一阶段称为对结果的预测或影响的评估。这一阶段会采用许多不同的方法或工具,如成本效益分析、成本效益、风险评估、决策分析、预测,影响评估和道德分析。

分析人员有可以有很多方法呈现政策备选方案,以便决策者和其他相关方面能够理解现有的分析和他们所面临的选择。例如,如果有三个政策方案可供考虑,分析人员可能会根据其可能的有效性、经济收益和公平性来呈现每个方案。在决策过程中,权衡是不可避免的。在所有评估标准中,给定的政策选项很少排序最高。因为有可能某一选项被认为是最有效的,但其他选项可能更廉价或更公平。因此,分析人员会重视每个评估标准。

例如,在促进危险废物场地的清理方面,公平比效率更重要吗?政府应该首先清理最危险的地方,还是试图同时改善几个地方?还是应该将资源用于对贫困和少数民族社区产生不利影响的地点的改进?这样做会促进更大的公平吗?由于分析人员考虑了评估政策选择的几个相互冲突的标准,因此会增加加权标准的必要性。

得出结论

分析人员对调查结果进行总结,根据相互竞争的政策建议的相对优点得出结论,并将政策行动的选择留给了决策者和公众。无论采取哪种方法,都必须牢记所有的分析都必然是局部的和有限的。也就是说,在涵盖提出的每个可能的问题的意义上,分析永远不会是完整的。它也不能不受到限制,因为可能使用的每种方法或工具都会受到一些限制。政策分析人员需要在这一过程中构建强大的能力来应对不确定性。

有时可能很难得出结论。在这种情况下,建议政策分析人员应学习如何提取所收集的信息中的关键问题,特别是关于其有效性的问题,例如:

信息来自哪里,信息来源的可靠性如何?

有没有办法对事实及其解释进行双重核实?信息和分析看上去可信吗?

是否存在任何可能影响研究结论的偏见?

如果两项或多项研究间相互矛盾,原因何在?

是因为政治意识形态、首选政策方案还是问题定义方式的差异?

在决定应该呈现哪些信息以及哪些信息可以被忽略时是否过于挑剔?

通过收集来自多个信源的信息并比较对其不同的解释,可能会发现哪些研究的可信度更容易确定。

6.3.2 政策分析过程框架

政策分析是如何进行的?迄今为止,并没有单一的、普遍认可的程序、框架或格式。许多研究者和实践者提出了各种分析过程框架,其中的大部分属于政策分析的理性主义模式。我们先来看一些比较有影响的观点,然后加以评论和综合。

(1)奎德的模型。奎德在《公共决策分析》一书中认为,政策分析的过程与其他系统过程一样,可以看作一个由初始阶段、持续阶段和终结阶段所组成的过程;政策分析过程中先做什么,后做什么依赖于被研究的问题及其脉络。分析过程一般包括如下五个逻辑上相联系的环节:规划、搜索、预测、模拟、综合。

(2)琼斯的模型。琼斯在《公共政策研究导论》一书中认为,政策分析过程包括如下一些功能因素:感知/定义、集合或累加、组织、代议、确定议程、规划、合法化、预算、执行、评估、调整/终结。

(3)巴顿和沙维奇的模型。巴顿和沙维奇在《政策分析和计划的基本方法》一书中提出了一个包括六步的过程。这六个步骤分别是:问题界定、评估标准的确定、备选方案的确认、备选方案的评估、备选方案的比较和结果的评估。

(4)斯托基和扎克豪斯模型。斯托基和扎克豪斯在《政策分析入门》一书中提出了一个五步的过程模型,即决定重要问题和追求目标、确定备选的行动过程、预测每个备选方案的结果、确定衡量备选方案成就的标准、表明偏好的行动选择。他们认为政策分析可能以从一步到另一步的顺序渐进的方式进行,并且必须在各个步骤中循环反复,但在分析过程中,这些基本步骤是不可或缺的。

（5）西蒙的模型。西蒙在《管理决策新科学》一书中对决策分析活动过程进行了分析，认为任何问题的解决，都可以分成如下三个阶段：情报活动——寻找需要做出决策的环境因素；设计活动——探索、发展和分析可能的行动方案；抉择活动——从可行的行动方案中选择较佳的一个。

（6）索伦森的模型。索伦森对美国白宫的决策实际进行了分析研究，发现了如下一套分析步骤：查明事实，确立目标，界定问题，根据可能牵涉的细节及其变化，对可能的解决方案作详细的分析，列举每个解决办法可能产生的后果，推介并抉择最后方案，抉择后的沟通，执行上的准备。

（7）城市研究所的模型。美国著名思想库之一的城市研究所提出了一种分析过程模型，它包括如下各步：界定问题，确认相关目的，选择评估标准，说明当事人群体，确认备选方案，估计每个备选方案的成本，决定每个备选方案的效果和提出有关的发现。

思考问题

1. 什么是政策分析？将科学知识带入政治过程意味着什么？
2. 政策分析的本质是什么？
3. 如何评估政策选择？
4. 有哪些不同类型的分析？
5. 政策分析的步骤是什么？

词　汇

政策目标
因果模型
政策工具
政策目标
政策实施
权威工具
诱导和制裁
能力建设工具
激励工具
学习工具
政治可行性
资源的可用性
行为假设

参考文献

Birkland, Thomas A. 2001. An Introduction to the Policy Process: Theories, Concepts, and Models of Public Policy Making. New York: M. E. Sharpe.

Dunn, N. William. 1981. An Introduction Public Policy Analysis. Englewood Cliffs, New Jersey: Prentice-Hall, Inc.

Kingdon, John W. 1995. Agendas, Alternatives and Public Policies. 2nd ed. New York: Harper Collins.

Kraft, Michael E. and Furlong, Scott R. 2004. Public Policy: Politics, Analysis, and Alternatives. Washington, D. C. CQ Press.

MacRae, Duncan, and Wilde, James. 1979. Policy Analysis for Public Decisions. North Scituate, Massachusetts: Duxbury.

Ministry of Employment and Labor. 2015. "Major Statistics," August 10, 2015, from http://www.moel.go.kr/english/pas/pas Major.jsp

Randall R. Bovbjerg. 1985. What Is Policy Analysis? Journal of Policy Analysis and Management, 5(1), Autumn: 154-158.

Stokey, Edith and Zeckhauser, Richard. 1978. A Primer for Policy Analysis. New York: W. W. Norton & Company.

Weimer, L. David, and Vining, R. Aidan. 2005. Policy Analysis: Concepts and Practice. Pearson, New Jersey: Prentice Hall.

Wilson, Edward O. 1998. Consilience: The Unity of Knowledge. New York: Knopf.

"Youth Unemployment in South Korea on the Rise." English Chosun, December 24, 2007, from http://english.chosun.com/w21data/html/news/200712/200712240012.html.

陈庆云. 公共政策分析. 北京:北京大学出版社,2006.

陈振明. 政策科学——公共政策分析导论. 2版. 北京:中国人民大学出版社,2003.

宁骚. 公共政策. 北京:高等教育出版社,2000.

谢明. 公共政策分析导论. 5版. 北京:中国人民大学出版社,2022.

张金马. 公共政策分析:概念·过程·方法. 北京:人民出版社,2004.

张国庆. 公共政策分析. 上海:复旦大学出版社,2004.

詹姆斯·E.安德森. 公共政策制定. 5版. 谢明,等,译. 北京:中国人民大学出版社,2009.

托马斯·R.戴伊. 理解公共政策. 12版,谢明,等,译. 北京中国人民大学出版社,2011.

保罗·A.萨巴蒂尔. 政策过程理论. 胡总超,钟开斌,等,译. 北京:生活·读书·新知三联书店,2004.

戴博拉·斯通. 政策悖论. 顾建光,译. 北京:中国人民大学出版社,2006.

Chapter 7
The Public Policy Process

Summary

Any problem definition represents one of many possible points of view. Defining a problem is not enough. Agenda setting is the process of bringing problems to the attention of elites and the public. Items on the agenda need to travel from systematic attention to the institutional agenda to the decision agenda before they are acted upon. Policy formulation may be routine, analogous, or creative and involves both formal and informal actors. Policy legislation is essential process for any political system as politics is based on legitimacy. It is both a simple and complex process at the same time and involves both formal and informal actors in a dynamic process. Implementation is the process of putting a policy into effect. Implementation involves interpretation, organization, and application. The techniques for affecting implementation include early planning, scheduling models, expenditures, incentives, participation, the case management system, and management by objectives. Implementation may be affected by internal and external factors and may be based on a top-down, bottom-up, or synthesis approach. Policy evaluation is an important part of policy process. Through policy evaluation, people can judge whether a policy has received the expected effect, so as to decide whether to continue, adjust or end the policy. Policy termination is the final step in the policy process, but should not bethe last step in terms of consideration. It includes functions, organizations, policies, and programs and is relatively rare.

7.1 Defining Problems and Agenda Setting

Figure 7-1 draws an overall picture of the policy process. Problem definition is a matter of representation because every description of a situation is a portrayal from only one of many points of view. Problem definition is strategic because groups, individuals, and government agencies deliberately and consciously fashion portrayals so as to promote their favored course of action. An individual's perspective and background determine how they define a problem and relate to it. Personal ideology and values are likely to influence how a problem is defined or even if the individual considers a situation to be a problem at all.

```
┌─────────────────────────────┐
│ Defining problem & Agenda   │
│ setting                     │
│ (How problems are perceived │◄──┐
│ and defined, command        │   │
│ attention, and get onto the │   │
│ political agenda)           │   │
└──────────────┬──────────────┘   │
               ▼                  │
┌─────────────────────────────┐   │
│ Policy formulation          │   │
│ (The design and drafting of │   │
│ policy goals and strategies │   │
│ for achieving them. Often   │   │
│ involves the use of policy  │   │
│ analysis.)                  │   │
└──────────────┬──────────────┘   │
               ▼                  │
┌─────────────────────────────┐   │
│ Policy legitimation         │   │
│ (The mobilization of        │   │
│ political support and       │   │
│ formal enactment of         │   │
│ policies. Includes          │   │
│ justification or rationales │   │
│ for the policy action.)     │   │
└──────────────┬──────────────┘   │
               ▼                  │
┌─────────────────────────────┐   ┌─────────────────────────────┐
│ Policy implementation       │   │ Policy termination          │
│ (Provision of institutional │   │ (Modification of policy     │
│ resources for putting the   │   │ goals and means in light of │
│ programs into effect within │   │ new information or shifting │
│ a bureaucracy)              │   │ political environment)      │
└──────────────┬──────────────┘   └──────────────▲──────────────┘
               ▼                                  │
                ┌─────────────────────────────┐
                │ Policy program and          │
                │ evaluation                  │
                │ (Measurement and assessment │
                │ of policy and program       │
                │ effects, including success  │
                │ or failure)                 │
                └─────────────────────────────┘
```

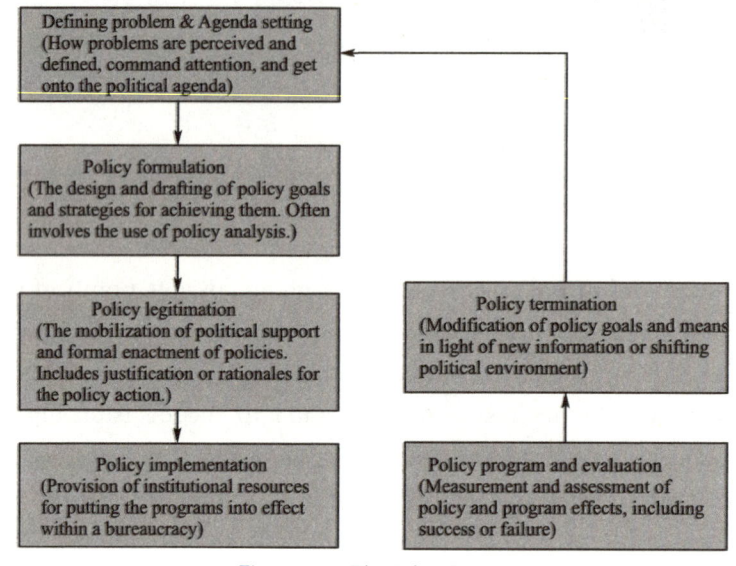

Figure 7-1　The Policy Process

For example, the issue of Internet pornography could be usually defined as one of public morality and child protection. Alternately, it could be defined in terms of free expression, as it often is in the United States, with very different implications. Family planning might be thought of as a simple public health issue, or it may be defined in moral and ethical terms and associated with abortion, or seen as a matter of women's rights and privacy. Making comparisons is part of problem definition.

By supplying new and often objective information on the nature of a problem and its implications, policy analysts can help to steer political debate toward a rational assessment of the scope of the problem, its causes, and possible solutions. For example, a study of urban sprawl might highlight adverse impacts on highway congestion, land use, and water supplies and suggest how better growth management could minimize those effects. The findings and recommendations of such a study would no doubt differ significantly from the arguments of real estate developers and pro-growth public officials.

Defining problems is not enough to find solutions, or formulate policy. A problem must rise high enough on the agenda. It is not easy for societal problems to reach agenda status because so many problems are competing for social and political attention at any particular time. Some make it onto the agenda and some do not. The agenda is a collection of problems, understandings of causes, symbols, solutions, and other elements of the public and government officials. An agenda can be as a concrete list of bills that are before a legislature, but also includes a series of beliefs about the existence and magnitude of problems and how they should be addressed by government, the private sector, nonprofit organizations, or through joint action by some or all of these institutions.

Agenda setting is the process by which problems and alternative solutions gain or lose public and elite attention. An agenda is a collection of understandings, causes, symbols, solutions, and other elements of public problems that come to the attention of members of the public and government officials. Agenda setting is central to the policy process. If an issue does not attract appropriate attention, chances are it will languish without a government response. Therefore, the public policy student needs to understand what facilitates the movement of certain issues onto the agenda.

The agenda is actually quite vast. It is useful to think of several levels of the agenda, as shown in Figure 7-2. The broadest level of the agenda is the agenda universe, which contains all ideas that could possibly be brought up and discussed in a society or a political system.

The vast numbers of ideas in the agenda universe are more or less "acceptable" in a political sense, and have the potential to move to and appear on the systemic agenda.

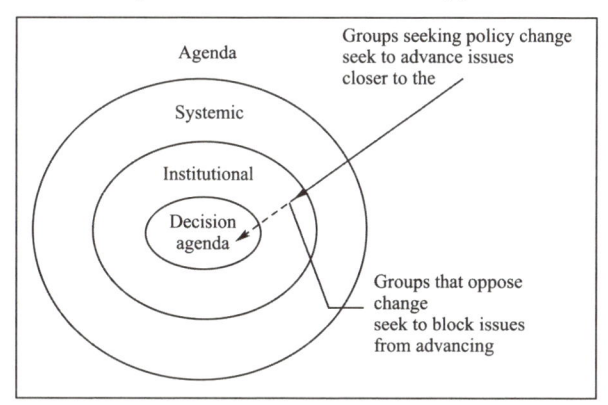

Figure 7-2 Levels of the Agenda

The systemic agenda consists of all issues that are commonly perceived by members of the political community as meriting public attention and as involving matters within the legitimate jurisdiction of existing government authority. The boundary between the systemic agenda and the agenda universe represents the current limit of the legitimate jurisdiction of existing government authority. That boundary can move in or out to accommodate more or fewer ideas over time. The institutional agenda is that list of items explicitly up for the active and serious consideration of authoritative decision makers. The limited amount of time or resources available to any institution or society means that only a limited number of issues are likely to reach the institutional agenda. The decision agenda contains items that are about to be acted upon by governmental body.

Figure 7-2 implies that, except for the limitless agenda universe, the agenda and each level within it is finite and no society or political system can address all the possible alternatives to all possible problems that arise at any time. The agenda is finite so interests must compete with each other to get their issues and their preferred policy alternatives on the agenda. Some issues automatically make it to the agenda. They are mandated or required actions that government must address. The annual budget, legislation to reauthorize existing programs, automatically make it on to the agenda.

Policy makers would rather deal with a problem that the public believes is important than with an issue that people are ignoring. The issue with the best chance of getting on the agenda would be one that is highly salient, but low in conflict, and issues with the worst chance would have low salience and high levels of conflict.

7.2 Policy Formulation

Formulation is a derivative of "formula" and means simply developing a plan, a method, or a prescription for alleviating some need or for acting on a problem. It is the first stage of policy development. There is no set method for it to proceed. Policy formulation is the development of proposed courses of action to help resolve a public problem. Formulation is a technical as well as a political process. Policies that are carelessly formulated are more likely to fail, for example, through using inadequate data, questionable projections, or unreasonable assumptions.

Types of Formulation

There are many types of formulation based on the classification criteria. For example, there can be any number of categories by subject matter-formulation of courses of action for economic problems, education problems, military problems, and so on. Three types are offered here:

— routine formulation

— analogous formulation

— creative formulation

Routine formulation means regularly reformulating similar proposals within an issue-area that has a well-established place on the government agenda.

Analogous formulation means treating a new problem by relying on what was done in developing proposals for similar problems in the past: searching for analogies.

Creative formulation means treating any problem with an essentially unprecedented proposal, one that represents a break with past practice.

Guidelines to Assist in Formulation Analysis

— Formulation does not need to be limited to one set of actors. There may be two or more groups of formulators producing competing (or complementary) proposals.

— Formulation may proceed without the problem ever being very clearly defined, or without formulators ever having much contact with the effected groups.

— There is no necessary connection between formulation and particular institutions, though it is a frequent activity of executive agencies.

— Formulation and reformulation may occur over a long period of time without ever building sufficient support for any single proposal.

— The formulation process itself is never neutral.

Who Is Involved in Policy Formulation?

It is not possible to list all actors involved in formulation across all issue areas. However, it is possible to identify the places to look for participation. Policy formulators can be categorized into two general groups (see Chapter 3):

— formal policy actors(government)

— informal policy actors(general public, interest groups)

Formal policy actors work in government such as legislators, chief executives, and agency officials, for example, who are especially influential in policy formulation. Appointed and career officials in a bureaucracy are among the most experienced and knowledgeable policy actors in most policy areas. They have the technical information needed to develop policy and the political knowledge that comes from working in the policy arena.

Interest groups, universities, professionals, and private research organizations are some of the informal policy actors. Each of them contributes substantially to formulating policy. Formal and informal policy actors correspond to official and unofficial actors.

The executive is typically seen as the source of planning. In the ROK, the president and close associates in the Blue House and the cabinet establish the goals and establish the priorities that set the boundaries for formulation of proposals. The actual development of plans and proposals normally occurs within the bureaucracy, with formal clearance of actions by the upper echelons of political decision making. Legislators are also frequently involved in formulation.

Interest groups are active contributors to policy formulation. Like the bureaucracy, interest groups have a great deal of information at their disposal to provide background or specific solutions to problems. This information ranges from technical details about the problem to judgments about whether a proposal is likely to have political support. Interest groups also attempt to shape policy to serve their own economic or political needs.

National Assembly	Executive	Judiciary
The Assembly plural acts on legislative proposals, appropriate money for all agencies, and oversee the operations of executive agencies.	Executive agencies implement public policies in part by establishing rules and regulations under the discretion granted to them by Congress.	The judiciary affects public policy through established precedent. The courts interpret constitutional and legislative provisions and settle disputes that arise as a result of executive agency decisions.

Lobby legislators; testify to committees; provide information	Participate in rule-making process; lobby for administrative appointments	Participate in rulemaking, has direct contact with agency personnel

Submit amicus briefs, bring court suits

Interest Group	Join interest group	General Public
There are many interest groups. Some focus on all levels of government, while others concentrate on one level only. Many participate in the electoral process through contributions, endorsements, and issue advocacy.		General public can participate in the policy process in a variety ways, including voting, joining interest groups, and contacting government officials directly. The public may have more opportunities to participate directly in policymaking through such channels as referendum and initiatives.

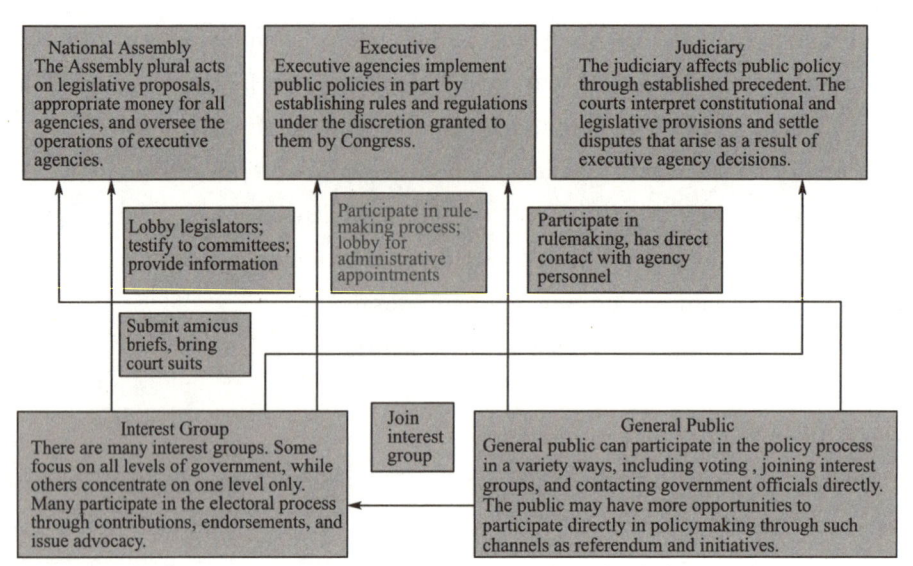

Figure 7-3 Agents of Policy Making and Avenues of Policy Formation

Policy makers are not faced with a single given problem at a time. Formulation is not institution-bound. It may result in one proposal or several and it may proceed with several clear definitions of the problem or no clear definition. It is also worth stressing that formulators make important linkages between problems and policies.

7.3 Policy Legitimation

After making a choice on the policy plan, we must legalize the plan into a truly authoritative policy so that it can be effectively implemented, which is the issue of policy legalization. Policy legalization is a necessary link in policy making, which has a wide range of contents, as well as one aspect that is not discussed enough in domestic policy science literature at present.

Process of Legitimation

Legitimation does not mean achievement of any particular measure of legitimacy. Officials must move ahead as though they knew what they are doing. The principle process of legitimation in a democracy is building a majority coalition. Majority rule is a cornerstone of democratic theory. It is a practical way of getting from political equality and popular sovereignty to a working government. While majority building is the principal process of legitimation, a number of sub processes also exist. For example, if an agency is authorized to establish standards, make contracts, grant resources, or make decisions of any other kind, it must develop legitimate processes by which choices are made.

An agency may, in fact, have the authority to create a complete policy process-defining the problem, formulating proposals, legitimating programs or standards etc. In many cases the choice of one alternative over another is made after consultation with affected groups or following public hearings similar to those conducted in a legislature. Legitimation is involved wherever methods have to be developed to authorize further action.

Who Is Involved?

The main body of policy legalization is the government agency that has the right to obtain the legal status of the policy program according to law. Subject and authority are two aspects of a problem. Whoever has the right to legalize the policy plan will become the subject of policy legalization. In other words, to become the subject of policy legalization, we must have the corresponding authority. This leads to two basic characteristics of the subject of policy legalization, that is, macro universality and micro specificity. At the same time, it must be noted that the subject is determined by the authority, and the authority is stipulated by law. The law stipulates corresponding and different functions and powers for different state organs, and the subject can only implement policy legalization within its legal authority. Legitimation is most closely identified in a democracy with the legislature. Therefore, legislators are surely involved, but majorities may also be put together through the efforts of bureaucrats, legislative staff, all levels local officials.

7.4 Policy Implementation

Implementation is the set of activities directed at putting a program into effect. Three of these activities are particularly important to successful implementation:
— interpretation
— organization
— application

Interpretation is translating a program's language into specific plans, directives, and regulatory requirements.

Organization is the establishment of offices and methods, and the provision of resources for administering a program.

Application represents the routine provision of services, payments, or other program objectives or instruments.

Who Is Involved?

The implementation system for any one program may be populated with a number of different types of actors so it is not easy to generalize. Those interacting for the purpose of putting a program into effect are involved in implementation. This generally includes bureaucrats, legislators, citizens, and private groups, who are all involved in implementation.

Techniques for Effective Implementation

There are some techniques that can make implementation more effective:
— early planning
— scheduling models
— expediters, incentives, and participation
— case management
— management by objectives

Early planning: Early planning is important for policy implementation. These questions are what need to be asked: What action has to be taken? Who is to take it? Do these people have the capacity to do it?

Scheduling models: These models facilitate the coordination of activities of an enterprise and help achieve a better utilization of resources. These models are useful for a wide range of activities, from the seemingly trivial task of scheduling a field office tour for high-ranking officials to the very complex technical job of scheduling intricate engineering processes. Three scheduling models are remarkable among the wide variety:

Expediters, incentives, and participation: The expediter is a single individual or an organizational unit whose position is a way for top executives to demonstrate that things can work, that there is someone who can take rapid action, representing their office and getting things done. Incentives are rewards for helping to move the process along. Participation makes it clear wherein the organization a certain answer to a question will be welcomed and when it will be resisted.

Case management: Most of the resources of a public sector organization are devoted to processing cases: patients in hospitals, welfare clients in a department of human resources, labor disputes in a labor relations board, grant proposals for a foundation, and so on.

Management by Objectives (***MBO***): MBO has four features:
• Establish overall objectives and priorities.
• Encourage executives to contribute maximum efforts to attaining the overall objectives.
• Coordinate planned achievement of all key objectives to promote greater total results for the whole organization.
• Establish control mechanisms for monitoring progress compared to objectives and feed the results back to higher levels.

Process of Influencing Implementation

External factors and internal factors affect implementation and are key in deciding whether it is successful.

External factors

External factors may skew the management effort and the implementing office cannot control many external factors. Among the most important external issues are:

— political vulnerability
— organizational location in the department
— relations with industry/the legislature/the public

Political vulnerability: Pressure by the legislature, individual legislators, industry spokesmen, and individual operators, as well as by executive branch officials may produce a policy in reaction to specific crises, circumstances, and interests.

Organizational location in department: Many decisions are actually made in the top layers of an agency by approval of the head of the office. Office managers are never safe from a decision being reversed as a result of pressure from somewhere else in the government.

Relations with industry/the legislature/the public: Related groups may try to solve problems on a joint basis or there may be conflict and disagreement.

Internal Factors

Even if all external factors were removed, management problems would not be solved and better performance would not automatically follow. The central issues are:

— lack of leadership
— lack of clarity
— lack of stability
— lack of field perspective
— lack of support
— external focus
— waste of staff resources
— lack of staff involvement
— poor communication

Lack of leadership: lack of strong direction leaves the operation vulnerable to whipsawing tactics of both the legislature and industry.

Lack of clarity: Confusion between the regulatory and educational functions creates problems that extend to the roles and functions of various staff members.

Lack of stability: Rearrangement of sections and changes of supervisors create program as well as policy uncertainty.

Lack of field perspective: The office does not recognize the crucial nature of field activity operating from a top-down hierarchical approach.

Lack of support: Staff members, particularly in the field, feel isolated and receive little support from the central office.

External Focus: External crises generated by pressures from the legislature and industry mean that the office chief pays little attention to program and personnel concerns.

Waste of staff resources: The office administration basically ignores professionals rather than use their experience and expertise.

Lack of staff involvement: Staff are not used for problem solving, and policy and program development or evaluation.

Poor communication: There is a lack of clearly-developed, articulated, and written policies throughout the system. Information sharing appears to be blocked to and from the field.

Implementation Approaches

There are three main eras of policy implementation research.

The first era (1960s and early 1970s) was characterized by works such as Derthick (1972) and Pressman and Wildavsky (1973). These studies focused on individual cases and did not create more generalizable theory that could be applied to and tested with other cases.

The second era of implementation studies (mid-1970s) sought to create systematic theories of the policy process that were generalizable to many cases, rather than focused on one or few cases. This can be divided into two separate research approaches:

— top-down approach

— bottom-up approach

The first of these approaches emphasizes a top-down perspective of policy implementation. It claims that policy implementation can be understood by looking at the goals and strategies adopted in the statute or other policy, as structured by the implementers of policy. This focuses on the gaps between the goals set by a policy's drafters and the actual implementation and outcomes of the policy.

The top-down approach is based on a set of important assumptions:

— Policies contain clearly defined goals against which performance can be measured. According to Ryan (1995), "Top-down implementation strategies greatly depend on the capacity of policy objectives to be clearly and consistently defined."

— Policies contain clearly defined policy tools for the accomplishment of goals.

— The policy has a single statute or other authoritative statement of policy.

— There is an "implementation chain" that starts with a policy message at the top and other steps following like links in a chain.

— Policy designers have good knowledge of the capacity and commitment of the implementers. Capacity includes the availability of resources for an implementing organization to carry out its tasks. These include monetary and human resources, legal authority and autonomy as well as the knowledge needed to implement policy effectively. Commitment includes the desire of the implementers to carry out the goals of policy designers. A high level of commitment means that the values and goals of the policy designers are shared by lower-level implementers such as teachers, police officers, or social workers.

The second approach emphasizes a bottom-up perspective, which suggests that implementation is best studied by starting at the lowest levels of the implementation system or chain and moving upward to see where implementation is more or less successful.

Bottom-up approaches recognize that goals are ambiguous rather than explicit and may conflict with other goals in the same policy area as well as with the norms and motivations of lower-level bureaucrats. Top-down models are most concerned with compliance, while bottom-up approaches value understanding how conflict can be overcome with bargaining and compromise.

The bottom-up approach does not require that there be a single defined policy in the form of a statute or other form. Rather, policy can be thought of as a set of laws, rules, practices, and norms that shape the ways government and interest groups address problems such as energy or crime. Thus, implementation can be viewed as a continuation of the conflicts and compromises that occur throughout the policy process, not just before and during enactment.

This bottom-up approach has a number of advantages. In particular, the lack of a focus on a specific program and a fixed top-to-bottom implementation chain means that the bottom-up approach can view implementation as working through a network of factors. This is much more like an issue network or policy community than a rigidly-specified process that fails to account for the richness of the policy-making environment.

On the other hand, there are also important shortcomings to consider in the bottom-up approach. First, the bottom-up approach overemphasizes the ability of low-level bureaucrats to frustrate the goals of top policy makers. Second, bottom-up models of implementation assume that groups are active participants in the implementation process even though this is not always true. The bottom-up approach also fails to take into account the power differences of target groups.

The third era: synthesis Researchers have sought to combine the benefits of the top-down and bottom-up approaches into one model or synthesis because of their relative strengths and weaknesses. They look for one model that can address both the structuring of policy from the top and the likelihood of its subversion or at least its alteration at the ultimate point of implementation. Sabatier (1991) argued that a conceptual framework should be developed that combines the best of the top-down and bottom-up approaches. The top-down approach is best where there is a dominant program (or law) that is well structured and where the researcher's resources for studying implementation are limited. The bottom-up approach is best when an analyst is interested in the dynamics of local implementation and where there is no single dominant program.

Sabatier's synthesis relies on a framework for studying public policy known as the Advocacy Coalition Framework, or ACF (see Chapter 4). Refining and reconciling the top-down and bottom-up approaches, Goggin et al. (1990) devised a theory of policy implementation that relies on sending messages between policy makers and implementers.

7.5 Policy Evaluation

Policy evaluation is an indispensable step in the whole process of policy analysis. It is a special research activity with specific standards, methods and procedures. Policy evaluation is a kind of evaluation behavior that judges the effectiveness, efficiency and value of a policy according to certain standards and procedures. The purpose is to obtain information about these aspects as a basis for comparison, selection, decision on policy changes, policy improvement and formulation of new policies. Evaluation is the measurement of the desirable and undesirable consequences of actions taken to forward some goal. This includes:

— the procedures of gathering information about the results of planned social actions

— measurement of the effectiveness of the program in terms of the fulfillment of the program's objective

— describing the effects of a program and thereby make progressive adjustments in order to reach goals more effectively

The six main uses of an evaluation study are:

— to discover whether and how well objectives are being fulfilled

— to determine the reasons for specific successes and failures

— to uncover the principles underlying a successful program

— to direct the course of experiments with techniques for increasing effectiveness

— to lay the basis for further research on the reasons for the relative success of alternative techniques

— to redefine the means to be used for attaining objectives, and even to redefine goals in the light of research findings

These purposes strongly suggest an almost intrinsic relationship between evaluation and program planning and development. Evaluative research provides the basic information for designing and redesigning action programs. Some questions that need to be asked for a satisfactory evaluation include:

— What kind of change is desired?
— How is change to be brought about?
— What is the evidence that the changes observed are due to the means employed?
— What is the meaning of the changes?
— Were there unexpected consequences?

The major concern in evaluation is with the reliability and validity of the measures of effectiveness and with an understanding of the reasons for success or failure. Six steps are essential for evaluation:

— identification of the goals to be evaluated
— analysis of the problems the activity must address
— description and standardization of the activity
— measurement of the degree of change
— determination whether the observed change is due to the activity or to some other cause
— some identification of the durability of the effects

Evaluation Process

Evaluation always starts with some value, either explicit or implicit. Then a goal is formulated based on this value. The selection of goals usually comes before or happens with value formation. A value may be defined as any aspect of a situation event, or object that is seen as being good, bad, desirable, or undesirable. Values are the principles by which people establish priorities and hierarchies of importance among needs, demands, and goals (Kingdon, 1995). Figure 7-6 illustrates the evaluation process.

Examples of goal-setting would be fewer people should die from cancer. Goal setting forces are always in competition with each other for money, resources, and effort. Next, there has to be some way of measuring goal attainment. If the goal is set that fewer people should die from cancer, then some means of discovering how many are presently dying from cancer is needed. The nature of the evaluation depends largely on the type of measures available to determine the attainment of objectives.

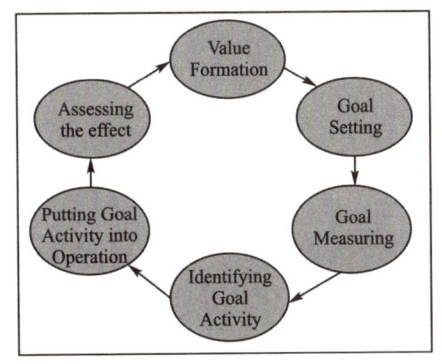

Figure 7-4　The Evaluation Process

The next step in the process is identification of some kind of goal-attaining activity. In the case of cancer, for example, a program of early detection and treatment might be considered. Then the goal-attaining activity is put into operation. Diagnostic centers would be set up and people urged to come in for check-ups.

This goal-directed operation is assessed at some point. This stage includes the evaluation of the degree to which the operating program has achieved the predetermined objectives. This assessment may be done scientifically.

Finally, a judgment is made on the basis of the assessment as to whether the goal-directed activity was worthwhile. This brings the process back to value formation. People may now say that it is good to have cancer diagnostic centers. At the end of the evaluation process, there may be a new value, or the process may reaffirm, reassess, or redefine an old value.

Objectives and Assumptions

The most identifying feature of evaluation is the presence of some goal or objective whose measure of attainment constitutes the main focus of the research problem. Evaluation must have a goal. Some of the more general considerations involved in the formulation of objectives for evaluation include:

— What is the nature of the content of the objectives?

Is the program interested in changing knowledge, attitudes, and/or behavior? Is it concerned with producing exposure, awareness, interest, and/or action? Answers to these questions permit the evaluator to determine within what regions the concepts are set.

— Who is the target of the program?

At which groups in the population is the program aimed? Is the program seeking to change individuals, groups, or whole communities?

— When is the desired change to take place?

Is the program seeking an immediate effect or gradually building toward some postponed effect?

— Are the objectives unitary or multiple?

Is the program aimed at a single change or at a series of changes? Are these changes the same for all people or do they vary for different groups of people?

— What is the desired magnitude of effect?

Is the program seeking widespread or concentrated results? Does any particular proportion of effectiveness need to be attained before the program can be considered a success? Are there any specified standards of accomplishment that have to be met?

— How is the objective to be attained?

What means are to be used to implement the program? Will the program depend primarily on voluntary cooperation or will an attempt be made to secure legal sanctions? Will personal or impersonal, formal or informal appeals be made?

These six considerations deal with basic questions that need to be answered in formulating the objectives of a program for the sake of evaluation.

Many of the answers to the questions raised above will require an examination of the underlying assumptions of the stated objectives. Assumptions may be divided into two types:

— value assumption

— validity assumption

Value assumptions pertain to the system of beliefs concerning what is good within a society or subgroup of society. There may be such almost universally accepted value assumptions as "human life is worth saving," "unnecessary suffering is bad," and "good health is desired."

Validity assumptions are much more specifically related to program objectives. Such assumptions, for example, underlie the belief that the cause for much prenatal morality may be found in lack of care during pregnancy and that prenatal clinics that supply information to expectant mothers can improve care and result in a reduction in prenatal mortality.

These validity assumptions help explain the move from mental institutions to home care based on the belief that people are better off at home than in institutions. The concepts of validity and reliability are important elements in the establishment of assumptions. Each assumption assumes the validity of an objective, meaning that each objective is valid for the achievement of some desired value.

Functions of Evaluation

Evaluation provides several functions that make it particularly useful to engage in the process.

Providing information: First and most important function of evaluation is providing reliable and valid information about policy performance, that is, the extent to which needs, values, and opportunities have been realized through public action.

Revealing particular goals: Evaluation reveals the extent to which particular goals and objectives have been attained and helps make practical inferences about the degree to which policy problems have been resolved.

Clarification and critique of values: Evaluation contributes to the clarification and critique of values that underlie the selection of goals and objectives. Values are clarified by defining and operationalizing goals and objectives. Values are also critiqued by questioning the appropriateness of goals and objectives in relation to the problem being addressed.

Creating alternative sources: In questioning goals and objectives, analysts may examine alternative sources of values (such as public officials, vested interests, and client groups) as well as their grounds in different forms of rationality (technical, economic, legal, social).

Contributing to other policy-analysis methods: Evaluation may contribute to the application of other policy-analysis methods, including recommendation and problem structuring. Information about inadequate policy performance may contribute to the restructuring of policy problems, for example, by showing that goals and objectives should be redefined.

Contributing to the definition of new or revised policy alternatives: Evaluation can also contribute to the definition of new or revised policy alternatives. For example, this can be done by showing that a previously favored policy alternative should be abandoned and replaced with another one.

Problems Approach and Experimentation

Evaluation is a technique for managing public organizations in which systematic data gathering and other research-like operations play a considerable role. From this angle, research-infused evaluation differs from other social research not in regard to the research designs and data-collection methods employed, but in the problems to be addressed. Problems, not designs or methods, provide the identity of evaluation.

There are eight primary evaluation problems. They can be expressed in the form of eight questions. Evaluators may consider some or all of the following eight problems:

— The purpose problem: What are the overall aims of the evaluation?

— The organization (evaluator) problem: Who should conduct the evaluation and how should it be organized?

— The intervention analysis problem: How is the objective of the evaluation to be characterized and described? Is the government intervention (normally a policy, a program, the components of policies and programs, or the provision of services and goods) regarded as a means or as a self-contained entity?

— The conversion problem: What does execution look like between the formal instigation of the intervention and the final outputs?

— The results problem: What are the outputs and outcomes-immediate, intermediate, and ultimate-of the intervention?

— The impact problem: What contingencies (causal factors, operating causal forces), the intervention included, explain the results?

— The criterion problem: What value criteria should be used to assess the merits of the intervention? What standards of performance can be used based on the value criteria to judge success or failure or satisfactory performance? What are the actual merits of the intervention?

— The utilization problem: How is the evaluation to be utilized? How is it actually used?

The first and second questions concern the evaluation of the intervention, three through seven are related to the intervention itself, and question eight concerns the feedback process.

Some Evaluation Techniques

Some techniques of evaluation such as Cost Benefit Analysis (CBA), Cost Effectiveness Analysis (CEA), and decision analysis have already been discussed. Here some other techniques are covered: network analysis, linear programming, simulation.

Network Analysis

Once a program or project has been decided, the problems of actually scheduling the components of the program remain: distributing resources to the various parts of the project, and rescheduling activities when conditions change. This phase of planning is especially difficult when dealing with non-repetitive tasks. These are jobs that have not been done before in exactly the same manner. Two similar network techniques have been developed for scheduling complex projects consisting of many interrelated tasks:

— program evaluation and review technique(PERT)
— critical path method(CPM)

***Program evaluation and review technique* (PERT)** defines and links together the various tasks that must be done as part of a project in a sequenced network. Time estimates for the completion of each task are used to examine the various ways of changing individual task times to speed up the completion of the entire project.

Suppose a city park department wants to set up a neighborhood playground. The first step is to define the tasks or activities necessary to complete the project. Four activities are necessary to build the proposed playground: (1) the necessary materials and equipment must be purchased; (2) the site must be cleaned of trash and weeds; (3) the playground equipment must be installed; and (4) some landscaping must be done.

The second step is to place these activities in a functional sequence as in the figure. Activities are represented as lines with arrowheads that connect events. Events are the beginnings and endings of activities and are represented as circles. Each project begins and ends with a single event, and each activity has a beginning event and an ending event.

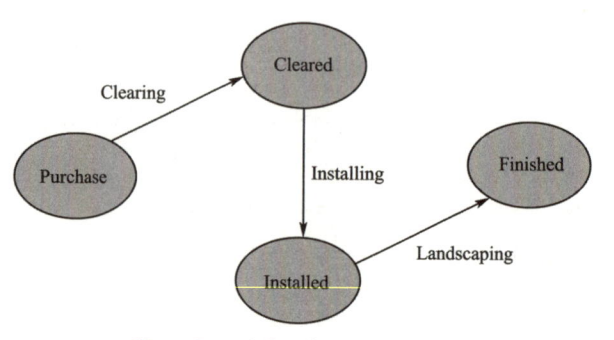

Figure 7-5 A Simple PERT Network

The third step consists of getting time estimates for each activity from the various work groups. Because getting only one-time estimate is risky, three estimates are requested for each activity. The most optimistic time, or *a*, is the time it could take under the best conditions, the time likely to happen only one out of 100 times. The most pessimistic time, or *t*, is the time it would take under the worst conditions, a time also having a one percent probability of happening. The most likely time, or *m*, is the time expected to be the most common (modal) if the activity is repeated many times under many conditions. These estimates are then combined algebraically to calculate the expected time or t_e, as represented in the following formula:

$$t_e = \frac{a + 4m + b}{6}$$

This formula weights the most likely time (*m*) more heavily than both the most pessimistic time (*t*) and the most optimistic time (*a*), which are given the same weight. If there is only a one in 100 chance of *t* or *a*, then they should have less influence on t_e than *m*, the most likely time.

The fourth step is to determine the earliest date by which the project can be completed by figuring out the earliest expected date at which each activity can be finished.

Critical path method (CPM): Like PERT, the critical path method uses networks and time estimates. CPM adds cost estimates to find the most efficient way of speeding up, or crashing, a project. The first steps are to estimate a normal time and a normal cost for each event and then to estimate a crash time and a crash cost for each activity.

Next step is to build the network and calculate t_e and the critical path, just as in PERT. Then the critical path is shortened by first crashing the activity with the cheapest crash cost. This provides a new time estimate for that activity, and the critical path is recalculated.

The next step is to un-crash the activities that do not lie on the critical path to the point where they become critical. Some of the crash projects have slack time and may be un-crashed to save money without changing the project completion date. Crashed activities are un-crashed until all are critical, a process that provides the optimum solution, the least cost, and minimum time to complete the project.

Who Can Do Evaluations?

Systematic evaluation studies are grounded in social science research techniques. Therefore, most evaluation specialists have social science training. At first glance, someone unacquainted with evaluation research would undoubtedly find professional discussions of evaluation difficult to comprehend. As in any other professional field, evaluators have developed their own vocabulary, shorthand expressions, and rules for doing the work. Some of the complexity of evaluation stems from the inherent tendencies of those in a professional field to develop their own language, but at least part of the need for special terminology derives from the unique concepts and insights developed in each field. At the most complex level, evaluation activities can be so technically complicated, sophisticated in conception, costly, and of such long duration that they require the dedicated participation of highly-trained specialists at ease with the latest in social science theory, research methods, and statistical techniques. Such highly complex evaluations are usually conducted by specialized evaluators. At the other extreme, there are many evaluation tasks that can be easily understood and can be carried out by persons of modest expertise and experience.

Evaluation, by contrast, is a policy analysis procedure used to produce information about the performance of policies in satisfying needs, values, or opportunities that constitute a defined problem.

In the main subject of policy evaluation, in addition to legislature, political parties, judicial organs, social organizations and citizens, more important evaluation subjects include policy makers and policy implementer, professional institutions and personnel, mass media.

Models of Evaluation

Different models of evaluation may help understand more about the process. This section considers several such models.

Effectiveness Models

The greatest number of models fall under the category of effectiveness models. These include the goal attainment, comprehensive, client-oriented, and stakeholder models (see Figure 7-6).

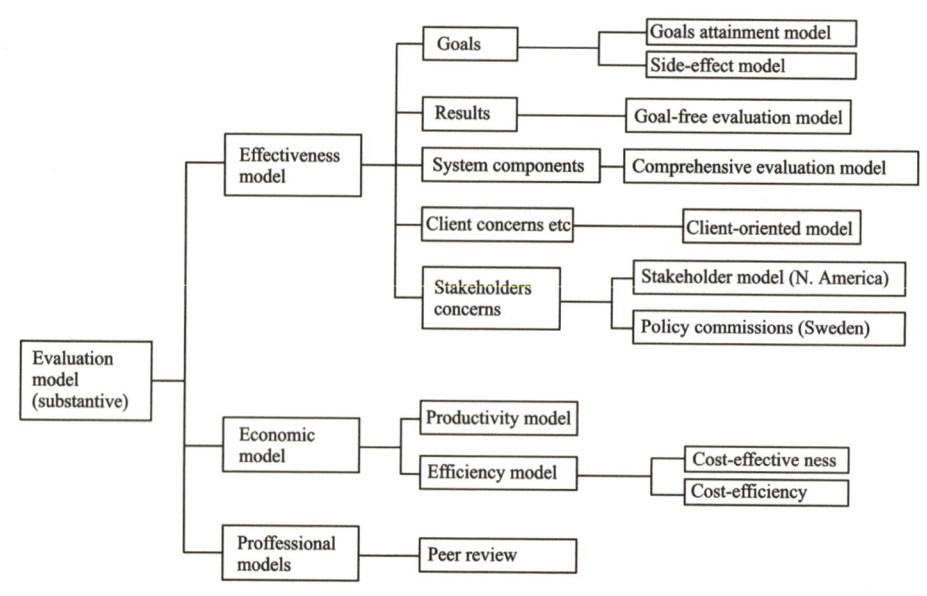

Figure 7-6 Models of Evaluation

Goal attainment evaluation: Goal attainment evaluation is an effectiveness model because it asks questions about the substantive content, output, and outcomes of the program, not about program procedures like equity of treatment or due process. It differs from economic and institutional models in that it raises substantive issues only, but neither pays heed to program costs nor to the organization of the evaluation.

Comprehensive evaluation: Comprehensive evaluation models are rooted in the conviction that evaluation should be more extensive than in the narrow goal-attainment model. The process of passing judgments should not be limited to achieved results but should at least include implementation and maybe even planning.

The first task of the evaluator in comprehensive evaluation is to contrast the intended results with the actual outcomes, the goals with the reality.

Client-oriented model: Proceeding from an entirely different point of departure, client-oriented evaluation takes the goals, expectations, concerns, or even needs of the program as its organizing principle and merit criteria. At the heart of the client-oriented evaluation is the question of whether the program satisfies client concerns, desires, or expectations.

Stakeholder model: The organizing principle of the stakeholder model is the concerns and issues of the people who have an interest in or are affected by the intervention. Stakeholder-based evaluation starts by mapping out the major groups who are involved or have an interest in the emergence, execution, and results of the program. The evaluator identifies the people who created the program, who initiated and funded it, and particularly those who are charged with its implementation.

Economic Models

The most typical feature of the economic model is to focus on cost, it includes productivity and efficiency.

The productivity model can be expressed through the mathematical formula:

$$\text{Productivity} = \frac{\text{output}}{\text{input}}$$

Productivity has some technical advantages as a measure of public sector activities. Costs are sometimes not very difficult to calculate since they reach agencies in terms of money. However, it may be hard at other times to trace the relevant costs because the funds allocated and spent are often indicated on the books as lump sums. Outputs, on the other hand, may be exacting to catch and compute, even though productivity only presupposes that they are indicated in physical, not monetary, terms.

Efficiency can be measured in two ways, as cost-benefit or cost-effectiveness. Efficiency assessments provide a frame of reference for relating costs to program results. In cost benefit analysis, both program inputs and outcomes are measured in monetary terms. Inputs are estimated in monetary terms and outcomes in terms of actual impact in cost-effectiveness analysis.

Professional Models: Peer Review

The professional models refer to that professionals evaluate the implementation of other personnel according to their own value criteria and quality standards, mainly including peer review, such as lawyers evaluating lawyers, professors evaluating professors, surgeons evaluating surgeons, etc. The peer review mostly refers to a screening procedure for the selection of contributions to scientific journals. Submitted articles are subjected to peer review in order to decide whether they ought to be accepted for publication. Peer review is also used to offer guidance to research foundations concerning which projects should get funding. Research proposals are submitted to a group of respected colleagues for screening. On top of that, peer review has also been used to investigate and judge supposed transgressions of rules of ethical conduct and inherited research practices. This model is constantly used in research evaluation. Peer review focuses on making a comprehensive quality judgment on the evaluation object. In some technical fields, political officials leave the planning and discussion of professional technical issues to well-educated professionals.

7.6 Policy Termination

Termination means ending, concluding, or cessation. Public policy termination is the deliberate conclusion or cessation of specific government functions, programs, policies, or organizations. Although termination represents the final step in the policy process, it should not conceptually be something to be considered last. The termination stage can be treated as both an end and a beginning: an end to a program that has served its purpose, and a beginning to correcting an errant policy or set of programs.

Types of Policy Termination

Policy termination refers to the behavior of policy makers to terminate unnecessary policies or projects after careful evaluation of policies or projects. Generic policy termination uses the term "policy" to include government functions, organizations, and programs as well as policies themselves.

Functions: A function is defined as a service provided by a government for its citizens. It transcends organization and policies. A number of agencies and their respective policies can all serve the same function.

The relative performance of functions is not difficult to understand. Generally speaking, the government will only dispense with services or functions if society lacks either the assets or judgment to provide itself with necessary services. Economists have identified the category of "public goods" that can be considered governmental functions. National defense is a function that has outlived any number of reorganizations of the national defense establishment. Jurisdiction over regulatory matters and the redistribution of wealth and income are other instances of government functions. These functions or obligations are assumed by the government as a result of the demands of its citizens, and are instituted because they fill a need not otherwise met. Terminating them would therefore cause hardship and even suffering, the effects of which would spread outward through society.

Organizations: Organizations are groups of individuals working together fora common purpose. Organizations are created to respond to specific needs although they may, and probably do expand their domain over time. They are designed to last and they do precisely that. Although organizations are rarely subjected to complete termination, it should be clear that they are more susceptible than governmental functions.

Policies: Organizations select and implement policies, which are generalized approaches or strategies toward solving particular problems. Although an organization can expend significant resources devising and executing appropriate policies, it should be stressed that policies are easier to terminate than the sponsoring organization itself.

This is true for four reasons. First, unless the policy and the institution are exactly coincident or inextricably interwoven, the organization will act to preserve itself before saving its components parts. The organization would prefer to forsake some of its policies rather than have the organization itself terminated. Second, a policy cannot usually find as many allies as the larger parent organization can. In the simple calculus of power politics, policies have fewer chips to expend on their survival. Third, policies are easier to evaluate relative to a given objective than an organization, which could have multiple policy objectives. Criteria are more available for the analyst to measure the policy's relative ineffectiveness and to support a case for termination. In this sense, it becomes much more vulnerable than the parent organization. Finally, most policies generate critics who can be expected to coalesce behind any termination proposal. Organizations, of course, also have a group of natural enemies. However, they are usually disposed against particular policies and therefore less likely to join a termination coalition against the organization.

Programs: Programs are the easiest of the four targets or levels of termination to end. Although they occupy the lowest stratum of the analyst's attention, individual programs have the fewest political resources to protect them and represent the smallest investment on the part of the organization. They are closest to the problem and therefore their impact can be most directly measured and, if found lacking, can most easily be blamed. On the other hand, the day-to-day minutia of program implementation might serve to shield them from the critical view of the analyst who may assume that the policy level is the appropriate focus of attention.

Ways of Policy Termination

In general, there are six ways to end policies:

Policy abolition: That is, to announce the abolition of a policy directly. According to the development and change of the political, economic and socialeconomic situation, the government irregularly cleans up and abolishes a large number of inappropriate and outdated policies. For example, after China's accession to the WTO, the Standing Committee of the National People's Congress and the State Council immediately announced the abolition of more than 830 national laws, regulations and policies that are inconsistent with WTO rules.

Policy substitution: It refers to replacing the old policy with a new one, but the policy problems and policy objectives have not changed basically. The new policy supplements and amends the old policy to better solve the problems that the old policy did not solve or could not solve at all, so as to meet the policy needs of target groups and achieve the policy objectives.

Policy consolidation: It means that although the old policy has been terminated, some of its actual functions have not been completely cancelled, but have been incorporated into other policy contents. The method is as follows: the terminated policy content is merged into an existing policy or two or more terminated policies are merged into a new policy.

Policy decomposition: It is to divide the content of the old policy into several parts according to certain rules, and each part forms a new policy. For example, social security-endowment insurance, unemployment insurance, life insurance, medical insurance, maternity insurance, etc.

Policy curtailment: It is to adopt a gradual approach to gradually end the policy. Its purpose is to effectively mitigate the huge impact brought by the end of the policy, gradually coordinate the relationship between all aspects, and reduce those unnecessary losses.

Policy legitimation: An effective policy, which has been implemented for a long time, is considered and adopted by the legislature or the administrative organ that authorizes legislation, and then becomes a law or administrative regulation. This is the end of policy in another sense.

Discussion Questions

1. What is policy analysis? What does it mean to bring scientific knowledge to the political process?
2. What is the nature of policy analysis?
3. How can policy alternatives be assessed?
4. What are the different types of analysis?
5. What are the steps of policy analysis?

Vocabularies

systematic agenda
institutional agenda
decision agenda
policy formulation
routine formulation
analogous formulation
creative formulation
formal policy actors
informal policy actors
legitimation
interpretation
organization
application
early planning
schedule models

expediters

incentives

participation

Case Management System

Management By Objectives

external factors

internal factors

political vulnerability

first era

second era

top-down approach

bottom-up approach

value assumption

validity assumption

network analysis

linear programming

simulation

Program Evaluation and Review Technique

Critical Path Method

productivity

efficiency

peer review

References

Allision, Graham. 1971. Essence of Decision: Explaining the Cuban Missile Crisis. Boston: Little, Brown.

Baumgartner, Frank and Jones, Bryan D. 1993. Agendas and Instability in American Politics. Chicago: University of Chicago Press.

Bendor, Jonathan and Hammond, Thomas H. 1992. "Rethinking Allison's Models." American Political Science Review, 86(2).

Berry, Jeffery M. 1989. "Subgovernments, Issue Networks, and Political Conflict." Remaking American Politics. Ed. Richard and Sidney Milkis Harris. Boulder, Colorado: Westview Press.

Birkland, Thomas A. 2001. An Introduction to the Policy Process: Theories, Concepts, and Models of Public Policy Making. New York: M. E. Sharpe.

Cigler, Allan J. 1991. "Interest Groups: A Subfield in Search of an Identity." Political Science, Looking to the Future: Volume IV: American Institutions. Ed. Evanston, IIIinois: Northwestern University Press.

Cohen, Michael D., March, James G., and Olson, Johan P. 1972. "A Garbage Can Model of Organization Choice." Administrative Science Quarterly, 17:1-25.

Derthick, Martha. 1972. New Towns in Town. Washington, DC: Urban Institute.

Easton, David. 1965. A Systems Analysis of Political Life. New York: John Wiley.

Goggin, Malcolm L., Bowman, Anne O'M., Lester, James P., and O'Toole, Laurence J. 1990. Implementation Theory and Practice: Toward a Third Generation. Glenview, Illinois: Scott Foresman/Little Brown.

Kingdon, John W. 1995. Agendas, Alternatives and Public Policies. 2nd ed. New York: Harper Collins.

Kraft, Michael E. and Furlong, Scott R. 2004. Public Policy: Politics, Analysis, and Alternatives. Washington, D.C. CQ Press.

Lindblom, Charles E. 1959. "The Science of Muddling Through." Public Administration Review, 19: 79-88.

Majone, Giandomenico. 1989. Evidence, Argument, and Persuasion in the Policy Process. New Haven: Yale University Press.

Nakamura, Robert T. 1987. "The Textbook Policy Process and Implementation Research." Policy Studies Journal, 7(1): 142-154.

Neustadt, Richard E. 1990. Presidential Power and the Modern Presidents: The Politics of Leadership from Roosevelt to Reagan. New York: Free Press.

Peters, B. Guy. 1999. American Public Policy: Promise and Performance. Chappaqua, New York: Chatham House/Seven Rivers.

Pressman, Jeffrey and Wildavsky, Aaron. 1973. Implementation. Berkeley, CA: University of California Press.

Ryan, Neal. 1995. "Unraveling Conceptual Developments in Implementation Analysis." Australian Journal of Public Administration, 54(1): 65-81.

Sabatier, Paul A. 1991. "Political Science and Public Policy." PS: Political Science and Politics, 24(2): 144-147.

Vedung, Evert. 2005. Public Policy and Evaluation Program. New Brunswick, New Jersey: Transaction Publishers.

Zahariadis, Nikolaos. 1993. "To Sell or Not to Sell? Telecommuni-cations Policy in Britain and France." Journal of Public Policy, 12(4): 355-376.

第 7 章

政策过程

　　对任何对问题的定义都代表了许多可能的观点之一。定义问题是不够的,议程设置是将问题引起精英或公众的关注的过程。议程上的项目需要在采取行动之前从系统的关注转移到政府议程再到决策议程。政策制定可能是常规的,相似的或创造性的,涉及正式和非正式的参与者。政策合法化是任何政治制度构建过程中的重要环节,因为政治是基于合法化的。政策合法化过程既简单又复杂,同时也是涉及正式和非正式参与者的动态的过程。政策实施是使政策生效的过程,政策执行涉及解释、组织和应用。政策有效执行的技巧包括前期规划、设计模型、监督、奖励、参与、案例管理,目标管理。政策执行受基于自上而下,自下而上或综合的内在、外在因素影响。政策评估是政策过程的一个重要环节。通过政策评估,人们才能够判断一项政策是否收到了预期效果,从而决定政策是继续、调整还是终结。政策终结是政策过程的最后一个环节,但也是承上启下的一环。政策终结包括将功能、组织、政策本身和计划予以终止或结束。

7.1　问题定义和议程设置

　　图 7-1 描述了政策过程的总体情况。问题定义是一个表征问题,因为对情境的每一种描述都只是众多观点中的一种。问题定义具有战略意义,因为团体、个人和政府机构有会意识地阐述并推动自己偏爱的议案。个人的观点和背景决定了他们如何定义问题并与之相关。个人的意识形态和价值观可能会影响问题的定义方式,即个人认为某种情况完全应该成为问题。

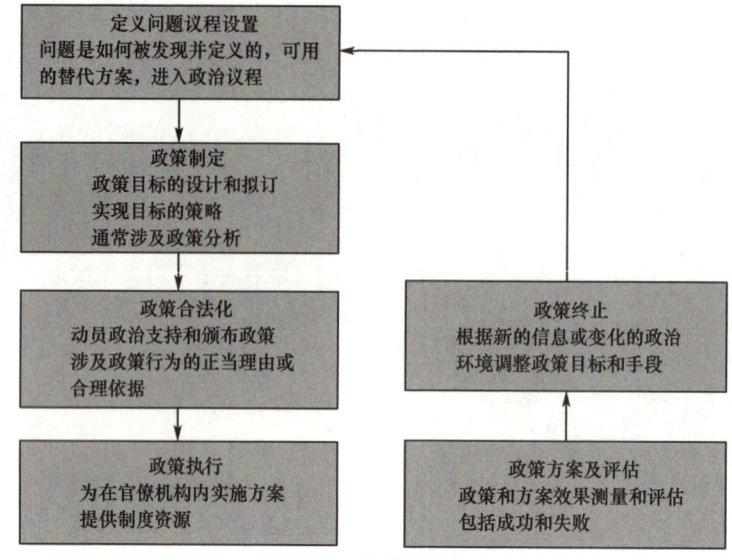

```
定义问题议程设置
问题是如何被发现并定义的，可用
的替代方案，进入政治议程
            ↓
政策制定
政策目标的设计和拟订
实现目标的策略
通常涉及政策分析
            ↓
政策合法化                    政策终止
动员政治支持和颁布政策        根据新的信息或变化的政治
涉及政策行为的正当理由或      环境调整政策目标和手段
合理依据
            ↓                       ↑
政策执行                      政策方案及评估
为在官僚机构内实施方案        政策和方案效果测量和评估
提供制度资源                  包括成功和失败
```

图 7-1　政策流程图

通过提供有关问题性质及其影响的新的、客观的信息，政策分析人员可以帮助引导政治辩论，以合理评估问题的范畴、原因和可能的解决方案。例如，对城市扩张的研究可能会强调对公路拥堵、土地使用和供水的不利影响，并建议为实现城市更好发展如何将这些负面影响降至最低。毫无疑问，这项研究的结果和建议在房地产开发商和支持发展的公职人员之间的观点会有很大不同。

定义问题不足以找到解决方案或制定政策。一个问题必须在议程上升到足够高，社会问题很难进入政策议程，因为许多问题在任何特定时间都在争夺社会和政府的关注。有些列入议程，有些则没有。议程是一系列问题，包括对问题成因的理解及解决方案以及公众和政府官员等其他因素。议程可以作为立法机构面前的具体议案清单，但也包括一系列对于问题的存在和重要性的认识，以及政府、私营部门、非营利组织或部分或全部这些机构应如何处理这些问题的联合行动。

议程设置是问题和备选方案获得或失去公众和精英关注的过程。议程是公众和政府官员关注的对公共问题、解决方案和其他要素的态度的集合。议程设置是政策过程的核心。如果一个问题没有引起适当的关注，在没有得到政府回应的情况下可能会被搁置。因此，学习公共政策学生需要了解如何促进某些问题进入政策议程。

政策议程的建立是一复杂的过程。各种问题能否进入正式的政策议程，取决于各种力量的交互影响力。一般来说，公众关心和讨论的各种问题叫公众议程，进入决策程序并被正式提出来讨论的各种问题，则是制度议程或政府议程。

议程实际上相当广泛。考虑议程的几个层级非常必要，如图 7-2 所示。最广泛的议程范围包含社会或政治社区的成员普遍认为值得公众注意，并由与现存政府权威中立法范围内的事物相关的一切问题组成。议程领域中的大量想法在政治意义上或多或少是"可接受的"，并且有可能转移并出现在系统议程中。

系统议程通常包括政府认为值得公众关注的所有问题，以及涉及现有政府机构合法管辖范围内的事项。系统议程与议程范围之间的界限代表了现有政府机构合法管辖权的局限。随着时间的推移,该边界可以移入或移出以容纳更多的想法。政府议程是明确提出权威决策者积极的和认真考虑的项目清单。任何制度或社会可用的时间或资源有限,意味着只有有限数量的问题可能会进入政府议程。决策议程包含即将由政府机构采取行动的议案。

图 7-2 表明,除了无限的议程体系外,议程及其中的每个层级都是有限的,任何社会或政治制度都无法提出解决可能出现的所有问题的所有可能替代方案。议程是有限的,因此利益群体间必须相互竞争,以便将他们的问题和他们的首选政策方案纳入议程。有些问题会自动提交至议程,因为需要政府必须采取强制性或必要的行动。如年度预算,重新授权现有计划的立法,以及执行总统提名的行政任命,都会自动被列入议程。

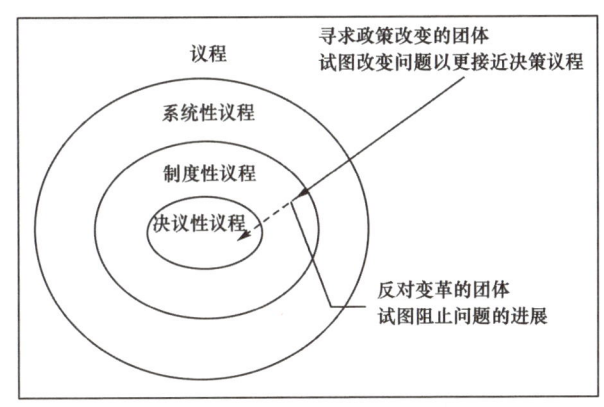

图 7-2　议程的层级

政策制定者选择处理公众认为重要而不是被人们忽视的问题。最有可能提上议程的问题通常是一个非常突出且冲突较少的问题,因为冲突双方势均力敌的问题具有较低的显著性和较高的冲突程度。

7.2　政策制定

制定是"方案"的衍生物,意味着简单地制订计划,方法或方案以减轻某些需求或对问题采取行动。这是政策展开的第一阶段。政策制定是制定帮助解决公共问题的拟议的行动方案。政策制定既是技术过程,也是政治过程。欠考虑的政策制定很有可能失败,例如,使用不充分的数据、不准确的预测或不合理的假设。

政策制定类型

基于不同的分类标准,可以有不同类型的政策制定。例如,按主题可以有多种类别——制定经济问题、教育问题、军事问题等的提案。这里提供三种类型:
——常规政策制定

——相似的政策制定

——创造性的政策制定

常规政策制定意味着在政府议程中具有明确地位的问题领域内需要定期重新制定的类似的提案。

相似的政策制定意味着依据过去对类似问题提出建议所做的工作来处理一个新问题；寻找类比。

创造性的政策制定意味着用一个前所未有的提议来处理问题，是对过去实践的一个突破。

辅助政策制定分析的指南

——制定不需要限定于某一群体，可能有两个或多个群体的制定者提出竞争（或补充）性的提案。

——制定可以在没有明确定义问题的情况下进行，或者制定者与受影响的群体没有很多接触。

——虽然制定是执行机构的一项经常活动，但在制定和特定机构之间没有必要的联系。

——制定和重新制定可能需要很长一段时间，因为没有任何一项提案获得足够的支持。

——制定过程本身永远不会中立。

谁参与政策制定？

不可能列出涉及所有问题领域的所有参与者，但是可以尝试识别和发现参与的主体。政策制定者可分为两大类（见第 3 章）：

——正式的政策参与者（政府）

——非正式的政策参与者（公众、利益集团）

官方政策主体是政府的工作人员，例如立法者、首席执行官和机构官员，他们在政策制定方面有影响力。政府中被任命的官员是大多数政策领域最有经验和知识渊博的政策参与者之一。他们拥有制定政策所需的技术信息以及政策领域的知识。

利益集团、大学、专业人士和私人研究组织是一些非正式的政策参与者，他们都对制定政策做出了重大贡献。正式和非正式政策参与者对应于官方机构和非官方机构。

通常将行政机关视为规划的源头。在韩国，总统和与之关系密切的青瓦台及内阁最高首长制定目标并确定优先事项，为制定提案设定了界限。规划和提案的实际发展——议案的正式批准——通常发生在政府内部的政治决策的高层。立法机关通常也参与政策制定。

利益集团是政策制定的积极贡献者。与官僚机构一样，利益集团可以随时提供大量信息，提供问题的背景信任或具体解决方案。这些信息包括问题的技术细节，以及对提案是否可能获得政治支持的判断。利益集团还试图设计政策以满足其自身的经济或政治需求。

第7章 政策过程

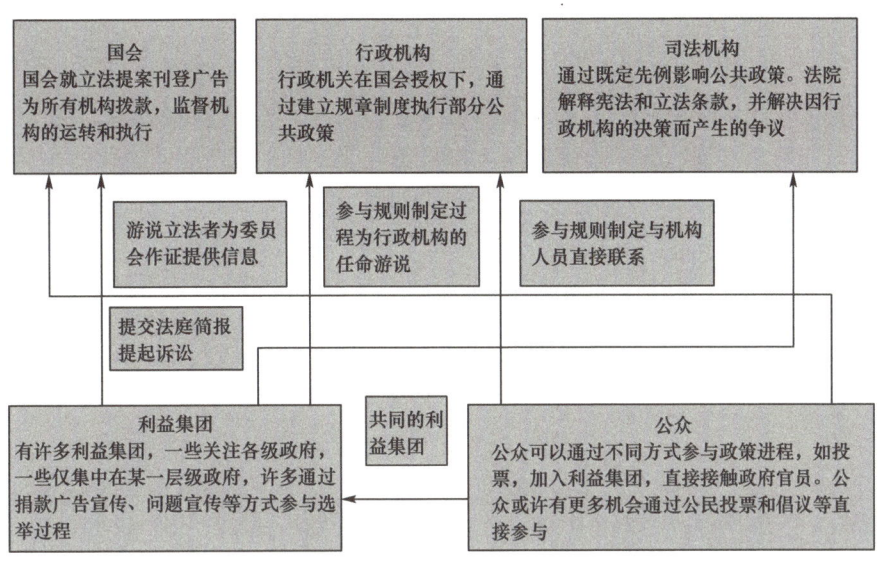

```
┌─────────────┐      ┌─────────────┐      ┌─────────────┐
│    国会     │      │  行政机构   │      │  司法机构   │
│国会就立法提案│      │行政机关在国会│      │通过既定先例影│
│刊登广告为所有│      │授权下,通过建│      │响公共政策。法│
│机构拨款,监督│      │立规章制度执行│      │院解释宪法和立│
│机构的运转和执│      │部分公共政策 │      │法条款,并解决│
│行           │      │             │      │因行政机构的决│
│             │      │             │      │策而产生的争议│
└─────────────┘      └─────────────┘      └─────────────┘
```

┌─────────────┐ ┌─────────────┐ ┌─────────────┐
│游说立法者为委│ │参与规则制定过│ │参与规则制定与│
│员会作证提供信│ │程为行政机构的│ │机构人员直接联│
│息   │ │任命游说   │ │系   │
└─────────────┘ └─────────────┘ └─────────────┘

┌─────────┐
│提交法庭简报│
│提起诉讼 │
└─────────┘

┌─────────────┐ ┌─────────┐ ┌─────────────┐
│ 利益集团   │ │共同的利 │ │   公众   │
│有许多利益集团│ │益集团   │ │公众可以通过不│
│,一些关注各级│ │   │ │同方式参与政策│
│政府,一些仅集│ │   │ │进程,如投票,│
│中在某一层级政│ │   │ │加入利益集团,│
│府,许多通过捐│ │   │ │直接接触政府官│
│款广告宣传、问│ │   │ │员。公众或许有│
│题宣传等方式参│ │   │ │更多机会通过公│
│与选举过程   │ │   │ │民投票和倡议等│
│   │ │   │ │直接参与   │
└─────────────┘ └─────────┘ └─────────────┘

图 7-3　政策制定机构和政策制定途径

政策制定者每次面对的不一定是给定的问题。政策制定不受制度约束,它可能会产生一个或多个提案,并且可能会对问题给出几个明确的定义或没有明确的定义。值得注意的是,政策制定者在问题和政策之间建立了重要的关联。

7.3　政策合法化

在对政策方案做出抉择之后,必须将该方案合法化为真正具有权威性的政策,使之能得到有效的执行,这就是政策合法化问题。政策合法化是政策过程的一个必要环节,它的内容广泛,是目前国内政策科学文献探讨得还不够的一个方面。

合法化的过程

合法化并不意味着取得任何特定的合法性。官员必须向前推进,知道自己在做什么。民主社会中合法化的基本过程是建立多数者联盟。多数人的统治是民主理论的基石,这是一种从政治平等和人民主权到执政的现实途径。多数构建是合法性的主要过程,但也存在一些子过程。例如,如果一个机构被授权制定标准、订立合同、提供资源或做出任何其他类型的决定,则必须制定合法的流程来进行选择。事实上,一个机构可能有权创建一个完整的政策过程——定义问题、制定提案、使方案或标准合法化等。在许多情况下,在与受影响群体协商后,或在类似于立法机构举行的公开听证会后才做出选择。在需要制定方案以授权采取进一步行动时,都涉及合法性。

谁参与？

政策合法化的主体是依法有权使政策方案获得合法地位的国家机关。主体与权限，是一个问题的两个方面。谁有权使政策方案合法化，谁就成为政策合法化的主体。换言之，成为政策合法化的主体，必须具有相应的权限。这就导致了政策合法化主体的两个基本特征，即宏观上的广泛性和微观上的特定性。同时，还必须注意，主体是由权限决定的，权限又是法律规定的。法律针对不同的国家机关规定了相应的、不同的职权，主体只能在其法定权限内实施政策合法化行为。合法性在民主制度中与立法机关的关系最为密切。因此，立法者肯定会参与其中，但多数人也可以通过努力与政府官员、立法人员、各级地方官员聚集在一起施加影响。

7.4 政策执行

执行是一系列旨在实施方案的活动。其中三项活动对方案成功执行尤为重要：
——解释
——组织
——应用

解释是将方案分解为具体的计划，指令和规范要求。

组织包括建立问询处和制度措施，以及为管理方案提供资源。

应用代表常规的服务提供、支付或其他方案目标或工具。

谁参与？

任何一个方案的执行都可能包含许多不同类型的参与者，因此很难加以概括。那些为了使方案生效而相互作用的主体都参与了执行过程。通常包括参与执行的政府机构、立法者、公民和私人团体等。

有效执行的技巧

有一些技巧可以让执行更加有效：
——前期规划
——设计模型
——稽查、激励和参与
——案例管理
——目标管理

前期规划：前期规划对政策实施很重要。需要考虑如下问题：必须采取什么行动？由谁来做？有能力做到吗？

设计模型：模型有助于协调组织的活动，更好地利用资源。模型广泛地适用于各种活动——从为高级官员安排实地考察这一看似琐碎的任务，到安排工作流程的非常复杂的技术工作。三种模型设计在种类繁多的模型中作用是最显著的：甘特图、关键路径方法（CPM）、计划评估审查（PERT）。

稽查、激励和参与：稽查员可以是单独的个人或组织单位，其职责是向高层管理人员证明事情可行，可以代表他们所在的办公室采取快速行动并完成工作。激励是对帮助推动流程的组织和个人的奖励。参与表明组织对某个问题的某种回答在什么时候会受到欢迎，什么时候会遭到抵制。

案例管理：公共部门组织的大部分资源都用于处理案例：医院的病人，人力资源部的福利对象，劳动关系委员会的劳资纠纷，基金会的拨款建议等等。

目标管理：目标管理有四个特征：
- 确定总体目标和优先事项
- 鼓励高管们为实现总体目标做出最大努力
- 协调所有关键目标的计划，以促进整个组织获得更好的成果
- 建立控制机制以监测与目标相比的进展情况，并将结果反馈给上级

影响执行的因素

外部因素和内部因素会影响执行，也是决定其能否成功的关键。

外部因素

外部因素可能会影响管理工作，执行办公室无法控制许多外部因素。最重要的外部问题包括：

——政治脆弱性
——部门中组织的位置
——与行业/立法机构/公众的关系

政治脆弱性：来自立法机构、个别立法者、行业代言人和个体经营者以及行政部门官员的压力可能会产生针对特定危机、环境和利益的政策。

部门中组织的位置：许多决策实际上是通过办公室负责人的批准在机构的顶层进行的。由于来自政府其他部门的压力，部门负责人永远不会顺利地做出决定。

与行业/立法机构/公众的关系：相关团体可能尝试在合作的基础上解决问题，否则可能会带来冲突和分歧。

内部因素

即使解决所有的外部因素，管理问题也可能无法解决，并且不会自动实现更好的绩效。核心问题在于：

——缺乏领导力
——缺乏明确性
——缺乏稳定性
——缺乏判断力
——缺乏支持

——注意力聚焦

——人力资源浪费

——缺乏员工参与

——沟通不畅

缺乏领导力:缺乏强有力的指导使得该行动容易受到立法机构和行业的双重打击。

缺乏明确性:监管和教育职能的混淆产生了一些问题,这些问题延伸到各个工作人员的角色和职能中。

缺乏稳定性:部门的重新设置和主管的变更带来了方案以及政策的不确定性。

缺乏判断力:办公室没有认识到从上到下分级进行现场活动的关键性。

缺乏支持:工作人员尤其是现场工作人员感到孤立,得不到核心领导人的支持。

注意力聚焦:立法机构和行业压力所产生的外部危机意味着办公室主管人员很少关注方案和人事问题。

人力资源浪费:办公室管理基本上忽略了专业人员而不是利用他们的经验和专业知识。

缺乏员工参与:员工没有参与解决问题、政策和方案的制定或评估。

沟通不畅:整个系统缺乏明确的、清晰的和书面的政策。与现场的信息共享被阻止。

执行路径

政策执行研究主要有三个阶段。第一个阶段(20世纪60年代和70年代初)以德西克(1972)和普雷斯曼和韦达夫斯基(1973)等人的著作为代表。这些研究侧重于个案研究,并没有创造出更广泛的理论以应用于其他案例并进行检验。

政策执行研究的第二个阶段(20世纪70年代中期)试图创建政策过程的系统理论,这些理论可以推广到许多案例当中,而不是集中在一个或几个案例上。可以分为两种不同的研究方法:自上而下的方法和自下而上的方法。

第一种方法强调自上而下的政策执行视角。认为可以通过审视由政策执行者构建的法规或其他政策中采用的目标和战略来理解政策执行。这种方法侧重于政策起草者设定的目标与政策的实际执行和结果之间的差距。自上而下的方法基于一系列重要假设:

——政策包含明确的已定义的目标,可据此衡量绩效。根据瑞安(1995)的观点,"自上而下的执行策略在很大程度上取决于政策目标的明确性和定义的一致性。"

——政策包含明确定义的政策工具以实现目标。

——政策有单一的法规或其他权威的政策声明。

——存在一个"执行链",它从顶部的政策信息开始,接下来按照链条中的链接依次进行。

——政策设计者对执行者的能力和承诺非常了解。能力包括执行组织任务所需的资源。这包括资金和人力资源、法律权威和自主权以及有效执行政策所需的知识。承诺包括执行者实现政策设计者目标的愿望。

第二种方法强调自下而上的观点,认为最好从执行系统或执行链的最低层次开始,向上看执行工作在哪些方面或多或少取得了成功。

自下而上的方法认识到有时候政策目标是模糊的而不是明确的,可能与同一政策领域的其他政策目标以及基层官僚的规范和动机相冲突。

自下而上的方法不要求以法规或其他形式定义单一的政策。相反,政策可以被视为一系列法律、规则、实践和规范,它们决定了政府和利益集团解决能源或犯罪等问题的方式。因此,执行可被视为在整个政策过程中,而不仅仅是在颁布之前和期间发生的冲突和妥协的延续。

这种自下而上的方法具有许多优点。特别是缺乏对具体方案和固定的自下而上的执行链的关注意味着自下而上的方法可以将执行视为通过各种因素组成的网络发挥作用。这更像是一个问题网络或政策共同体,不同于一个严格指定的流程,无法解释政策制定环境的丰富性。

另一方面,自下而上的方法也有一些缺点需要考虑。首先,自下而上的方法过分强调基层官僚能够挫败最高决策者的目标的能力。其次,自下而上的实施模型假设群体是实施过程中的积极参与者,但事实并非总是如此。自下而上的方法也未考虑目标群体的力量差异。

第三阶段:研究人员寻求将自上而下和自下而上两种方法的优势结合到一个模型或一种综合方法中,因为它们各自具有相对的优势和劣势。他们寻找一种模式,既能从最高层解决政策的结构问题,又能解决政策被颠覆的可能性,或至少在最终执行时改变政策的可能性。萨巴蒂尔(1991)认为,应制定一个概念框架,将自上而下和自下而上两种方法结合起来。在有结构良好的主导方案(或法律)且研究人员执行研究资源有限的情况下,采用自上而下的方法是最好的。当分析人员对实施的动力感兴趣并且没有单一的主导计划时,自下而上的方法是最好的。

萨巴蒂尔的综述依赖于一个被称为支持(倡导)联盟框架(ACF)的公共政策研究框架(见第四章)。戈金等人(1990年)提出了一种政策执行理论,该理论依靠在决策者和执行者之间进行信息传递。

7.5 政策评估

政策评估是整个政策分析过程中不可或缺的一步。是一种具有特定标准、方法和程序的专门研究活动。政策评估是依据一定的标准和程序,对政策的效益、效率和价值进行判断的一种评价行为,目的在于取得有关这些方面的信息,作为比较、择优、决定政策变化、政策改进和制定新政策的依据。评估是衡量为实现某些目标而采取的行动的可取和不可取的后果。包括:

——收集有关方案的社会行动结果的信息的程序
——在方案目标实现方面衡量计划的有效性

——说明方案的效果,并逐步调整以便更有效地实现目标

评估研究的六大用途:

——了解目标是否实现和如何实现

——确定成功和失败的具体原因

——揭示成功方案的基本原则

——旨在提高效率的技术指导实验过程

——为进一步研究备选方案相对成功的原因奠定基础

——重新定义用于实现目标的手段,甚至根据研究结果重新界定目标

这些目标强烈地暗示了评估与项目规划和开发之间的内在关系。评估研究为设计和重新设计行动方案提供了基本信息。为取得满意的评估效果,需要考虑一些问题包括:

——需要什么样的改变?

——如何改变?

——有何证据表明所观察到的变化是由于方案实施造成的?

——变化意味着什么?

——会有意想不到的后果吗?

评估的主要关注点是措施的可靠性和有效性,以及对成功和失败的原因的了解。六个步骤对评估至关重要:

——确定要评估的目标

——分析活动需要解决的问题

——活动的说明和标准化

——测量变化程度

——确定观察到的变化是由于活动还是由于某些其他原因引起的

——确认效果的持久性

评估过程

评估总是基于价值,不管是明确的或是隐含的,然后根据价值制定一个目标。目标的选择通常出现或发生在价值形成之前。价值可以被定义为情境事件或目标的任何方面,被认为是好的、坏的、可取的或不可取的对象。价值观是人们在需要、需求和目标之间建立优先级和重要性等级依据的原则(金登,1995)。图 7-4 说明了评估过程。

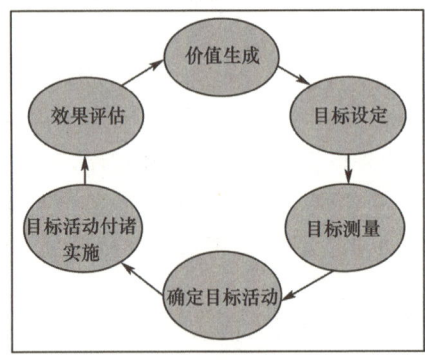

图 7-4 评估程序

目标设定——减少癌症患者。目标设定的各方力量总是在金钱、资源和努力方面相互竞争。其次，需要有一些衡量目标实现的方法。如果确定的目标是减少患癌症的人数，则需要获得目前有多少人死于癌症的数据。评估的性质在很大程度上取决于可用于确定目标实现情况的措施类型。

下一步是确定某种达到目标的活动。例如，在上面减少癌症患者的例子中，可以考虑一个早期发现和治疗的方案。然后目标实现活动开始运作——建立诊断中心并敦促人们来检查。

目标导向的操作在某一时刻被评估，该阶段包括评估运行程序实现预定目标的程度，评估需要科学地进行。

最后，根据评估结果判断目标导向活动是否值得。这使得该过程回归到价值的确立。现在人们可能会觉得拥有癌症诊断中心是件好事。在评价过程结束时，可能有新的价值出现，或者流程可能会被重新确认，需要对已有的价值重新评估或定义。

目标和假设

评估的最主要特征是存在某种目的或目标，其实现程度是研究问题的主要焦点。评估需要有一个目标。在制定评价目标时涉及的一些较为一般性的考虑因素包括：

目标性质是什么？

该方案是否对改变知识、态度或行为感兴趣？是否涉及被报道、认识、利益和行为？对这些问题的回答可以帮助评估人员确认概念的设置区域。

谁是这个方案的目标群体？

该方案的目标人群包括哪些群体？该方案是否试图改变个人、团体或整个社区？

预期的变化何时发生？

该方案是寻求即时效果，还是逐渐形成某种延迟效应？

目标是单一的还是多个的？

该方案的目标是单一改变还是一系列改变？这些变化对所有人都一样，还是针对不同的群体而有所不同？

预期效果怎么样？

该方案是寻求广泛的还是聚焦的结果？在该方案被认为是成功的之前，是否需要达到一定的有效性？是否有任何必须满足的特定的标准？

如何实现这一目标？

用什么方法来实施该方案？该方案主要依靠自愿合作还是法律制裁？是否会提出个人或非个人，正式或非正式的上诉？

这六个需要考虑的因素涉及在为评估而制定计划目标时需要回答的基本问题，上述问题的许多答案都需要审视所述目标的基本假设。假设可分为两种类型：价值假设和有效性假设。

价值假设

适用于信仰体系——对一个社会或一个社会群体中什么是好的的判断。可能存在一些几乎被普遍接受的价值假设如"人的生命值得拯救"，"不必要的苦难是糟糕的"，"身体健康是必要的"等。

有效性假设

与方案目标的相关性要更强。例如,假设使人相信,产前死亡率问题的主要原因可能是怀孕期间缺乏护理,那么诊所可以向孕妇提供信息以改善护理,进而降低产前死亡率。

这些有效的假设有助于解释从精神病院到家庭护理的转变,因为人们相信在家里比在精神病院更好。有效性和可靠性的概念是建立假设的重要因素。每个假设都假定了一个有效性的目标,也就是说,每个目标都对实现某种期望值是有效的。

评估的功能

评估提供了一些对参与政策过程特别有用的功能:

提供信息:评估的第一个也是最重要的功能是提供有关政策执行情况的可靠的和有效的信息,即通过公共行为实现需求、价值和机会的程度。

揭示特定目标:评估揭示了特定目标和目标的实现程度,并有助于对政策问题的解决程度做出实际推断。

对价值观的澄清和批判:评估有助于澄清和批判作为目标和目的选择基础的价值观。通过定义和执行目的和目标来阐明价值观。通过质疑与所解决问题相关的目的和目标的适当性,也会对价值观进行批判。

创造替代来源:在质疑目的和目标时,分析人员可审查替代价值的来源(如公职人员、既得利益者和客户群体)及其以不同形式存在的合理性(技术的、经济的、法律的、社会的)。

有助于界定新的或经修订的政策选择:评估也有助于界定新的或经修订的政策选择。例如,可以通过表明应放弃先前偏爱的政策选择,代之以另一种政策选择来实现。

问题方法和实验

评估是一种管理公共组织的技术,系统的数据收集和其他类似研究的操作在其中发挥了相当大的作用。从这个角度看,融入研究的评估与其他社会研究的不同之处不在于所采用的研究设计和数据收集方法,而是在于需要解决的问题,问题而不是设计或方法决定了评估的特征。

评估的八个主要问题可以通过以下八个问题来呈现,评估人员可考虑其中的一些或全部:

——目标问题:评估的总体目标是什么?
——组织(评估人员)问题:应该由谁来进行评估以及如何组织评估?
——干预分析问题:评估的目标如何被定性和描述?
——问题转换:干预(措施)的正式启动与最终产出之间的执行情况如何?
——结果问题:干预措施的直接、中间和最终的产出和结果是什么?
——影响问题:干预措施包括哪些突发事件(因素、因果力的控制)和解释结果?
——标准问题:应采用何种价值标准来评估干预措施的优点?根据价值标准可以使用哪些绩效标准来判断成功或失败或令人满意的绩效?干预的实际好处是什么?

——效用问题：如何利用？实际是如何操作的？

第一个和第二个问题涉及对干预的评价，三至七个问题涉及干预本身，问题八涉及反馈过程。

一些评估技巧

前面对成本效益分析(CBA)、成本效果分析(CEA)、决策分析等评估方法进行了探讨。这里还有一些其他技巧：网络分析、线性规划、模拟，这里主要介绍网络分析。

网络分析

一旦一个方案或项目被决定了，实际安排方案要素的问题仍然存在：分配资源到项目的各个部分，以及在条件改变时重新安排活动等。在处理非重复任务时，这一阶段的规划尤其困难，因为工作以前从未以同样的方式完成。为安排由许多相互关联的任务组成的复杂项目，开发了两种类似的网络分析方法：计划评审技术（PERT）、关键路径方法（CPM）。

计划评审技术（PERT）定义并链接在有序网络中作为项目的一部分必须完成的各种任务，每个任务的完成时间估计值用于检查改变单个任务时间的各种方式，以加快整个项目的完成。

假设一个城市公园部门想建立一个社区游乐场。第一步是确定完成项目所需的任务或活动。兴建游乐场需要四项活动：需要购买必要的材料和设备；清理场地的垃圾和杂草；安装游乐场设备；进行一定程度的园林绿化。

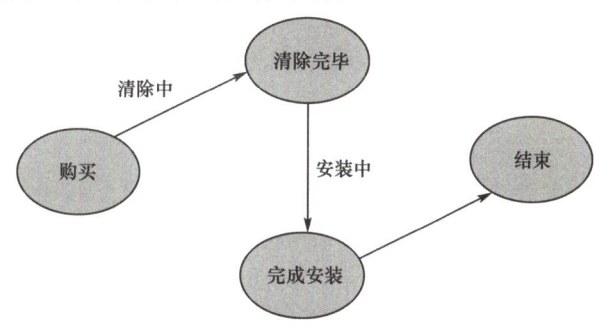

图 7-5 程序评估与审查技术的例子

第二步是将这些活动按图中的功能顺序排列，活动以带有连接事件的箭头的线表示，事件活动的开始和结束，以圆圈的形式表现。每个项目都以单个事件开始和结束，每个活动都有一个开始事件和结束事件。

第三步是从各个工作组获得对每项活动所需时间的估计。因为只得到一次估计值是不可取的，所以要求对每项活动所需时间进行三次估算。最乐观的时间 a，或者说，是在最好的情况下可能需要的时间，发生的概率是百分之一。最悲观的时间 b，或者说，是在最糟糕的情况下所需要的时间，发生的概率也是百分之一。最可能的时间 m，或者说，如果在不同情况下活动重复多次，预期时间是最常见的（模态）。然后用代数方法将这些估计值组合起来，计算出预期时间 t_e，或者，如下面的公式所表示的：

$$t_e = \frac{a + 4m + b}{6}$$

这个公式对最可能的时间(m)的权重要比最悲观的时间(b)和最乐观的时间(a)的权重都要大,而后者的权重是相同的。如果只有百分之一的可能性,或者说,他们应该比最可能的时间的影响要小。

第四步是确定项目完成的最早日期,确定每项活动完成的最早预期日期。

关键路径方法(CPM)。和 PERT 方法一样,关键路径法使用网络和时间估计。CPM 增加了成本估算,以找到最有效的会加速或延误项目的方法。第一步是估计每个事件的正常时间和正常成本,然后估计每个活动的崩溃时间和崩溃成本。

下一步是构建网络并计算 t_e 和关键路径,就像在 PERT 中一样。然后通过首先以最低的崩溃成本使活动崩溃来缩短关键路径。这为该活动提供了新的时间估计值,并重新计算了关键路径。

下一步是取消对那些不在关键路径上的活动的延误,直到它们成为关键点。有些延误项目有空闲时间,为了节省资金而不改变项目完成日期,可能会进行非延误。这个过程可以提供最佳的解决方案,最低的成本和完成项目的最短时间。

谁可以做评估?

系统的评估研究以社会科学研究技术为基础。因此,大多数评估专家都受过社会科学培训。乍一看,不熟悉评估研究的人无疑会发现对评估的专业讨论难以理解。与其他任何专业领域一样,评估人员开发了自己的词汇、速记符号和工作规则。评估的复杂性部分源于专业领域中人们开发自己语言的固有倾向,这来自于每个领域发展出来的独特概念和见解。在最复杂的层面上,评估活动可能在技术和构思上很复杂,成本高昂且持续时间长,需要训练有素的专家专门参与学习最新的社会科学理论、研究方法和统计技术,所以这种高度复杂的评估通常由专业评估人员进行。另一方面有许多评估任务很容易理解,并且可以由具有适度专业知识和经验的人员执行。相比之下,评估是一种政策分析程序,用于提供有关政策在满足构成既定问题的需求、价值观或机会方面的绩效的信息。

在政策评估主体中,除立法机关、政党组织、司法机关、社会组织和公民外,比较重要的评估主体还有政策制定者和执行者、专业机构和人员、大众传播媒介等。

政策评估模式

不同的评估模式有助于我们更多地了解该评估过程。本节主要介绍这样几个模式。

有效性模式

大多数模式属于有效性模式的范畴。其中包括目标实现评估模式、综合评估模式、顾客导向评估模式和利益相关者模式(图7-6)。

目标实现评估模式:目标实现评估是一种有效性模式,因为它关注的是方案的实质内容、输出和结果,而不是方案的程序,如公平待遇或正当程序。它不同于经济和制度模式,因为它只提出实质性问题,但既不关注方案成本,也不关注评估的组织。

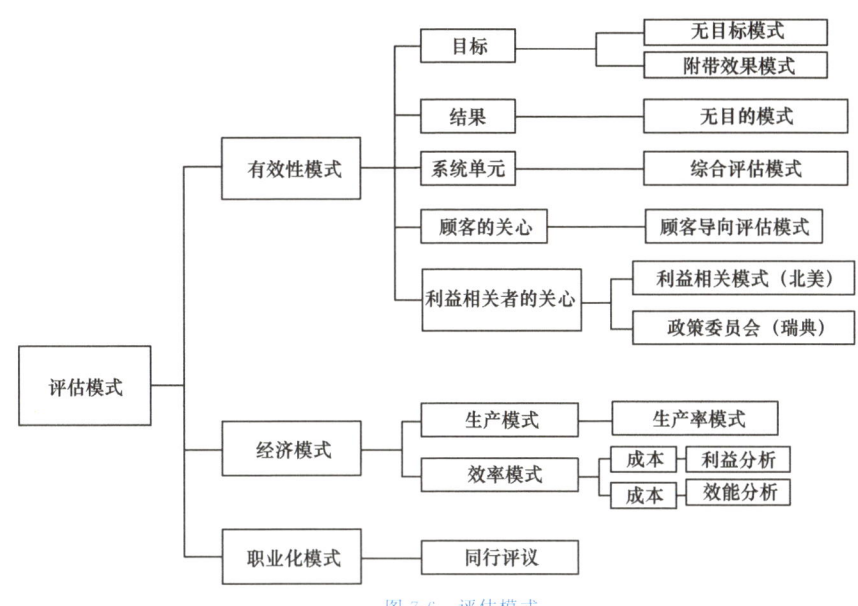

图 7-6 评估模式

综合评估模式:综合评估模式的评估范围比目标实现评估模式更广泛。该模式认为,评估不应仅限于取得的成果,而应至少包括执行甚至规划。评估者在全面评价中的首要任务是将预期结果与实际结果、目标与现实情况进行对比。

顾客导向评估模式:从完全不同的出发点出发,顾客导向评估模式将政策干预对象的目标、期望、关注甚至需求作为评估的组织原则和价值标准。顾客导向的核心是程序是否满足客户的关注、愿望或期望。

利益相关者模式:利益相关者模式的组织原则是利益相关方或受干预影响方的关切和问题。以利益相关者为基础的评估首先要列出参与该方案的提出、执行和或对其结果感兴趣的主要群体。评估人员确定方案的创建者、发起者和资助者,特别是负责其执行的人。

经济模式

经济模式最典型的特征是关注成本,包括生产率模式和效率模式。

生产率模式可以用如下的数学公式来表示:

$$\text{Productivity} = \frac{\text{output}}{\text{input}}$$

作为衡量公共部门活动的指标,生产率具有一些技术上的优势。成本有时不是很难计算,因为它们是以货币的形式到达相关部门的。然而,在其他时候追踪相关成本可能很困难,因为分配和支出的资金往往在账面上显示为一次性付款。另一方面,产出可能是很难获得和计算的,即使生产力也预先假设它们是以物理而非货币的方式来表示。

效率模式可以用两种方法来衡量,即成本利益或成本效能。效率评估为将成本与方案结果联系起来提供了一个参考框架。在成本利益分析中,方案投入和结果都是用货币来衡量的。在成本效能分析中,投入按货币价值和实际影响结果估算。

职业化模式:同行评议

职业化模式指职业人员根据他自己的价值准则和执行的质量标准来评估其他人员的

执行情况，主要是同行评议，如律师评估律师、教授评估教授、外科医生评估外科医生等。同行评议主要是指学术期刊投稿的筛选程序，提交的文章将接受同行评审，以决定是否可以发表，也用于指导研究基金会哪些项目应该获得资助。研究计划提交给一组受人尊敬的同行进行筛选，除此之外，同行评议还被用于调查和判断涉嫌违反道德行为规则和继承的研究实践，该模式经常用于评估研究评估。同行评议特别着力于对评估对象作一个全面的质量判断，在一些技术性领域，政治官员们把规划和讨论专业性的技术问题留给受过良好教育的专业人员去完成。

7.6 政策终止

终止意味着结束或停止。公共政策终止是对特定的政府职能、计划、政策或组织的结束或停止。虽然终止是政策过程的最后一步，但在概念上不应成为最后考虑的问题。终止阶段可以被看作是一个方案的结束和另一个方案的开始：一个已经达到目的的方案的结束，一个纠正错误的政策或方案的开始。

政策终止的类型

政策终止指的是政策决策者在通过对政策或项目的审慎评估后，终止那些不必要的政策或项目的一种行为。一般一项被终止的"政策"包含政府职能、组织和项目以及政策本身。

功能：功能是指政府为其公民提供的服务，它超越了组织和政策。一些机构及其各自的政策都可以发挥同样的作用。

功能的终止不难理解。一般来说，只有当社会缺乏资源或判断力，无法为自己提供必要的服务时，政府才会放弃提供服务的职能。经济学家已经确定了可被视为政府职能的"公共产品"的类别，如国防是一项比国防机构的任何重组都要持久的职能。对监管事项的管辖权以及财富和收入的重新分配是政府职能的另一个例子。这些职能是由政府根据公民的要求义务承担，并且由于满足了其他方面的需要而被制定。因此，政策终止很困难甚至是痛苦的，其影响将通过社会向外扩散。

组织：组织是为了共同的目的而一起工作的个人组成的团体。创建组织是为了响应特定的需求，尽管组织可以并且可能随着时间的推移而扩展它们的领域。组织旨在持久性，并且也是这样做的。尽管组织很少被完全终止，但我们应该清楚组织比政府职能更容易受到影响。

政策：组织选择并执行政策，这些政策是解决特定问题的一般方法或策略。虽然组织花费大量资源来设计和执行适当的政策，值得一提的是，政策比组织本身更容易终止。

这主要有四个原因。首先，除非政策和组织完全一致或不可分割地交织在一起，否则组织将在保留其组成部分之前采取行动保护自己。组织宁愿放弃其一些政策，也不愿组织本身被终止。其次，一项政策通常不能像上级组织那样找到那么多的盟友。在权力政治的简单计算中,政策用于生存的筹码较少。第三,相对于某一特定目标而言,政策比组织更容易被评估,因为组织可以有多重组织目标,其标准更便于政策分析者衡量政策的相对无效,并支持其终止的理由。最后,大多数政策会招致批评,在任何终止提案的背后,人们可以被预期会联合起来,当然,组织也有一群天敌,但是他们通常反对特定的政策,因此不太可能加入反对组织的终止联盟。

项目:项目是四个终止类型中最容易实现的。个别项目在分析人员的注意力中所占的比例最低,它们获得的政治资源也最少,无法保护自己,也代表了组织方面最小的投资。项目最接近问题,因此,它们的影响可以被直接衡量,如果发现存在缺陷,也最容易受到指责。另一方面,日常项目实施的一些细节可能有助于保护它们免受政策分析人员的批评,因为政策分析人员可能认为政策层面才是适当的关注焦点。

政策终止的方式

一般说来,政策终结的方式有以下六种:

政策废止。即直截了当宣布一项政策的废止。政府根据政治、经济和社会经济形势的发展变化,不定期地清理、废止大量不合时宜、过时了的政策。例如,我国加入世贸组织后,全国人大常委会和国务院当即宣布废止了830余项与WTO规则不相符合的国家法律、法规和政策。

政策替代。指用新政策替代旧政策,但所面对的政策问题和政策目标基本没有改变。新政策对旧政策的补充、修正,目的是更好解决旧政策没有解决或根本解决不了的问题,以满足目标群体的政策需求,实现政策目标。

政策合并。指旧的政策虽被终止,但部分实际功能并没有被完全取消,而是将其合并到其他政策内容中去。其方式为:终止的政策内容合并到一项现有的政策中或者把两项或以上终止的政策合并为一项新政策。

政策分解。就是将旧政策的内容按照一定的规则分解成几部分,每一部分形成一项新的政策。例如:单位保障—养老保险、失业保险、人寿保险、医疗保险、生育保险等。

政策缩减。就是采用渐进的方式,逐步对政策进行终结,其目的是有效缓解因政策终结所带来的巨大冲击,逐步协调各方面的关系,减少那些不必要的损失。例如:物价政策改革。

政策法律化。一项长期实行确立的有效的政策,经过立法机关或授权立法的行政机关审议通过,上升为法律或行政法规。这是另一种意义的政策终结。

思考问题

1. 议程设定的过程是什么?
2. 举例说明对问题定义的不同可以衍生出不同的解决方案。
3. 常规的,类似的和创造性的政策制定之间有什么区别?
4. 什么是政策合法化?为什么它是重要的?
5. 政策实施需要哪些技术?

6. 评估过程的步骤是什么？它们的功能是什么？
7. 为什么终止比较少见？

词　汇

系统议程
制度议程
决策议程
政策制定
常规的政策制定
相似的政策制定
创造性的政策制定
正式的政策主体
非正式的政策主体
合法化
解释
组织
应用
早期规划
调度模型
稽查员
激励
参与
案例管理系统
目标管理
外在因素
内部因素
政治脆弱性
第一阶段
第二阶段
自上而下的方法
自下而上的方法
价值假设
有效性假设
网络分析
线性规划
模拟
计划评估审查和技巧

关键路径方法

生产率

效率

同行评审

参考文献

Allision, Graham. 1971. Essence of Decision: Explaining the Cuban Missile Crisis. Boston: Little, Brown.

Baumgartner, Frank and Jones, Bryan D. 1993. Agendas and Instability in American Politics. Chicago: University of Chicago Press.

Bendor, Jonathan and Hammond, Thomas H. 1992. "Rethinking Allison's Models." American Political Science Review, 86(2).

Berry, Jeffery M. 1989. "Subgovernments, Issue Networks, and Political Conflict." Remaking American Politics. Ed. Richard and Sidney Milkis Harris. Boulder, Colorado: Westview Press.

Birkland, Thomas A. 2001. An Introduction to the Policy Process: Theories, Concepts, and Models of Public Policy Making. New York: M. E. Sharpe.

Cigler, Allan J. 1991. "Interest Groups: A Subfield in Search of an Identity." Political Science, Looking to the Future: Volume IV: American Institutions. Ed. Evanston, IIlinois: Northwestern University Press.

Cohen, Michael D., March, James G., and Olson, Johan P. 1972. "A Garbage Can Model of Organization Choice." Administrative Science Quarterly, 17: 1-25.

Derthick, Martha. 1972. New Towns in Town. Washington, DC: Urban Institute.

Easton, David. 1965. A Systems Analysis of Political Life. New York: John Wiley.

Goggin, Malcolm L., Bowman, Anne O'M., Lester, James P., and O'Toole, Laurence J. 1990. Implementation Theory and Practice: Toward a Third Generation. Glenview, Illinois: Scott Foresman/Little Brown.

Kingdon, John W. 1995. Agendas, Alternatives and Public Policies. 2nd ed. New York: Harper Collins.

Kraft, Michael E. and Furlong, Scott R. 2004. Public Policy: Politics, Analysis, and Alternatives. Washington, D. C. CQ Press.

Lindblom, Charles E. 1959. "The Science of Muddling Through." Public Administration Review, 19: 79-88.

Majone, Giandomenico. 1989. Evidence, Argument, and Persuasion in the Policy Process. New Haven: Yale University Press.

Nakamura, Robert T. 1987. "The Textbook Policy Process and Implementation Research." Policy Studies Journal, 7(1): 142-154.

Neustadt, Richard E. 1990. Presidential Power and the Modern Presidents: The Politics of Leadership from Roosevelt to Reagan. New York: Free Press.

Peters, B. Guy. 1999. American Public Policy: Promise and Performance. Chappaqua, New York: Chatham House/Seven Rivers.

Pressman, Jeffrey and Wildavsky, Aaron. 1973. Implementation. Berkeley, CA: University of California Press.

Ryan, Neal. 1995. "Unraveling Conceptual Developments in Implementation Analysis." Australian Journal of Public Administration, 54(1): 65-81.

Sabatier, Paul A. 1991. "Political Science and Public Policy." PS: Political Science and Politics, 24(2): 144-147.

Vedung, Evert. 2005. Public Policy and Evaluation Program. New Brunswick, New Jersey: Transaction Publishers.

Zahariadis, Nikolaos. 1993. "To Sell or Not to Sell? Telecommuni-cations Policy in Britain and France." Journal of Public Policy, 12(4): 355-376.

陈庆云. 公共政策分析. 北京:北京大学出版社,2006.

陈振明. 政策科学——公共政策分析导论. 2版. 北京:中国人民大学出版社,2003.

宁骚. 公共政策. 北京:高等教育出版社,2000.

谢明. 公共政策分析导论. 5版. 北京:中国人民大学出版社,2022.

张金马. 公共政策分析:概念·过程·方法. 北京:人民出版社,2004.

张国庆. 公共政策分析. 上海:复旦大学出版社,2004.

詹姆斯·E.安德森. 公共政策制定. 5版. 谢明,等,译. 北京:中国人民大学出版社,2009.

托马斯·R.戴伊. 理解公共政策. 12版,谢明,等,译. 北京中国人民大学出版社,2011.

保罗·A.萨巴蒂尔. 政策过程理论. 胡总超,钟开斌,等,译. 北京:生活·读书·新知三联书店,2004.

戴博拉·斯通. 政策悖论. 顾建光,译. 北京:中国人民大学出版社,2006.

Chapter 8
Public Problems and Policy Alternatives

Summary

> The creation of policy alternatives begins with the description of a problem. This is a problem of definition. Policy arguments may be decided on operational measures that are based on how a problem is defined. Statistical information is abundantly available, but not everything can be reduced to quantitative measures. The problem must be defined, measured, its extent and magnitude determined, its caused considered, goals set, and what can be done must be determined.
>
> Most studies focus on the immediate causes of problems. Solving problems can begin with an explicit list of the goals of the various actors and possible ways of achieving those goals. Policy analysis should look at costs and benefits and at how they are distributed. Different alternatives include the things government has in its power to do. Government may regulate, subsidize, ration, tax and spend, contract out, use market incentives, privatize, charge fees, educate, hold in trust, and research. Assessing alternatives is a process of looking at a criterion for evaluation.

8.1 Public Problems: Definition and Components

The beginning of any policy study involves the description of a problem. Sometimes the problem, and perhaps even its causes, are obvious. For example, if the problem is teenage smoking and how to limit it, one can find abundant information about the number of teenage smokers, why they choose to smoke, and the implications for lifelong smoking habits and the associated health problems. Many governments use that information to adopt educational programs aimed at prevention and other policies that successfully reduce the rate of teenage smoking.

Problem analysis involves trying to answer the basic questions about:

— The nature of the problem

— The extent or magnitude of the problem
— How the problem came about
— The major causes of the problem
— The importance of the problem as a public policy matter
— What the problem entails
— What is already known about the problem
— Possible solutions to the problem

Any copy of a daily newspaper contains information about a large number of potential policy problems such as crime, pollution, inflation, energy, welfare, and unemployment. Very few people argue that these are not problems, that is, that each of these conditions interferes with the attainment of some value or need. This may be personal security, health, consumption or some other desired state of affairs. Yet this everyday understanding of the meaning of problem is frequently inadequate, since it obscures the fact that the same problem (for example, crime) is viewed in radically different ways by different segments of the population. For some, crime is a natural condition of all human societies while for others it is an understandable response to poverty and exploitation. The way people view crime as a problem depends on several factors.

First, different people may agree that crime is a problem but may disagree about the kinds of behaviors that are criminal. One person may define crime solely in terms of illegal acts against people (homicide, armed robbery, rape) while another may focus on illegal acts involving property (theft, fraud, embezzlement, government corruption).

Second, people may also disagree about the kind/class of problem represented by criminal activities. Some people see crime as an economic problem. Therefore, the potential resolution lies in restructuring the production and distribution of goods and services in society. Others see it as a social, psychological, or even administrative problem that may be resolved by providing greater opportunities for social mobility, by changing attitudes through education, or by strictly enforcing existing criminal laws. The way people classify a problem generally determines the way they will explain and attempt to resolve it.

Finally, people may agree on the definition, classification, and explanation of a problem and yet disagree about its scope, severity, and importance. Judgments about the severity of a problem largely depend on what values and needs are deemed to be most important. People with a strong need for physical security, or those committed to values of law and order, are more likely to view crime as a policy problem than those with a strong commitment to social justice.

An essential step in the policy process is defining the problem. For example, analysts need to define what poverty means if they are studying the plight of the poor. Is being poor only a matter of having insufficient money or income, or does it include other characteristics, such as the lack of certain skills or abilities? Should poverty be defined in relative terms or in absolute terms? Public policy arguments also depend on operational measures or operational indicators of problems. Rather than refer to poverty in the abstract, analysts want to know how many people live in poverty and their demographics. When discussing quality of education in the public schools, analysts want to see test scores and other student evaluations to determine whether a problem exists in the schools and how one community's schools compare to another's. If the subject is violent crime, the analysts need statistics about the number of crimes committed nationally and in local communities, and whether the crime rate is increasing or decreasing.

Quantitative measures are abundant for most contemporary public problems. How much statistical information needs to be provided is a matter of judgment. At a minimum, most issue papers or problem analyses include some basic descriptive statistics. One type is the frequency count, such as the percentage of the population at different income levels or the number of people in a survey who respond one way or another. Another type is the mean (average) measure of a group or category, such as the average score on an examination. An alternative is the median of a variable, which is the point where one half of the group is above and one half is below. One example is the median price of homes sold in different regions of the nation. Some idea of the range of variation or the correlation or relationship between two variables, such as age and income, may be useful as well.

Statistical information can be displayed in many ways in a report. These include tables that show frequency counts or percentages of what is being studied, such as the percentage of different age groups who smoke. Information can be superimposed on maps to show geographic variations such as rates of urban growth or the income levels for adjacent urban and suburban areas. Graphic figures such as pie charts or bar charts are common, as are line figures that show how the magnitude of a problem changes over time, such as the number of people without jobs from 1980 to 2020.

There is an art to choose how best to display quantitative information. At a minimum, reports should aim for clarity. Even so, some visual displays are more likely to capture the reader's attention than others. The use of computer-generated color graphics allows a range of different formats, both in written form and in a PowerPoint or similar presentation. The best advice is generally to keep the audience and purpose clearly in mind when choosing the format of a report or presentation. The use of quantitative data also carries some risks. Analysts need to be alert to the possibility of inaccurate data in a report or an invalid measurement that does not truly capture the problem.

Naturally, not all human concerns, such as happiness or sense of well-being, can be reduced to quantitative measures. Analysts can, however, make use of surveys that ask people things like whether they are happy, enjoy living in their communities, and believe the schools are doing a good job. Where public problems cannot be measured directly, this kind of survey may be useful substitute. Economists also say that people can be asked to estimate the dollar value of many activities for which no market value exists. Their responses can help to calculate whether certain actions, such as preserving open space or planting trees, are justifiable uses of tax dollars.

Anticipating the Future

One other aspect of defining and measuring problems deserves mention. Any consideration of the present state of affairs must be grounded in an assessment of how a problem is likely to change over time. What will the problem look like in several years or decades? Forecasts, or projections, usually involve an extrapolation of current trends, but that is only one method for looking ahead.

Examples of forecasting include economic forecasting (will the nation have a surplus or deficit in five years?), population projections (how large will the country's population be by 2025 or 2050?), and energy needs (what kind, how much, and where?). Such projections are especially helpful if they reveal how that change will likely unfold with or without policy intervention. For example, to what extent would the nation adopting energy conservation measures reduce the reliance on imported oil?

Major Components of Public Problems

The flow chart in Figure 8-1 summarizes the basic elements of problem analysis. The list can also be a guide to what questions might be addressed in preparing a problem analysis or issue paper.

Define the Problem

If the problem is educational quality, what does educational quality mean exactly? In other words, what is the exact nature of the education problem under the study? Has quality declined? Is it lower than many people believe it ought to be?

Measure the Problem

Find a way to measure the problem that is consistent with the way it is defined. This step is sometimes called developing an operational definition. What kinds of quantitative indicators are available from reliable sources? What is the best measurement to use for educational quality? Student scores on standardized examinations? Other measures of student learning? Indicators of the quality of a school's faculty?

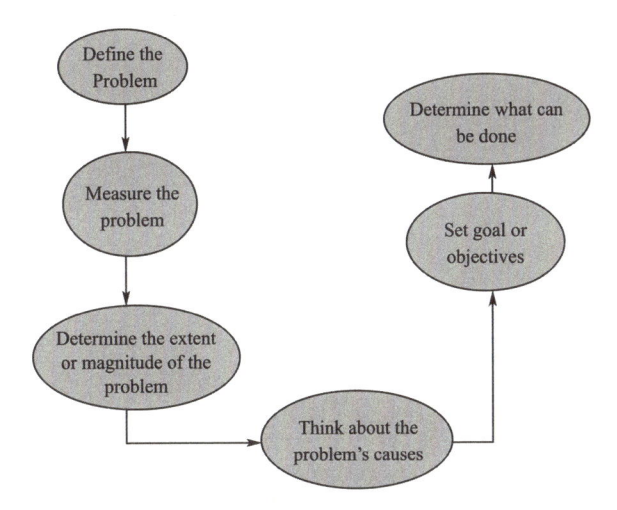

Figure 8-1 Flow Chart of Problem Analysis

Determine the Extent or Magnitude of the Problem

Using indicators that are available, try to determine who is affected by the problem and by how much. Try to answer these kinds of questions: what groups in the population suffer from the problem being studied, how long have they been affected by it, and to what extent are they affected? For example, how does educational quality vary from one school district or region to another? From urban districts to rural districts? From schools in less-affluent neighborhoods to those in more-affluent areas?

Think about the Problem's Causes

How did the problem come about, and why does it continue? What are the leading causes of the problem, and what other causes should be considered? Knowing the causes of a problem is critical to developing solutions to it. How has educational quality changed over the past several decades, and why?

Set Goals or Objectives

What should be done about the problem and why? Are certain goals and objectives of paramount importance, widely agreed upon, and economically or socially feasible? Over what period of time the goals and objectives should be sought? For educational quality, what goals or objectives are most appropriate? If quality is to be improved, how much progress should be expected for a given period of time?

Determine What Can Be Done

What actions might work to solve the problem or reach the specified goals and objectives? What policy efforts might be directed at the causes of the problem? What variables can be affected by such efforts? If the goal is improving educational quality to a certain extent, what needs to be done? Improving teacher quality? Reducing class sizes? Changing the curriculum?

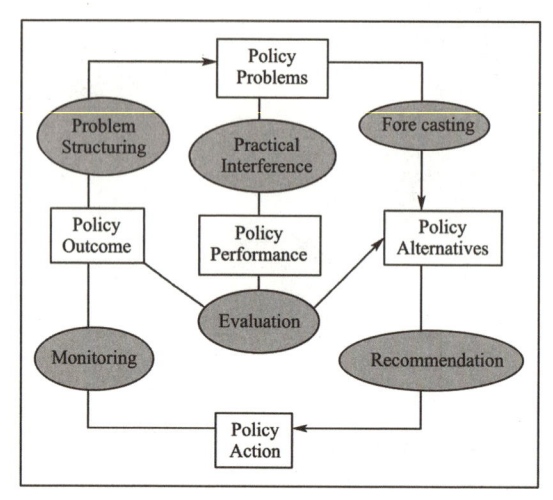

Figure 8-2　Structure of Policy Problems

Thinking about Causes and Solutions

　　Any assessment of a public problem requires thinking about its causes, how it came about, and why it continues. The answers make a big difference in whether and how public policy might resolve the problem. For example, if the question is why youth unemployment increased dramatically from 2000 to 2020, part of the answer is that employment security overall decreased through the period. In many companies, there even have been mass layoffs of long-term employees. If there is a general problem in job security, there is likely to be a specific problem for youth as well.

　　Most policy studies focus on what can be called proximate, or immediate, causes of public problems. The greater challenge is to deal with the root causes of problems. Taking policy action might be more difficult because of long-standing public attitudes and habits that are resistant to change. Think about urban traffic congestion. Why does it exist? The obvious answer is that too many people are driving their cars on a limited number of roads at any given time. Is the solution to build more highways? Or is it to think about ways to reduce the use of automobile in urban areas where congestion is the greatest? Some urban designers and environmentalists offer a more radical solution, at least for new communities. They suggest building cities with adequate mass transit where people can live closer to where they work. Many states and communities are adopting "smart growth" policies with similar ambitions for managing anticipated growth over the next several decades. Most public problems have multiple causes, and therefore people disagree over which is the most important and which ought to be the object of public policy. The astute student of public policy learns how to deal with the politics and overheated rhetoric that can sometimes cloud an objective review of the evidence.

Public problem solving can begin with making an explicit list of the goals and objectives of various policy actors and a determination of what might be done to reach them. The objectives may include a specific measure of what is to be achieved, such as improving access to health care services or reducing the rate of teenage smoking. When analysts think of potential solutions to public problems, they try to identify the opportunities for policy intervention. They try to imagine how a change in public policy might affect the problem. For example, would raising the price of cigarettes reduce the teenage smoking rate?

Analysis sometimes want to describe the benefits and costs of trying to solve a problem. They look at how the consequences of policy action, positive or negative, are distributed across population subgroups, such as those in certain regions, occupations, or social groups—in other words, who gains and who loses if the problem is resolved. Politicians and other major policy actors are sometimes very clever about addressing these kinds of distributive concerns. They are almost always interested in knowing about them. They may speak about solving public problems as though the entire nation will benefit equally, but the reality is that some segments of the population are more likely than others to enjoy the benefits of acting on a problem, and some are more likely than others to pay the costs. It is wise to think about how to present such information.

8.2 Constructing Alternatives

Constructing alternatives focuses on how to develop the list of alternatives that merit further consideration. It emphasizes learning how to think creatively about public policy, particularly when ineffective policies and programs need to be replaced. How do analysts know which alternatives to consider?

What Can Governments Do?

The starting point for constructing alternatives is to see what governments are doing or can do. Among their options, governments can regulate, subsidize, ration, tax and spend, contract out, use market incentives, privatize, charge fees for service educate, create public trust, and commission research. Table 8-1 summarizes these activities and illustrates them with examples.

Analysts might suggest modifying the present policies or trying a different policy approach or strategy when current policies are not working well enough and a change is needed. Present policy could be strengthened. For example, the national government could raise standards for clean air or water policies. Policy makers could fund programs at a higher level, which might permit improved research, better enforcement, and better public information campaigns. Analysts and policy makers also consider alternatives to conventional regulatory policies. This might include a combination of market-based incentives, public information campaigns, and various forms of regulatory reinvention, which are more flexible and efficient policy reforms.

For some policies and agencies policy makers might try different institutional approaches, such as a new way to organize the bureaucracy in charge. For example, in 2018, the State Council made departmental adjustments. It integrated the responsibilities of the Ministry of Science and Technology and the State Administration of Foreign Experts Affairs, and reorganized the Ministy of Science and Technology as a component department of the Ministries of the People's Republic of China. The establishment of the Ministry of Ecology and Environment has highlighted the government's role in ecological and environmental protection, and the Ministry of Environmental Protection will no longer be retained.

Table 8-1   What Can Governments Do?

Action	Illustrations	Specific Examples
Regulate	Licensing, inspection, enforcement of standards, application of sanctions.	Environmental, health, and workplace safety regulation; corporate financial regulations.
Subsidize	Loans, direct payments or benefits, tax credits, price supports.	Student loans, subsidies to farmers; low-interest loans for disaster recovery.
Ration	Limit access to scarce resources.	Charge fees for museum entrance; limit services covered by national health insurance.
Tax and spend	Tax an activity at a level that encourages or discourages it. Spend money on preferred programs.	Allowing insurance deductions to encourage purchase; imposing cigarette taxes to discourage smoking. Defense weapons, prisons, public higher education.
Contract out	Contract government services from the private sector or buy products for government agencies.	Defense contracts for weapons procurement; purchase of computers and fleet vehicles for government or public schools.
Use market incentives	A special category of taxation or imposition of fees that creates incentives for changing behavior and achieving goals and objectives.	Raising gasoline taxes to encourage conservation of fuel and reduce carbon dioxide emissions; tax rebates for purchasing hybrid vehicles
Privatize	Transferring public services from government to the private sector.	Turning over management of public schools to private companies.

(续表)

Action	Illustrations	Specific Examples
Charge fees	Fees for select services.	Requiring students to pay to ride the school bus; charging for parking at public facilities.
Educate	Provide information to the public through formal programs or other actions.	Formal public meetings; public education services; food safety labels; information on toxic chemical releases; automobile fuel efficiency labels.
Create public trusts	Holding public property in trust for citizens indefinitely.	Local land conservation trusts, national parks and recreation areas.
Conduct research	Conduct or support research and development.	Support for government research institutes and think tanks.

Governments are trying another interesting institutional reform option. They make routine government services available online, everything from providing tourists information to supplying government forms that people can fill out on their computers. Governments report improved efficiency, and the users say they are more satisfied with the results and think more highly of the agencies than before.

Actions in many policy areas are rooted in one of two views of the problem being confronted. These might be called the supply and demand perspectives. If analysts believe a problem such as energy scarcity results from an insufficient supply of energy, they would likely recommend the policy alternative of increasing supply. They would consider actions to boost supplies of energy, whether from fossil fuels (oil, natural gas, and coal), nuclear energy, or alternative energy such as wind or solar power. Conversely, the demand perspective would recommend addressing demand. To consider which policy option will work best or be more efficient or fair, policy makers also have to think about the philosophical and ideological aspects.

8.3　Assessing Policy Alternatives

Assessing policy alternatives is about applying evaluative criteria. Analysts have many ways to present the alternatives so that policy makers and other interested parties can understand the analysis and the choices they face. For example, if three policy options are offered for consideration, the analyst might present each in terms of its likely effectiveness, economic efficiency, and equity. Trade-offs are inevitable in this kind of decision making. Only rarely does a particular policy option rank highest on all of the evaluative criteria. It is far more likely that one option is judged to be most effective, but another cheaper or more equitable in its effects. Analysts, therefore, attach weight to each criterion. For example, is equity more important than efficiency in promoting cleanup of hazardous waste sites? Should governments clean up the most dangerous sites first or try to ameliorate the conditions at several sites at once? Or should the resources be directed to sites that have a disproportionate impact on poor and minority communities? Would doing so promote greater equity? As analysts consider more than a few conflicting bases for assessing policy options, the necessity for weighting criteria increases.

Discussion Questions

1. Why is the process of problem definition important?
2. What are the major components of public programs?
3. What are the different categories of alternatives?
4. How are policy alternatives assessed?

Vocabulary

quantitative
qualitative
statistics
goal
objective
proximate causes
regulatory reinvention

References

Anderson, James E. 2003. Public Policy Making. 5th ed. Boston: Houghton Mifflin.

Birkland, Thomas A. 2001. An Introduction to the Policy Process: Theories, Concepts, and Models of Public Policy Making. New York: M. E. Sharpe.

Dunn, N. William. 1981. An Introduction Public Policy Analysis. Englewood Cliffs, New Jersey: Prentice-Hall, Inc.

Kraft, Michael E. and Furlong, Scott R. 2004. Public Policy: Politics, Analysis, and Alternatives. Washington, D. C. CQ Press.

Patton, Carl V. and Sawicki, David S. 1993. Basic Methods of Policy Analysis and Planning. 2nd ed. Englewood Cliffs, New Jersey: Prentice Hall.

Starling, Grover. 1988. Strategies for Policy Making. Chicago: Dorsey Press.

Ringquist, Evan J. 1993. Environmental Protection at the State Level: Politics and Progress in Controlling Pollution. Armonk, New York: M. E. Sharpe.

第8章

公共问题与政策备选方案

　　政策备选方案的提出始于对问题的描述即问题的定义,政策争论可能取决于基于问题定义的操作措施。统计信息十分丰富,但并非所有内容都可以简化为定量指标。除了需要对问题加以定义,还需要考虑问题如何测量,确定问题的影响范围和重要程度,问题的成因,设定目标以及确定可以做什么。

　　大多数研究关注问题的直接原因。解决问题可以从明确列出各个参与者的目标以及实现这些目标的可能方式开始。政策分析应着眼于成本和收益及如何分配。不同的备选方案包括了政府有权做的事情。政府可以通过监管、补贴、定额、税收和支出、外包、使用市场激励措施、私有化、收费、教育、信托和研究的方式做出选择。评估备选方案是发现评估标准的过程。

8.1　公共问题:定义及基本要素

　　任何政策研究的开始都涉及对问题的描述。有些问题,可能原因是显而易见的。例如,如果问题是青少年吸烟以及如何限制吸烟,我们可以找到关于青少年吸烟者的人数,他们选择吸烟的理由以及终身的吸烟习惯和相关健康问题的影响等丰富信息。许多政府利用这些信息制定旨在预防的教育方案和其他成功降低青少年吸烟率的政策。

　　问题分析尝试回答以下基本问题:

——问题的本质

——问题的程度或规模

——问题是如何产生的

——问题存在的主要原因

——问题作为公共政策问题的重要性

——问题将导致的风险

——关于问题已经了解到什么

——问题可能的解决方案

任何一份日报都包含有关大量潜在政策问题的信息，如犯罪、污染、通货膨胀、能源、福利和失业。很少有人认为这些不是问题，也就是说，这些情况的每一个都会影响某些价值或需求的实现。可能是个人安全、健康、消费或者其他某种需要。然而，这种对问题含义的日常理解往往是不充分的，因为它模糊了这样一个事实，即不同的群体可能会以截然相反的态度看待同一问题（例如犯罪）。对一些人来说，犯罪是人类社会普遍的社会现象，而对另一些人来说，犯罪是对贫困和剥削的一种可以理解的回应。人们将犯罪视为问题的方式取决于以下几个因素。

首先，不同的人可能都同意犯罪是一个问题，但可能对犯罪行为的种类有不同的看法。一个人可能仅仅从对人的非法行为（杀人、持械抢劫、强奸）来定义犯罪，而另一个人可能把重点放在涉及财产的非法行为（偷窃、欺诈、贪污、政府腐败）上。

其次，人们也可能不同意犯罪活动所代表的问题类型/类别。有些人认为犯罪是一个经济问题。因此，潜在的解决方案在于重组社会中商品和服务的生产和分配。也有人认为这可以通过提供更多的社会流动机会，通过教育改变人们的态度或严格执行现有刑法来解决社会、心理甚至管理问题。人们对问题分类的方式通常决定了他们解释和尝试解决问题的方式。

最后，人们可能就问题的定义、分类和解释达成一致，但对其范围、严重性和重要性却存在分歧。关于问题严重性的判断很大程度上取决于哪些价值观和需求被认为是最重要的。与那些坚决致力于社会正义的人相比，对人身安全有强烈需求的人或致力于法律和秩序价值观的人更有可能将犯罪视为一个政策问题。

政策过程的一个重要步骤是定义问题。例如，如果分析人员研究贫困人口的困境，他们需要定义贫困的含义。贫困仅仅是缺钱或收入不足的问题？是否包括其他特征，如缺乏某些技能或能力？贫困究竟是相对的还是绝对的？公共政策的争论还取决于问题的操作措施或运行指标。分析人员需要知道有多少人生活在贫困之中，他们的人口结构如何，而不仅仅是抽象地提到贫困。在讨论公立学校的教育质量时，分析人员希望看到考试成绩和其他对学生进行的相关评估的数据，以确定学校是否存在问题，以及一个社区的学校与另一个社区的学校相比如何。如果研究对象是暴力犯罪，分析人员需要全国和当地犯罪数量的统计数据，以及犯罪率是上升还是下降了。

对大多数当代公共问题而言，存在大量的量化指标，所以需要对提供多少统计信息进行判断。至少，大多数议题文件或问题分析都包括一些基本的描述性统计数据。其中一种是频率计数，例如不同收入水平的人口所占百分比或调查中以某种方式做出答复的人数。另一种是一个群体或类别的平均的（平均值）量度，例如考试的平均分数。一个替代方法是变量的中位数，即该组的一半在中位数以上，一半在中位数以下。例如全国不同地区房屋销售的中位价格。对变化区间或两个变量之间的相关性或关系，如年龄和收入，也可能是有益的。

统计信息可以在报告中以多种方式呈现。其中包括显示频率计数或现有研究的百分比的表格，例如不同年龄组吸烟人数的百分比。也可以在地图上叠加信息以显示地理差异，例如城市增长率或邻近城市和郊区的收入水平。饼状图或条形图这样的图表就很常见，而条形图可以显示问题的严重程度是如何随时间变化的，例如 1980 年至 2020 年失业的人数。

如何选择以最好的方式呈现量化信息是一门艺术，报告至少应该是清晰的。即便如此，一些视觉呈现方式可能更吸引读者的注意力，例如使用计算机生成的各种不同格式的彩色图形，包括书面形式和幻灯片或类似的演示文稿。在选择报告或演示文稿的格式时，通常好的建议是将观众和目标铭记于心。定量数据的使用也会带来一些风险，分析人员需要警惕报告中数据不准确的可能性或者无法真正解决问题的无效测量。

当然，并不是所有人类关注的问题都可以用量化指标来衡量，如幸福或幸福感。然而，分析人员可以利用调查来询问人们是否快乐，是否喜欢生活在自己的社区里，是否相信学校会做得很好。如果是不能直接量化的公共问题，这种调查可能是有益的替代方案。经济学家也认为人们可以被要求评估许多没有市场价值的活动。他们的反馈有助于判断某些行动，例如保护开放空间或种植树木，是否合理地使用税收资金等。

展望未来

此外，还应提及定义和测量问题的另一个方面。对现状的任何考虑都必须基于对问题可能随着时间的推移而变化的前提。几年或几十年后问题会发生怎样的变化？预测或预判通常涉及对当前趋势的推断，但这只是展望未来的一种方法。

预测包括经济预测（国家会在五年内出现盈余还是赤字？）、人口预测（到 2025 年或 2050 年，国家人口将达到多少？）和能源需求（哪种，多少，在哪里等）。如果这些预测揭示了在有或没有政策干预的情况下可能发生的情况，那这些预测非常有用。例如，采取节能措施的国家将在多大程度上减少对进口石油的依赖？

公共问题的基本要素

图 8-1 中的流程图总结了问题分析的基本要素。该图可以指导在准备对问题或议案进行分析时可能涉及的问题给予指导。

定义问题。如果问题是教育质量，教育质量究竟意味着什么？换言之，研究中教育问题的确切性质是什么？质量下降了？是否比很多人认为的还要低？

衡量问题。找到一个与定义方式相适配的方法来衡量问题。这个步骤有时被称为发展一个操作性定义。可靠来源提供了哪些定量指标？教育质量最好的衡量标准是什么？学生在标准化考试中的分数？学生学习的其他考量方法？还是学校教师的素质指标？

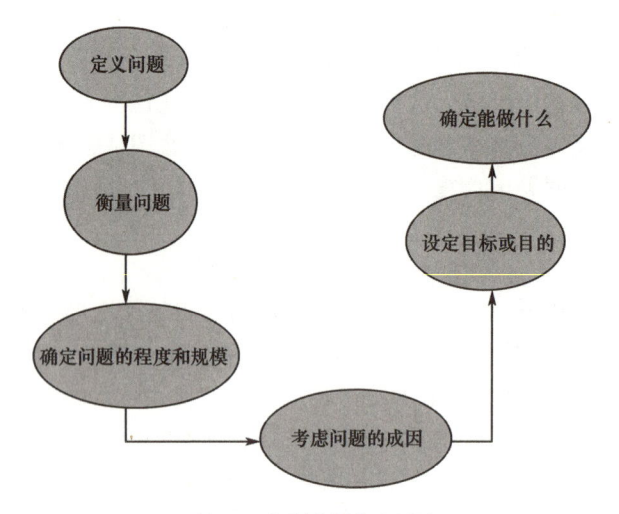

图 8-1　问题分析的流程图

确定问题的程度和规模。使用可用的指标确定受问题影响的人及数量。试着回答这些问题：有哪些群体受到正在研究的问题的影响，受影响的时间有多长？以及受影响的程度如何？例如，不同学区或地区——从城市到农村的教育质量有何不同？从贫困地区的学校到较富裕地区的学校。

考虑问题的成因。问题是如何产生的，为什么会继续？问题的主要原因是什么，还有哪些其他原因需要考虑？了解问题的原因对制定解决方案至关重要。在过去的几十年里，教育质量发生了怎样的变化？为什么？

设定目标或目的。如何做才能解决问题？为什么？某些目的和目标是否至关重要，是否得到广泛认同，在经济或社会方面是否可行？应该在什么时间内寻求目标的实现？在教育质量方面，最合适的目标是什么？如果要提高质量，在一定时期内应该取得多大的进展？

确定能做什么。哪些行动可能有助于解决问题或实现既定目标？针对问题的根源可以采取哪些政策措施？这些努力可以影响哪些变量？如果目标是在一定程度上提高教育质量，还需要做些什么？提高教师素质？减少班级规模？改变课程？

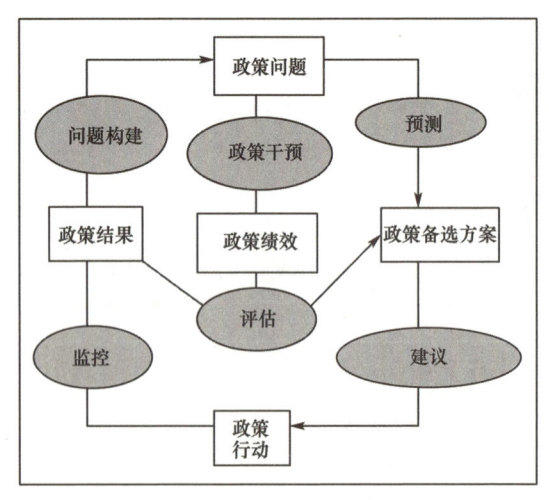

图 8-2　政策问题构建

考虑问题成因及解决方案

对公共问题的任何评估都需要考虑其成因即问题是如何产生的，以及它为何会继续存在。问题的答案对公共政策是否能够以及如何解决问题有很大影响。例如，如果问题是为什么青年失业率从 2000 年到 2020 年急剧增加，部分答案可能在于就业保障在整个期间整体下降。在许多公司中，甚至有大规模的长期雇员被解雇。如果就业保障存在普遍问题，那么青年也可能面临特定问题。

大多数政策研究都集中在所谓的公共问题的近因或直接原因上。更大的挑战是找到解决问题的根本原因。由于公众长期以来形成的态度和习惯难以改变，采取政策行动可能会更加困难。想想城市交通拥堵的问题，为什么存在？答案显而易见，在任何特定时间里有太多人在有限数量的道路上开车。那么建设更多高速公路是解决方案吗？是否考虑在拥堵最严重的城市地区减少汽车的使用？一些城市设计师和环保人士提供了一个更激进的解决方案，至少对新社区而言。他们建议在城市中建设足够的公共交通，让人们离工作地点更近一些。许多国家和地区正在采取"智能增长"政策，对未来几十年的预期增长进行管理。大多数公共问题都有多种成因，因此人们在哪些问题是最重要的，哪些应该成为公共政策研究的对象上存在分歧。

公共问题的解决可以从明确列出各种政策参与者的目的和目标开始，并确定为实现这些目标可采取的行动。目标可包括具体衡量要实现的标准，例如改善获得医疗保健服务的机会或降低青少年吸烟率。当分析人员考虑公共问题的潜在解决方案时，他们会试图找出政策干预的机会。他们试图想象公共政策的改变会对这个问题产生怎样的影响。例如，提高香烟的价格会降低青少年的吸烟率吗？

分析人员有时试图描述解决问题的好处和成本。他们研究了政策行为（积极或消极）的后果如何在人口分组之间分配，例如在某些地区、职业或社会群体——换言之，如果问题得到解决，谁是受益者，谁是受害者。一些政治家和其他主要政策参与者有时非常精明地解决这些分配问题，他们几乎总是对了解自己感兴趣。他们看似在谈论解决公共问题，好像整个国家都将平等受益一样，但现实情况是，某些群体比其他人更有可能享受对某一问题采取行动的好处，有些人比其他人更有可能支付这些费用，所以考虑如何呈现这样的信息是充满智慧的选择。

8.2 构建备选方案

构建备选方案的重点是如何制定值得进一步考虑的备选方案清单。它强调学习如何创造性地思考公共政策，特别是当无效的政策和方案需要被替换的时候。分析人员需要了解如何对备选方案进行考量？

政府可以做什么？

构建备选方案的出发点是了解政府正在做什么或可以做些什么。在他们的选择中，政府可以使用监管、补贴、定额、税收和支出、外包，使用市场激励、私有化、收费、教育、建立公共信任和调研等手段。表 8-1 概述了这些活动，并通过示例进行了说明。

表 8-1　　　　　　　　　　政府可以做什么？

行为	示例	具体例子
监管	许可，审查，执行标准，实施制裁	环境，健康和工作场所安全法规，公司财务规定
补贴	贷款，直接支付或福利，税收抵免，价格补贴	助学贷款，对农民的补贴，用于灾难恢复的低息贷款
定额	限制对稀缺资源的使用权	博物馆门票，限制国民健康保险所涵盖的服务
税收和支出	通过征税在某种程度上对某一活动加以鼓励或阻止 对优先项目的投资	扣除保险金以鼓励购买；征收香烟税以阻止吸烟 防御武器，监狱，公立高等教育
外包	与私营部门签订政府服务合同或为政府机构购买产品	国防武器采购合同 为政府或公立学校购买计算机和校车
使用市场激励	通过特殊类别的税收或收费，可以鼓励人们改变行为方式进而实现政策目标	提高汽油税以节约燃料和减少二氧化碳排放，为购买混合动力汽车的退税
私有化	将公共服务从政府转移到私营部门	将公立学校的管理权交给私人教育集团
收费	特定服务收费	要求学生付费乘坐校车，对一些公共场所实施停车收费
教育	通过正式计划或其他行动向公众提供信息	正式的公开会议；公共教育服务；食品安全标签；有关有毒化学物质释放的相关信息；汽车燃油效率标签
建立公共信任	保障公民可以无限期持有信托财产	国家公园以及休闲区的土地保护信托基金
调研	进行或支持研发	支持政府研究机构和智囊团

政策分析人员可能会建议修改现行政策，或在现行政策运行不佳且需要调整时，尝试不同的政策方针或策略。现行政策可以加强，例如，中央政府可以提高清洁空气或水政策的标准。政策制定者可以为更高级别的方案提供资金，这可能有助于改善研究，更好地执行政策和更好的开展宣传活动。分析人员和政策制定者也会考虑替代传统的监管政策，这可能包括基于市场的激励措施、公共宣传活动和各种形式的监管改革相结合，这些都是更加灵活和有效的政策改革。

对于一些政策和机构，政策制定者可能会尝试不同的制度方法，例如组织机构改革。

2018年，国务院部门进行调整，将科学技术部、国家外国专家局的职责整合，重新组建科学技术部，作为国务院组成部门。组建生态环境部，突出了生态环境保护的政府职能，不再保留环境保护部。

政府正在尝试另一项改革方案——在网上提供日常的政府服务，从提供信息给用户到用户可以在政府的门户网站上填写相关业务申请的表格。政府部门的服务效率提高了，用户表示他们对政府提供的服务更满意，并且对政府机构的评价比以前更高了。

许多政策领域的行动会面临两种基于不同的观点的选择。例如供需观点，如果政策人员认为能源短缺问题是能源供应不足造成的，他们可能会推荐增加供应的政策选择去增加能源供应，无论是化石燃料（石油，天然气和煤炭）、核能还是风能、太阳能等替代能源。反过来，从需求的视角来看，则建议解决需求问题。为了考虑哪种政策选择最有效或更公平，政策制定者还必须考虑哲学和意识形态的因素。

许多政策领域的行动根植于所面临问题的两种观点之一。这可能被称为供需观点。如果政策人员认为能源短缺问题是能源供应不足造成的，他们可能会推荐增加供应的政策选择，增加能源供应。无论是来自化石燃料（石油，天然气和煤炭），核能还是风能、太阳能等替代能源。反过来，从需求的视角来看，则建议解决需求问题。为了考虑哪种政策选择最有效或更有效或更公平，政策制定者还必须考虑哲学和意识形态方面。

8.3　政策备选方案评估

评估政策备选方案需要采用评估标准。分析人员有很多方法来提出备选方案，以便决策者和其他相关方能够理解他们所面临的选择。例如，如果有三种政策备选方案可供考虑，分析人员可能就其可能的有效性、经济效率和公平性对每一项政策备选方案进行比较。在这种决策中，权衡是不可避免的。在所有评估标准中，特定的政策备选方案很少排在首位。更可能的是一种备选方案被认为是最有效的，而另一种备选方案被认为更便宜或更公平。因此，分析人员重视每一项标准。例如，在促进清理危险废物场地方面，公平是否比效率更重要？政府应该首先清理最危险的地方，还是同时改善几个地方的情况？或者是否应将资源用于对贫困和少数社区产生过大影响的地方？这样做会促进更大的公平吗？分析人员认为，在评估政策备选方案时，存在许多相互冲突的依据，因此增加了加权标准的必要性。

思考问题

1. 为什么问题定义的过程很重要？
2. 公共项目的主要组成部分是什么？
3. 不同类别的替代选择有哪些不同？
4. 如何评估政策选择？

词 汇

定量的
定性的
统计的
目标
目的
近因
监管改革

参考文献

Anderson, James E. 2003. Public Policy Making. 5th ed. Boston: Houghton Mifflin.

Birkland, Thomas A. 2001. An Introduction to the Policy Process: Theories, Concepts, and Models of Public Policy Making. New York: M. E. Sharpe.

Dunn, N. William. 1981. An Introduction Public Policy Analysis. Englewood Cliffs, New Jersey: Prentice-Hall, Inc.

Kraft, Michael E. and Furlong, Scott R. 2004. Public Policy: Politics, Analysis, and Alternatives. Washington, D. C. CQ Press.

Patton, Carl V. and Sawicki, David S. 1993. Basic Methods of Policy Analysis and Planning. 2nd ed. Englewood Cliffs, New Jersey: Prentice Hall.

Starling, Grover. 1988. Strategies for Policy Making. Chicago: Dorsey Press.

Ringquist, Evan J. 1993. Environmental Protection at the State Level: Politics and Progress in Controlling Pollution. Armonk, New York: M. E. Sharpe.

陈庆云. 公共政策分析. 北京:北京大学出版社,2006.

陈振明. 政策科学——公共政策分析导论. 2版. 北京:中国人民大学出版社,2003.

宁骚. 公共政策. 北京:高等教育出版社,2000.

谢明. 公共政策分析导论. 5版. 北京:中国人民大学出版社,2022.

张金马. 公共政策分析:概念·过程·方法. 北京:人民出版社,2004.

张国庆. 公共政策分析. 上海:复旦大学出版社,2004.

詹姆斯·E.安德森. 公共政策制定. 5版. 谢明,等,译. 北京:中国人民大学出版社,2009.

托马斯·R.戴伊. 理解公共政策. 12版. 谢明,等,译. 北京中国人民大学出版社,2011.

保罗·A.萨巴蒂尔. 政策过程理论. 胡总超,钟开斌,等,译. 北京:生活·读书·新知三联书店,2004.

戴博拉·斯通. 政策悖论. 顾建光,译. 北京:中国人民大学出版社,2006.

Chapter 9 Creative Thinking about Policy Action

Summary

Analysis may go beyond policy typologies and evaluations on existing policies. They may also gather ideas through brainstorming. They may do quick surveys. They may conduct literature reviews to discover what is known about a problem. They may also compare existing situation against ideal standard.

Beyond considering policy typologies or variations on existing policies analysts can try other techniques to expand their list of policy alternatives. Here the discussion is centered on how to apply creative thinking on policy action. Among other strategies some scholars suggest the following: no-action analysis, quick surveys, literature reviews, comparison to real world situations, passive collection and classification, use of analogies and metaphors, brainstorming, and comparison with an ideal. This chapter will discuss:

— Brainstorming
— Quick Surveys
— Literature Reviews
— Comparison with an Ideal

9.1 Brainstorming

Brainstorming is a method for generating ideas, goals, and strategies that help identify and conceptualize problematic situations. It may be used to generate a large number of suggestions about potential solutions for problems.

Brainstorming is a popular technique for encouraging creative thinking in public policy or in organizational change. It usually takes place in an informal meeting of people who share an interest in finding solutions to a given problem.

The participants in a brainstorming session bounce idea around with the goal of producing a list of possibilities. Ideas are offered and recorded as they are made, with no attempt to criticize or evaluate them. This freewheeling discussion of the issues should produce creative thinking and numerous suggestions. In the second phase of the meeting, the participants reduce the number of suggestions to come up with a shorter list of alternatives worthy of further consideration.

Brainstorming can also take the form of written suggestions rather than an open meeting with verbal responses. Some variations on the brainstorming theme suggest that creativity is enhanced when some structure is introduced into the discussions.

Brainstorming involves several simple procedures:

— Brainstorming groups should be composed in accordance with the nature of the problematic situation being investigated. This usually means the selection of particularly knowledgeable experts.

— The process of idea generation and idea evaluation should be kept strictly apart, since intense group discussion may be inhibited by premature criticism and debate.

— The atmosphere of brainstorming activities should be kept as open and permissive as possible in the idea-generating phase.

— Idea evaluation should begin only after the first phase of generating ideas has been exhausted.

— The group should prioritize ideas at the end of the idea-evaluation phase and incorporate them into a proposal that contains a conceptualization of the problem and its potential solutions.

Brainstorming is a highly versatile procedure that may involve relatively structured or unstructured activities, depending on the analyst's aims and the practical constraints of the situation. Relatively unstructured brainstorming activities occur frequently in government agencies and public and private "thinktanks."

The main difference between brainstorming and other techniques for problem structuring is that the focus is on collective groups of experts rather than on individuals. Moreover, brainstorming activities are assessed, not in terms of logical consistency or the plausibility of comparisons, but according to consensus among members of brainstorming groups.

9.2 Quick Surveys

Quick surveys involve talking with people in a particular policy network or searching through hearings transcripts, minutes of meetings, newspaper accounts, and the like for pertinent information about a problem and policy alternatives. The idea here is that people familiar with the issues have probably raised many alternatives. Interviewing them, distributing questionnaires to them, or reviewing what they have written or said on the issues should produce a short list of possible policy alternatives. This technique could be particularly useful at the local level where gaining access to principal policy actors is a real possibility.

9.3 Literature Review

A literature review is an examination of library sources such as books, journal articles, in addition to other sources like internet sites. The purpose here is to look for policy alternatives that have been proposed or considered previously. This kind of search could extend to a survey of the options that policy makers have considered or adopted in other policy area as well.

For example, the Environmental Impact Assessment Act required that government agencies conduct an environmental impact analysis, and make it public, before making a major decision such as building highways. Can an impact analysis be applied elsewhere? In other words, why not require that specific studies or reports be conducted and made public prior to reaching a final decision in other areas of public policy? Rather than think about abstract ideas, analysts might ask what has worked well in specific or real world situations, and therefore what might be considered an effective policy alternative for the present policy. Analysts also want to know which alternatives have been tried elsewhere and found wanting. Analysts can look to and evaluate what other nations have tried to do about a particular problem.

9.4 Comparison with an Ideal

Analysts sometimes compare policy alternatives with an ideal situation. For example, as part of smart growth planning or sustainability efforts, many communities hold "visioning" meetings at which residents are encouraged to think about the community they want for the future. What kind of residential neighborhoods, what kind of downtown, what kind of recreational opportunities? The goal is to envision an ideal future and use that vision to generate ideas for moving in the desired direction.

Participants in public policy debates too often assume that an ideal situation is unattainable and therefore not worthy of consideration. However, excluding ideals guarantees that they will be never come about. By encouraging the expression of an ideal, analysts can ensure that at least the more pragmatic ideas that do receive consideration are evaluated in terms of how close they come to the ideal.

Any of these strategies for generating a list of policy alternatives should help an analyst think clearly about how to solve a problem. At this point in the process, neither the cost nor the political feasibility of a particular option is the primary concern. Rather, the goal is to think critically about the problem and try to imagine the various ways of addressing it.

Discussion Questions

1. How should brainstorming be conducted to be most effective?
2. When are quick surveys the most useful? How should they be conducted?
3. What is the purpose of a literature review? Where should a policy analyst look in order to conduct one?
4. What kinds of ideals can be the basis for a policy comparison?

Vocabularies

brainstorming

questionnaire

quick surveys

transcripts

literature reviews

environmental impact

comparison with an ideal

visioning

References

Birkland, Thomas A. 2001. An Introduction to the Policy Process: Theories, Concepts, and Models of Public Policy Making. New York: M. E. Sharpe.

Baumgartner, Frank R., and Jones, Bryan D. 1993. Agendas and Instability in American Politics. Chicago: University of Chicago Press.

Dunn, N. William. 1981. An Introduction Public Policy Analysis. Englewood Cliffs, New Jersey: Prentice-Hall, Inc.

Goldenberg, Jacob, David Mazursky, and Sorin Solomon. 1999. "Creative Sparks." Science, 3 (September): 1495-1496.

Kraft, Michael E. and Furlong, Scott R. 2004. Public Policy: Politics, Analysis, and Alternatives. Washington, D. C.: CQ Press.

Patton, Carl V. and Sawicki, David S. 1993. Basic Methods of Policy Analysis and Planning. 2nd ed. Englewood Cliffs, New Jersey: Prentice-Hall, Inc.

第 9 章

政策分析的创造性思维

政策分析人员可能会超越现有政策的政策类型和政策变迁,通过头脑风暴来收集更多想法,可以做调查,可以做文献研究以发现已有的对该问题的研究,也可以对现实和理想愿景进行比较。

除了考虑政策类型或现有政策的变化外,分析人员还可以尝试其他方式来扩展其政策选择清单。我们这里的讨论集中在如何将创造性思维应用于政策行动。在其他策略中,一些学者提出以下建议:快速调查,文献综述,与现有情况的比较,被动收集和分类,类比和隐喻,头脑风暴以及与理想愿景的比较。本章将讨论:

——头脑风暴
——快速调查
——文献综述
——与理想愿景的比较

9.1 头脑风暴

头脑风暴是一种产生想法来解决设计问题的方法,集中一组人来同时思考某事的方式。它可以用来产生大量关于问题的潜在解决方案的建议。

头脑风暴是一种在公共政策或组织变革中鼓励创造性思维的流行技术。它通常在非正式的会议上进行,与会者都希望找到一个特定问题的解决办法。

头脑风暴会议的参与者反复思考以列出各种可能性。对生成和记录下来的创意想法不去批评或评估。这种畅所欲言的讨论会产生创造性思维和众多建议。在会议的第二阶段，与会者减少了提出建议的数量，以便提出一份值得进一步审议的较短的备选方案清单。

头脑风暴也可以采取书面建议的形式，而不是公开会议或口头答复。头脑风暴主题的一些变化表明，在讨论中引入某种制度可以加强创造力。

头脑风暴包括如下一些步骤：

——头脑风暴小组成员应根据所调查的问题情况的性质组成。这通常意味着挑选知识渊博的专家。

——思想产生和评价过程应该严格分开，因为过早的批评可能使得激烈的小组讨论受到限制。

——在创意阶段，头脑风暴活动的氛围应尽可能保持开放和宽容。

——应在产生想法的第一阶段用尽之后，才开始进行想法评估。

——小组应在理性评估阶段结束时对想法进行优先排序，并将其纳入一个包含问题定义及其潜在解决方案的提案中。

头脑风暴是一个高度通用的方法，可能涉及相对结构化或非结构化的活动，这取决于分析人员的目标设定和实际情况的限制。在政府机构以及公共和私人"智囊团"中，相对没有组织的头脑风暴活动经常发生。

头脑风暴和其他问题构建技术上的主要区别在于，重点是集体的专家小组而不是个人。此外，对头脑风暴的评估，不是根据逻辑一致性或比较的可行性，而是根据头脑风暴小组成员的共识。

9.2 快速调查

快速调查包括在特定的政策网络中与人交谈，或通过听证会记录、会议记录、报纸报道等来搜索有关问题和政策选择的相关信息。这样做的想法是，熟悉这些问题的人可能已经提出了许多替代方案。与他们进行面谈，向他们分发调查问卷，或者审视他们在这些问题上所写或所说的内容，应该可以得到一份简短的备选政策清单。这种方法在地方一级尤其有用，因为真正有可能接触到主要的政策主体。

9.3 文献研究

文献研究是对图书馆资源的检阅，如书籍、期刊文章以及其他来源，如互联网网站。这样做的目的是寻找先前提出或考虑过的政策选择。这种搜索可以扩展到政策制定者在其他政策领域考虑或采用的选项的调查。

例如，《环境影响评估法》要求政府机构在做出诸如建设高速公路等重大决策之前进行环境影响分析,并将其公之于众。环境影响分析能否在其他地方应用?换言之,为什么不要求在其他公共政策领域做出最终决定之前进行具体的研究或报告?分析人员或许会问,在特定或现实情况下哪些方法行之有效,因此哪些方法可被认为是当前政策的有效替代方案。分析人员还想知道哪些替代方案已在其他地方实践,但却被发现有缺陷。分析人员可以关注并评估其他国家对某个特定问题上所做的努力。

9.4 与理想愿景的比较

分析人员有时会将政策选择与理想愿景进行比较。例如,作为理性增长规划或可持续性发展的一部分,许多社区举行"愿景"的会议,鼓励居民思考他们未来所需要的社区。如需要什么样的住宅,什么样的市中心,什么样的娱乐机会?我们的目标是设想一个理想的未来,并利用这一愿景产生朝着理想方向前进的想法。

公共政策的参与者往往认为理想的情况是无法实现的,因此不值得考虑。然而,如果排除理想那么它们则永远不会实现。通过鼓励对理想的表达,政策分析人员确保至少可以得到对更务实的想法进行评估,看看它们与理想的距离。

这些策略中的任何一个都可以生成一个政策选择列表,帮助分析人员清晰地思考如何解决问题。在此过程中,一个特定方案的成本和政治可行性都不是主要关注点。相反,我们的目标是批判性地思考这个问题,并设法想象各种解决方法。

思考问题

1. 如何进行头脑风暴最有效?
2. 什么时候快速调查最有用?应如何进行?
3. 文献研究的目的是什么?政策分析人员应该在哪里开始工作?
4. 什么样的理想愿景可以作为政策比较的基础?

词 汇

头脑风暴

快速调查

文献研究

与理想愿景的比较

调查问卷

记录

对环境的影响

参考文献

Birkland, Thomas A. 2001. An Introduction to the Policy Process: Theories, Concepts, and Models of Public Policy Making. New York: M. E. Sharpe.

Baumgartner, Frank R., and Jones, Bryan D. 1993. Agendas and Instability in American Politics. Chicago: University of Chicago Press.

Dunn, N. William. 1981. An Introduction Public Policy Analysis. Englewood Cliffs, New Jersey: Prentice-Hall, Inc.

Goldenberg, Jacob, David Mazursky, and Sorin Solomon. 1999. "Creative Sparks." Science, 3 (September): 1495-1496.

Kraft, Michael E. and Furlong, Scott R. 2004. Public Policy: Politics, Analysis, and Alternatives. Washington, D.C.: CQ Press.

Patton, Carl V. and Sawicki, David S. 1993. Basic Methods of Policy Analysis and Planning. 2nd ed. Englewood Cliffs, New Jersey: Prentice-Hall, Inc.

巴比. 社会研究方法. 邱泽奇,译. 北京:华夏出版社,2005.

Chapter 10
▶▶▶ Policy Failure and Learning from It

Summary

> Explanations for policy failure are complicated. Success and failure are not precise concepts. They are highly subjective and are related to the goals of the different policy actors. Policies may fail due to untried alternatives, the impact of changing circumstances, the relationship between policies, political boundaries, excessive policy demands, unrealizable expectations, the inaccuracy of causal theories, the choice of policy tools, the complexity of the implementation process, and the failure of political institution. Analysts should learn from the failure of policies. Instrumental policy learning concerns the viability of policy designs and tools. Social policy learning concerns the social construction of policies. Political learning is about political strategy.

10.1 Explanations for Policy Failure

No doubt you have complained and heard others complain that a policy has failed. A lot of people complain about traffic congestion and public transportation. Why might a policy be a failure? It might be argued that there are not enough roads, or that the bus fare is too high. Maybe gas prices are not high enough to discourage automobile use and public transportation is not convenient enough.

Ingram and Mann (1980) provided a number of useful ways to think about policy failure. They argued that "success and failure are slippery concepts, often highly subjective and reflective of an individual's goals, perception of need, and perhaps even psychological disposition toward life." In other words, failure is often in the eye of the beholder. Further, it is affected by immediate perception of the policy in question. One person might argue that a policy has failed, while another person might look at it as a tentative first step toward a larger goal. The current level of public transportation may have failed some, but another person may think it just needs more support. Ideology plays a role. Conservative successes are often liberal failures and vice versa.

Table 10-1　　　　　　　　　**Explanations for Policy Failure**

Alternatives to policies tried	Failure needs to be assessed in terms of the do-nothing option and in terms of the likelihood that other options would have been more or less successful.
The impact of changing circumstances	Changing circumstances can render policies less successful, such as energy policies that provide price relief before they create dependency on oil and natural gas.
Relationships of one policy to another	Policies are related and these relationships must be considered. For example, a stricter policy against unauthorized immigrants may endanger broader policy goals surrounding American's relations with China, such as trade or security.
The boundary question	Political boundaries (between provinces, for example) influence policy success.
Realizable policy expectations	Policies sometimes fail when they go beyond what can be achieved now though ambitious policy making can be the result of 'speculative argumentation' that seeks to induce innovation. The stated purpose of a policy may not be the actual purpose. There may be more symbolic goals than substance.
Accurate theory of causation	Policy will fail if it is not based on sound causal theory.
Choice of effective policy tools	The choice of ineffective tools will likely yield failure. However, the choice of tools is often a function of compromise or ideological predisposition.
The vagaries of implementation	The problems inherent in policy implementation can contribute to policy failure.
Failure of political institutions	Policy failure is a symptom of problems within political institutions such as the breakdown of political party power or devolution of power from legislative leaders to the committees and subcommittees.

Other reasons for policy failure are listed in Table 10-1. If you are active in politics and policy making or even reasonably attentive to politics, you may recognize these reasons for policy failure. There are many possible reasons policy failure and many possible problems that can cause or contribute to policy failure. Thus, simple storytelling about policy failure may reflect popular dissatisfaction with a policy in particular, or government in general, but fails to consider the multiple reasons why policies can at least be perceived as failures.

10.2　Policy Success, Failure, and Learning

Given that policies fail or at least appear to fail relatively often, it is likely that some sort of policy change will result from these failures if failure provides an opportunity to learn from mistakes. It is useful to think about how policy failure induces policy change through a learning process. Indeed, many experts and commentators on important public issues claim that certain phenomena can induce organizations to learn from their mistakes.

Bennet and Howlett(1992) note that learning can be a more active and "deliberate attempt to adjust the goals and techniques of policy in the light of the consequences of past policy and new information so as to better attain" policy goals. Indeed, organizations make concerted efforts to improve their learning capacity by creating systems to store and disseminate information. Sabatier(1988) provides a more specific definition of policy-oriented learning as "relatively enduring alternations of thought or behavioral intentions which result from experience and which are concerned with the attainment (or revision) of policy objectives."

You can think of learning at the organizational and individual level, but it is most useful to consider people as the agents of learning. People apply what they have learned in group policy-making processes.

Types of Learning
May (1990) divides learning into three categories:
— instrumental policy learning
— social policy learning
— political learning

Instrumental policy learning concerns learning about the "viability of policy interventions or implementation designs" (May, 1990). This sort of learning centers on implementation tools and techniques. Learning seems to have happened and been successful when feedback from implementation is analyzed and changes to the design are made that improve its performance.

Social policy learning involves learning about the social construction of a policy or program. This type of learning goes beyond simple adjustments of program management to the heart of the problem itself, including attitudes toward program goals and the nature and appropriateness of government action. Social policy learning can result in better understanding of the underlying casual theory of a public problem if successfully applied, leading to better policy responses.

Political learning is considerably different from instrumental and social learning. Political learning involves learning better strategies for advocating for or against particular policies. Political learning is learning about effective political advocacy. It can be assumed to have occurred when advocates for or against policy change alter their strategy and tactics to conform to new information that has entered the political system.

Given the complexity of the South Korean political system, it seems that policy failure would be the inevitable outcome of any public program. This may not be true, however, because failure is, like so much else in public policy, a subjective condition that is more often grounded in the perceptions of a particular interest than in empirical "fact." However, it can be stipulated that some policies are much less successful than others and that policy makers and others concerned with the management of public programs will learn from the purported failure of a policy. In this way, policy development is an ongoing process with no discernible beginning and no obvious end, but with plenty of opportunities for refinement and fine-tuning.

Discussion Questions

1. Why do some policies fail?
2. Should policy standards be objective or subjective?
3. What can be learned from policy failure?
4. How can policy failure contribute to political development?

Vocabularies

alternatives to policies tried
the impact of changing circumstances
relationships between policies
the boundary questions
excessive policy demand
realizable policy expectations
accurate theory of causation
choice of effective policy tools
the vagaries of implementation
failure of political institutions
instrumental policy learning
social policy learning
political learning

References

Anderson, James E. 2000. Public Policy Making. 4th ed. Boston: Houghton Mifflin.

Birkland, Thomas A. 2001. An Introduction to the Policy Process: Theories, Concepts, and Models of Public Policy Making. New York: M. E. Sharpe.

Bennet, Colin J. and Howlett, Michael. 1992. "The Lessons of Learning: Reconciling Theories of Policy Learning and Policy Change." Policy Sciences, 25 (3):

275-294.

Ingram, Helen and Mann, Dean. 1980. "Policy Failure: An Issues Deserving Attention." In Why Policies Succeed or Fail. Ingram, Helen, and Mann, Dean. ed. Beverly Hils, California: Sage.

Kraft, Michael E. and Furlong, Scott R. 2004. Public Policy: Politics, Analysis, and Alternatives. Washington, D. C. CQ Press.

May, Peter. 1990. "Reconsidering Policy Design: Policies and Publics." Journal of Public Policy, 11(2): 187-206.

Ryan, Neal. 1995. "Unraveling Conceptual Developments in Implementation Analysis." Australian Journal of Public Administration, 54(1): 65-81.

Sabatier, Paul A. 1988. "An Advocacy Coalition Framework of Policy Change and the Role of Policy-Oriented Learning Therein." Policy Sciences, 21: 129-168.

第 10 章

决策失误与误区

决策失误的原因是非常复杂的。成功和失败不是精确的概念。它们具有很强的主观性并且与不同的政策主体的目标相关。决策失误或许在于还未试用的备选方案,不断变化的环境的影响,政策、政治边界、过多的政策需求、无法实现的期待、不准确的因果理论,政策工具的选择、政策实施过程的复杂性、政治制度的失败等。

政策分析人员应从政策失误中获得教训。工具性的政策学习包括政策设计和政策工具的可行性。社会性政策学习包括政策的社会建构。政治性政策学习包括政治策略。

10.1 对政策失误的解释

毫无疑问,你抱怨过也听到其他人抱怨政策失误。很多人抱怨交通拥堵和公共交通。为什么会政策失误?有人认为没有足够的道路,或者公交车票价太高。也许汽油价格还不足以抑制私家车的使用,公共交通也不够方便。

英格拉姆和曼(1980)为思考政策失误提供了很多有用的方法。他们认为"成功和失败是不明确的概念,往往是高度主观的,反映了个人的目标、对需求的感知,甚至可能是对生活的心理倾向。"换言之,失败往往在旁观者的眼中。此外,它还受到对有关政策的直接看法的影响。

有些人可能会认为是政策失误,而另一些人可能将其看作朝着更大目标迈出的试探性的第一步。目前的公共交通水平可能有些失败,但也有人可能认为它只是需要更多的支持。意识形态起着重要作用。保守的成功往往是自由主义的失败,反之亦然。

表10-1列出了政策失误的其他原因。如果你积极参与政治和政策制定,甚至相当关注政治,你可能会了解政策失误的原因。政策失误的原因有很多,有许多因素可能导致或导致政策失误。因此,关于政策失误的片面理解反映了公众对某项政策的不满,或是对政府的普遍不满,但却没有考虑到导致政策失误存在多种原因。

表 10-1　　　　　　　　政策失误的解释

政策替代尝试	政策失败需要根据"无为"选项和其他选项或多或少成功的可能性来进行评估失败
政策环境的变化	不断变化的政策环境会降低政策的成功率,例如能源政策应该在对石油和天然气产生依赖性之前提供价格优惠
政策之间的关系	策略是相关的,而且必须充分考虑这些关系。例如,对非法移民采取更严格的政策可能会危及围绕中美关系的更广泛的政策目标,例如贸易或安全
边界问题	政治边界(例如省之间的边界)影响政策的成功
政策需求过多	人们对政策抱有太多的期望
准确的因果关系理论	如果政策没有基于合理的因果关系理论,也可能失败
有效的政策工具的选择	选择无效的政策工具可能会导致政策失败。但是工具的选择通常具有妥协性或意识形态倾向
政策实施的难以预测	政策实施中固有的问题也可能导致政策失败
政治制度的失败	政策失败是政治机构内部问题释放的信号,例如政党权力丧失或权力从立法机构人下放到委员会和小组委员会

10.2　决策成功、失误和教训

如何看待政策失误或至少看起来相对失误?如果失误提供了从中吸取教训的学习机会,那么这样的失误可能会带来某种政策变迁,政策失误对于如何通过学习过程引发政策的变迁是有益处的。事实上,许多重要公共问题的专家和评论家认为,某些现象可以促使组织从错误中吸取教训。

班纳特和豪利特(1992)指出,学习可以是一种更加积极和"有意识的尝试,根据过去政策和新信息的后果调整政策的目标和技术以便更好地实现"政策目标。实际上,组织通过建立存储和传播信息的系统,共同努力提高学习能力。萨巴蒂尔(1988)对面向政策的学习做了更具体的定义,即"相对持久的思想或行为意图的变化,这些变化来自于经验,并关系到政策目标的实现(或修订)。"

我们可以从组织和个人层面来思考学习,但是将人看作是学习的推动者是最有意义的,因为人们在群体决策过程中会应用他们所学到的知识。

学习的类型

梅(1990)将学习分为三类：
——工具性政策学习
——社会政策学习
——政治学习

工具性政策学习涉及了解"政策干预或执行设计的可行性"(梅,1990)。这种学习以实施工具和技术为中心。当对现实的反馈进行分析并对政策设计进行修改以改善其性能时,学习似乎已经发生并取得了成功。

社会政策学习包括学习政策或方案的社会建构。这种类型的学习超越了简单的将方案管理调整到问题本身,包括对方案目标的态度以及政府行为的性质和适当性的关注。如果可以很好地加以利用,社会政策学习可以帮助人们更好地理解公共问题的潜在随意性,从而产生更好的政策反应。社会政策学习有很多例子。例如政府解决腐败的方式。政府传统上试图通过逮捕罪犯来控制腐败,并且经常这样做以阻止人们受贿或行贿。现在可以通过利用信息技术开放采购系统以减少腐败的机会,也可以开放政府系统以提高透明度。

政治学习与工具和社会政策学习有很大不同。政治学习涉及学习更好的策略来倡导或反对特定政策,同时政治学习会学习有效的政治宣传。可以假设,当支持或反对政策变革的倡导者改变他们的战略和战术,以适应进入政治系统的新信息时,就会发生这种情况。

鉴于政治体制的复杂性,决策失误似乎是任何公共计划(项目)的必然结果。然而如同公共政策中的许多其他因素一样,失败是一种主观条件,通常基于对特定利益的认识,而不是基于经验的"事实"。一些政策不如其他政策成功,政策制定者和其他与公共管理有关的人将从所谓的决策失误中吸取教训。通过这种方式,政策制定是一个持续的过程,没有明显的开始和结束,但有很多机会进行完善和调整。

思考问题

1. 为什么有些政策失败了?
2. 政策标准应该是主观的还是客观的?
3. 从政策失败中可以学到什么?
4. 政策失败如何能促进政策发展?

词 汇

替代政策尝试
环境变化的影响
政策之间的关系
边界问题
过度的政策需求
可实现的政策预期

准确的因果理论

有效的政策工具选择

实施的变化无常

政治制度的失败

工具性政策学习

社会政策学习

政治学习

参考文献

Anderson, James E. 2000. Public Policy Making. 4th ed. Boston：Houghton Mifflin.

Birkland，Thomas A. 2001. An Introduction to the Policy Process：Theories, Concepts, and Models of Public Policy Making. New York：M. E. Sharpe.

Bennet, Colin J. and Howlett, Michael. 1992. "The Lessons of Learning：Reconciling Theories of Policy Learning and Policy Change." Policy Sciences, 25 (3)：275-294.

Ingram，Helen and Mann，Dean. 1980. "Policy Failure：An Issues Deserving Attention." In Why Policies Succeed or Fail. Ingram, Helen, and Mann, Dean. ed. Beverly Hils，California：Sage.

Kraft, Michael E. and Furlong, Scott R. 2004. Public Policy：Politics, Analysis, and Alternatives. Washington, D. C. CQ Press.

May, Peter. 1990. "Reconsidering Policy Design：Policies and Publics." Journal of Public Policy, 11(2)：187-206.

Ryan, Neal. 1995. "Unraveling Conceptual Developments in Implementation Analysis." Australian Journal of Public Administration，54(1)：65-81.

Sabatier, Paul A. 1988. "An Advocacy Coalition Framework of Policy Change and the Role of Policy-Oriented Learning Therein." Policy Sciences，21：129-168.

陈庆云. 公共政策分析. 北京：北京大学出版社，2006.

陈振明. 政策科学——公共政策分析导论. 2版. 北京：中国人民大学出版社，2003.

宁骚. 公共政策. 北京：高等教育出版社，2000.

谢明. 公共政策分析导论. 5版. 北京：中国人民大学出版社，2022.

张金马. 公共政策分析：概念·过程·方法. 北京：人民出版社，2004.

张国庆. 公共政策分析. 上海：复旦大学出版社，2004.

詹姆斯·E.安德森. 公共政策制定. 5版. 谢明，等，译. 北京：中国人民大学出版社，2009.

托马斯·R.戴伊. 理解公共政策. 12版. 谢明，等，译. 北京中国人民大学出版社，2011.

保罗·A.萨巴蒂尔. 政策过程理论. 胡总超，钟开斌，等，译. 北京：生活·读书·新知三联书店，2004.

戴博拉·斯通. 政策悖论. 顾建光，译. 北京：中国人民大学出版社，2006.

Chapter 11　Policy Capacity and Participation

Summary

> Policy analysis can improve the performance of government and its responsiveness to citizens. The commonplace criticisms of government are based on popular assessments and not on objective evidence, which usually shows that government is functioning well. The policy process can help strengthen the capacity for citizens to participate in the public spheres.

11.1　Improving Policy Capacity

Policy analysis can help improve the performance of government and its responsiveness to citizen concerns. How can policy analysis contribute to improving the policy capacity of government? One way is through the analysis of proposed institutional reforms, such as changes in the electoral process, campaign finance, term limits for legislators, and opportunities for citizens to participate in decision making. This is a task at which political scientists excel. Yet their analysis too often fails to reach the public or even policy makers, who then act without the benefit of what analysis has uncovered. Policy capacity can also be improved through better evaluation of the agencies charged with implementing policies and programs. Evaluation of government institutions and processes sometimes comes from citizen groups.

One of the central tasks for improving government policy capacity is in the hands of the people. Government will continue to respond to organized groups and special interests if citizens lack interest in public affairs and fail to educate themselves on the issues. What citizens see as faulty performance in government sometimes reflects the influence of organized groups that work to ensure that policies affecting their operations are not effective or that they inflict minimum constraints on their activities. The best way to counter self-serving actions by special interests is for citizens to get involved.

11.2 Citizen Participation in Decision Making

The decision-making process affects what kinds of decisions are made and, ultimately, what impacts they have on society. Policy outcomes reflect who participates in the process, who does not, and the different resources that each policy actor brings to the decision-making arena. Public policies in a democracy maybe expected to be consistent with public preferences and meet the needs of citizens. As noted, however, policy makers are often more responsive to organized interests such as big private companies and industries than they are to the general public.

One way to overcome this is to strengthen citizen capacity to participate in policy making processes. The level of public participation in policy processes, whether voting in elections or taking an active role in civic affairs, has improved over the past several decades. Of all age groups, the youngest, including college students, have the lowest level of interest in politics and policymaking and have the least active participation in these processes. It remains clear that citizen participation has a long way to go to be truly effective.

Public participation in the policy process can go well beyond voting, writing letters or e-mail messages to policy makers, and talking with others about policy issues. Historically, only a small percentage of the public is even this active. Even so, the percentage could rise as technology makes public involvement easier and as policy makers become more interested in having a higher level of public participation in government. Most government agencies already make a concerted effort to promote the use of their web sites, to offer information and public services through e-government, and to invite the public to engage the issues.

Nearly universal access to the Internet should make it easier for citizens to become active in public affairs. However, like public policy students, every citizen must also be alert to bias in Internet-based information. Each person must learn to ask about the source of the data and how reliable it is. Despite the difficulties, there are reasons to be optimistic about the potential of the Internet and citizen access to information about government and public policy.

Policy analysts have long recognized different social goals furthered by public involvement in policy making and the criteria by which participation can be evaluated. Beierle and Cayford (2002) identify five goals: (1) incorporating public values into decisions; (2) improving the substantive quality of those decisions (for example, by suggesting alternatives and findings errors of incorporate assumptions underlying policy proposals); (3) resolving conflict among the various competing interests (by emphasizing collaborative rather than adversarial decision making); (4) building trust in institutions and processes (thereby improving their ability to solve public problems); (5) educating and informing the public (raising public understanding of the issues and building a shared perspective on possible solutions).

Government agencies and public officials are often unclear about what they expect public participation to accomplish, and citizens might be puzzled as well. Some agencies feign interest in public involvement to appear to be doing the "right thing" and to comply with legal mandates while greatly limiting the degree to which citizens can affect decision making. Responding to that common practice, some analysts have suggested that there are four quite different models of citizen involvement, with increasing degrees of public influence on decision making. The first is the commentary model, in which agencies and proponents dominate. Second is the social learning model, in which citizens learn about policy proposals and provide advice on them. Third is the joint planning model, in which citizens engage in a dialogue with policy makers and planners and work collaboratively with them. Fourth is the consent and consensus model, in which citizens share authority with government and work together to solve problems.

Discussion Questions

1. How can policy analysts impact government?
2. How can you explain the discrepancy between popular and evidence-based assessments of government?
3. What can the policy process do for citizen participation?

Vocabularies

policy capacity
public participation
commentary model
joint planning model
consent and consensus model

References

Beierle, Thomas C. and Cayford, Jerry 2002. Democracy in Practice: Public Participation in Environmental Decisions. Washington, D.C.: Resources for the Future.

Bok, Derek. 2001. The Trouble with Government. Cambridge: Harvard University Press.

Kraft, Michael E. and Furlong, Scott R. 2004. Public Policy: Politics, Analysis, and Alternatives. Washington, D.C.: CQ Press.

Mackenzie, G. Calvin, and Labiner, Judith M. 2002. "Opportunity Lost: The

Rise and Fall of Trust and Confidence in Government after September 11." Washington, D. C.: Brookings Institution, Center for Public Service. Available at www.brook.edu.

Putnam, Robert D. 1995. "Tuning In, Tuning Out: The Strange Disappearance of Social Capital in America." PS: Political Science and Politics, 28 (December): 664-683.

Schneider, Anne L. and Ingram, Helen 1997. Policy Design for Democracy. Lawrence, Kansas: University Press of Kansas

第 11 章

公共决策能力与公民参与

政策分析人员可以提高政府绩效和对公民关注的响应能力。对政府的普遍批评是基于大众的评估,而不是客观的证据,这通常表明政府运作良好。政策过程可以增强公民参与公共领域事务的能力。

11.1　提高公共决策能力

政策分析有助于提高政府绩效及其对公民关注的回应能力。政策分析如何有助于提高政府的决策能力?一种方法是通过分析拟议的体制改革,例如选举过程的变化、竞选资金、立法者的任期限制以及公民参与决策的机会等,这是政治学家最擅长的工作。然而,他们的分析往往未能触及公众,甚至政策制定者,他们没有在政策分析中得到好处。还可以通过更好地评估负责执行政策和方案的机构来提高政策能力。对政府机构和程序的评估有时来自公民团体。

改善政府决策能力的核心任务之一掌握在人民手中。如果公民对公共事务缺乏兴趣并且未能就这些问题进行自我教育,政府将继续对有组织的团体和特殊利益集团做出回应。公民认为政府表现不佳的情况有时反映了有组织的团体的影响力,这些团体致力于确保影响其运作的政策无效,或对其活动施加最低限度的限制,打击特殊利益集团自私行为的最佳方式是公民参与。

11.2 公共决策中的公民参与

公共决策过程影响决策的类型,最终影响到这些决策对社会的影响。政策结果反映了谁参与这一过程,谁没有参与,以及每个政策主体为决策领域带来的不同资源。民主国家的公共政策可能与公众偏好一致并满足公民的需求。然而,如上所述,决策者往往对大型私营公司和行业等有组织的利益集团的反应比对一般公众的反应更为积极。

克服这个问题的一种途径是加强公民参与决策过程的能力。在过去的几十年里,公众参与政策过程的程度,无论是选举投票还是在公民事务中发挥积极作用都有所提升。在所有年龄组中,包括大学生在内的最年轻群体,对政治和政策制定的兴趣有所提高,并且积极参与这些过程。然而,公民参与要取得真正的成效还有很长的路要走。

公众对政策过程的参与远远不止投票、给决策者写信或发电子邮件、以及与他人讨论政策问题等方式。从历史上看,只有一小部分公众是活跃的。即便如此,由于技术的发展使得公众更容易参与决策,而且决策者对提高公众参与政府的行为更感兴趣,这一比例仍可能会上升。大多数政府机构已做出一致的努力,推广其网站的使用,通过电子政务提供信息和公共服务,并邀请公众参与到这些事务中来。

现在几乎人人都能使用互联网,这使得公民更容易参与公共事务。但是,与公共政策的学生一样,每个公民也必须对基于互联网的信息的偏见保持警惕,每个人都必须学会对数据的来源以及它的可靠性保持警惕。尽管困难重重,但仍有理由对互联网和公民获取政府和公共政策信息的潜力感到乐观。

长期以来,政策分析人员认识到,公众参与决策和评价会促进不同的社会目标的实现。Beierle 和 Cayford(2002)确定了五个目标:(1)将公共价值纳入决策;(2)提高这些决策的质量(例如,通过提出备选方案并纳入政策建议所依据的假设);(3)解决各种竞争利益团体之间的冲突(强调合作决策而不是对抗决策);(4)建立对机构和过程的信任(从而提高其解决公共问题的能力);(5)对公众进行教育和宣传(提高公众对问题的理解,并就可能的解决方案达成共识)。

政府机构和公职人员往往不清楚他们通过公众参与能够实现什么,而公民也可能会感到困惑。一些机构假装对公众参感兴趣,以显示其做了"正确的事情"并遵守法律规定,同时却极大地限制了公民可以影响决策的程度。针对这一普遍做法,一些分析人员提出,公民参与有四种截然不同的模式,公众对决策的影响力越来越大。第一个是评论模式,在这一模式中,机构和支持者占主导地位。其次是社会学习模式,公民了解政策并提供建议。第三是联合规划模式,公民与政策制定者和规划者进行对话,并与他们合作。第四是公民与政府分享权力共同解决问题的共识模式。

思考问题

1. 政策分析人员如何影响政府？
2. 你如何解释公众对政府的评估和基于证据的政府评估之间的差异？
3. 政策过程可以为公民参与做些什么？

词 汇

政策能力
评论模式
公众参与
联合规划模式
赞同和共识模式

参考文献

Beierle, Thomas C. and Cayford, Jerry 2002. Democracy in Practice: Public Participation in Environmental Decisions. Washington, D. C.: Resources for the Future.

Bok, Derek. 2001. The Trouble with Government. Cambridge: Harvard University Press.

Kraft, Michael E. and Furlong, Scott R. 2004. Public Policy: Politics, Analysis, and Alternatives. Washington, D. C.: CQ Press.

Mackenzie, G. Calvin, and Labiner, Judith M. 2002. "Opportunity Lost: The Rise and Fall of Trust and Confidence in Government after September 11." Washington, D. C.: Brookings Institution, Center for Public Service. Available at www. brook. edu.

Putnam, Robert D. 1995. "Tuning In, Tuning Out: The Strange Disappearance of Social Capital in America." PS: Political Science and Politics, 28 (December): 664-683.

Schneider, Anne L. and Ingram, Helen 1997. Policy Design for Democracy. Lawrence, Kansas: University Press of Kansas.

陈庆云. 公共政策分析. 北京:北京大学出版社, 2006.

陈振明. 政策科学——公共政策分析导论. 2版. 北京:中国人民大学出版社, 2003.

宁骚. 公共政策. 北京:高等教育出版社, 2000.

谢明. 公共政策分析导论. 5版. 北京:中国人民大学出版社, 2022.

张金马. 公共政策分析:概念·过程·方法. 北京:人民出版社, 2004.

张国庆. 公共政策分析. 上海:复旦大学出版社, 2004.

詹姆斯·E.安德森. 公共政策制定. 5版. 谢明,等,译. 北京:中国人民大学出版社, 2009.

托马斯·R.戴伊. 理解公共政策. 12版. 谢明,等,译. 北京中国人民大学出版社，2011.

保罗·A.萨巴蒂尔.政策过程理论.胡总超，钟开斌，等，译.北京：生活·读书·新知三联书店，2004.

戴博拉·斯通.政策悖论.顾建光，译.北京：中国人民大学出版社，2006.

Bibliography

Affholter, Dennis P. 1994. "Outcome Monitoring." In Handbook of Practical Program Evaluation. Ed. Joseph S. Wholey, Harry P. Harty, and Kathryn E. Newcomer. San Francisco: Josse Bass.

Allision, Graham. 1971. Essence of Decision: Explaining the Cuban Missile Crisis. Boston: Little, Brown.

Anderson, James E. 2000. Public Policy Making. 4th ed. Boston: Houghton Mifflin.

Anderson, James E. 2003. Public Policy Making. 5th ed. Boston: Houghton Mifflin.

Bardach, Eugene. 2000. A Practical Guide for Policy Analysis: The Eightfold Path to More Effective Problem Solving. New York: Chatham House.

Baumgartner, Frank R. and Jones, Bryan D. 1993. Agendas and Instability in American Politics. Chicago: University of Chicago Press.

Beierle, Thomas C. and Cayford, Jerry 2002. Democracy in Practice: Public Participation in Environmental Decisions. Washington, D. C. : Resources for the Future.

Bendor, Jonathan and Hammond, Thomas H. 1992. "Rethinking Allison's Models." American Political Science Review, 86(2).

Bennet, Colin J. and Howlett, Michael. 1992. "The Lessons of Learning: Reconciling Theories of Policy Learning and Policy Change." Policy Sciences, 25 (3): 275-294.

Berry, Jeffery M. 1989. "Subgovernments, Issue Networks, and Political Conflict." Remaking American Politics. Ed. Richard Sidney and Milkis Harris. Boulder, Colorado: Westview Press.

Bickers, Kenneth N. and Williams, John T. 2001. Public Policy Analysis: A Political Economy Approach. Boston, Massachusetts: Houghton-Mifflin.

Birkland, Thomas A. 2001. An Introduction to the Policy Process: Theories, Concepts, and Models of Public Policy Making. New York: M. E. Sharpe.

Bok, Derek. 2001. The Trouble with Government. Cambridge: Harvard University Press.

Cigler, Allan J. 1991. "Interest Groups: A Subfield in Search of an Identity." Political Science, Looking to the Future: Volume IV: American Institutions, ed. Evanston, Illinois: Northwestern University Press.

Cochran, Clarke E., Mayer, Lawrence C., Carr, T. R., Cayer, N. Joseph, McKenzie, Mark J., and Peck, Laura R. 1999. American Public Policy: An Introduction. 6th ed. New York: St. Martin's Press.

Cohen, Michael D., March, James G. and Olson, Johan P. 1972. "A Garbage Can Model of Organization Choice." Administrative Science Quarterly, 17:1-25.

"Constitution of the Republic of South Korea" from http://South Korea.na.go.kr/res/low_01_read.jsp

"Consumer Groups Urge Lotte Boycott." 2015. English Chosun, August 5, 2015 from http://english.chosun.com/site/data/html_dir/2015/08/05/2015080501247.html

Derthick, Martha. 1972. New Towns in Town. Washington, DC: Urban Institute.

Dery, David. 1984. Problem Definition in Policy Analysis. Lawrence, Kansas: University Press of Kansas.

Dunn, N. William. 1981. An Introduction to Public Policy Analysis. Englewood Cliffs, New Jersey: Prentice-Hall, Inc.

Dye, Thomas R. 1992. Understanding Public Policy. 7th ed. Englewood Cliffs, New Jersey: Prentice-Hall, Inc.

Dye, R. Thomas. 1995. Understanding Public Policy. 8th ed. Englewood Cliffs, New Jersey: Prentice-Hall, Inc.

Easton, David. 1965. A Systems Analysis of Political Life. New York: John Wiley.

Elazar, Daniel J. 1984. American Federalism: A view from the States. 3rd ed. New York: Harper and Row.

Fischer, Frank, Miller, Gerald J., and Sidney, Mara S. (eds.). 2007. Handbook of Public Policy Analysis: Theory, Politics, and Methods. Boca Raton, Florida: CRC Press.

Frohock, Fred M. 1979. Public Policy: Scope and Logic. Englewood Cliffs, New Jersey: Prentice Hall.

Gerston, Larry N. 2010. Public Policy Making: Process and Principles. Armonk, New York: M. E. Sharpe.

Goggin, Malcolm L., Bowman, Anne O'M., Lester, James P., and O'Toole, Laurence, J. 1990. Implementation Theory and Practice: Toward a Third Generation. Glenview, Illinois: Scott Foresman/Little Brown.

Goldenberg, Jacob, David Mazursky, and Sorin Solomon. 1999. "Creative

Sparks." Science, 3 (September): 1495-1496.

Gupta, Dipak K. 2001. Analyzing Public Policy: Concepts, Tools, and Techniques. Washington, DC: Congressional Quarterly.

Ingram, Helen, and Mann, Dean. 1980. "Policy Failure: An Issues Deserving Attention." In Why Policies Succeed or Fail. Ingram, Helen, and Mann, Dean. Ed. Beverly Hils, California: Sage.

Jansson, Bruce K. 2003. Becoming an Effective Policy Advocate. Pacific Grove, California: Brooks/Cole.

Katz, Daniel and Kahn, Robert L. 1966. "Organizations and the System Concept." pp. 206-216, in Shafritz, Jay, Hyde, Alan and Parkes, Sandra (eds). 2004 Classics of Public Administration, 5th ed. Belmont, California: Wadsworth.

Kim, Heejin. 2015. "Jobless Rate for Young South Koreans Rises to 11.1%." South Korea Joong Ang Daily. March 19, 2015 from http://South Korea joong ang daily. joins. com/news/article/Article. aspx? aid=3002087

Kingdon, John W. 1995. Agendas, Alternatives and Public Policies. 2nd ed. New York: Harper Collins.

Kraft, Michael E. and Furlong, Scott R. 2004. Public Policy: Politics, Analysis, and Alternatives. Washington, D.C.: CQ Press.

Laumann, Edward O. and Knoke, David. 1987. The Organizational State: Social Choice in National Policy Domains. Madison: University of Wisconsin Press.

Lee, Jong Youl and Anderson, Chad. 2008. Policy Analysis. Seoul: Daeyoung Moonhwasa.

Levi, Edward. 1949. An Introduction to Legal Reasoning. Chicago: University of Chicago Press.

Levine, Charles H., Peters, B. Guy, and Thompson, Frank J. 1990. Public Administration: Challenges, Choices, Consequences. Glenview, Illinois: Scott, Foresman/Little Brown.

Lindblom, Charles E. 1959. "The Science of Muddling Through." Public Administration Review, 19: 79-88.

Lowi, Theodore J. 1964. "American Business, Public Policy, Case Studies, and Political Theory." World Politics, 16 (July): 667-715.

Lowi, Theodore. 1979. The End of Liberalism: The Second Republic of the United States. 2nd ed. New York: W. W. Norton.

Mackenzie, G. Calvin, and Labiner, Judith M. 2002. "Opportunity Lost: The Rise and Fall of Trust and Confidence in Government after September 11." Washington, D.C.: Brookings Institution, Center for Public Service. Available at www. brook.

edu.

MacRae, Duncan and Wilde, James. 1979. Policy Analysis for Public Decisions. North Scituate, Massachusetts: Duxbury.

Majone, Giandomenico. 1989. Evidence, Argument, and Persuasion in the Policy Process. New Haven: Yale University Press.

May, Peter. 1990. "Reconsidering Policy Design: Policies and Publics." Journal of Public Policy, 11(2): 187-206.

Mazmanian, Daniel A. and Kraft, Michael E. eds. 1999. Toward Sustainable Communities: Transition and Transformations in Environmental Policy. Cambridge: MIT Press.

Ministry of Employment and Labor. 2015. "Major Statistics," August 10, 2015, from http://www.moel.go.kr/english/pas/pas Major.jsp

Nagel, Stuart S. 2002. Handbook of Public Policy Evaluation. Thousand Oaks, California: Sage.

Nakamura, Robert T. 1987. "The Textbook Policy Process and Implementation Research." Policy Studies Journal, 7(1): 142-154.

Neustadt, Richard E. 1990. Presidential Power and the Modern Presidents: The Politics of Leadership from Roosevelt to Reagan. New York: Free Press.

Olson, Mancur. 1971. The Logic of Collective Action. Cambridge: Harvard University Press.

Parsons, Wayne. 1995. Public Policy: An Introduction to the Theory and Practice of Policy Analysis. Northampton, Massachusetts: Edward Elgar.

Patton, Carl V. and Sawicki, David S. 1993. Basic Methods of Policy Analysis and Planning. 2nd ed. Englewood Cliffs, New Jersey: Prentice Hall, Inc.

Percy-Smith, Janie. 1996. Needs Assessments in Public Policy. Bristol, Pennsylvania: Open University Press.

Peters, B. Guy. 1999. American Public Policy: Promise and Performance. Chappaqua, New York: Chatham House/Seven Rivers.

"Powers of the National Assembly" from http://South Korea.na.go.kr/int/aut_01.jsp?leftid=CA

Pressman, Jeffrey and Wildavsky, Aaron. 1973. Implementation. Berkeley, California: University of California Press.

Putnam, Robert D. 1995. "Tuning In, Tuning Out: The Strange Disappearance of Social Capital in America." PS: Political Science and Politics, 28 (December): 664-683.

Randall R. Bovbjerg. 1985. "What Is Policy Analysis?." Journal of Policy Analysis and Management, 5(1), Autumn: 154-158.

Ringquist, Evan J. 1993. Environmental Protection at the State Level: Politics and Progress in Controlling Pollution. Armonk, New York: M. E. Sharpe.

Ripley, Randall and Franklin, Grace. 1991. Congress, the Bureaucracy and Public Policy. 5th ed. Pacific Grove, California: Brooks-Cole.

Ryan, Neal. 1995. "Unraveling Conceptual Developments in Implementation Analysis". Australian Journal of Public Administration, 54(1): 65-81.

Sabatier, Paul A. 1988. "An Advocacy Coalition Framework of Policy Change and the Role of Policy-Oriented Learning Therein." Policy Sciences, 21: 129-168.

Sabatier, Paul A. 1991. "Political Science and Public Policy." PS: Political Science and Politics, 24(2): 144-147.

Sabatier, Paul A. 2007. "The Need for Better Theories," pp. 3-17 in Sabatier, Paul A. (ed), Theories of the Policy Process, 2nd ed. Boulder, Colorado: Westview Press.

Schneider, Anne L. and Ingram, Helen. 1997. Policy Design for Democracy. Lawrence, Kansas: University Press of Kansas.

Schneider, Anne and Ingram, Helen. 1993. "The Social Con-struction of Target Populations: Implications for Politics and Policy." American Political Science Review, 87(2): 334-348.

Simon, Christopher A. 2009. Public Policy: Preferences and Outcomes, 2nd ed. New York, New York: Routledge.

Starling, Grover. 1988. Strategies for Policy Making. Chicago: Dorsey Press.

Steinberger, Peter J. 1980. "Typologies of Public Policy: Meaning Construction and the Policy Process." Social Science Quarterly, 61 (September): 185-197.

Stillman, Richard J. 1996. The American Bureaucracy. Chicago: Nelson-Hall.

Stone, Deborah. 1997. Policy Paradox: The Art of Political Decision Making. New York: W. W. Norton & Company.

Stokey, Edith and Zeckhauser, Richard. 1978. A Primer for Policy Analysis. New York: W. W. Norton & Company.

Theodoulou, Stella Z. and Cahn, Matthew A. 1995. Public Policy: The Essential Readings. Upper Saddle River, New Jersey: Prentice-Hall, Inc.

Vedung, Evert. 2005. Public Policy and Evaluation Program. New Brunswick, New Jersey: Transaction Publishers.

Weimer, L. David and Vining, R. Aidan. 2005. Policy Analysis: Concepts and Practice. Pearson, New Jersey: Prentice-Hall, Inc.

Wildavsky, Aaron. 1964. The Politics of Budgetary Process. Boston: Little, Brown.

Wilson, Edward O. 1998. Consilience: The Unity of Knowledge. New York: Knopf.

Wilson, Woodrow. 1887. "The Study of Administration." pp. 22-37, in Shafritz, Jay, Hyde, Alan, and Parkes, Sandra (eds). 2004 Classics of Public Administration, 5th ed. Belmont, California: Wadsworth.

Wood, B. Dan. 1991. "Federalism and Policy Responsiveness: The Clean Air Case." Journal of Politics, 53(3): 851-859.

Zahariadis, Nikolaos. 1993. "To Sell or Not to Sell? Telecommuni-cations Policy in Britain and France." Journal of Public Policy, 12(4): 355-376.